50 Hikes North of the
White Mountains

Hurlbert Swamp, meandering bog bridges

50 *Hikes*

North of the
White Mountains

**New Hampshire's Great North Woods
to the Canadian Border**

KIM ROBERT NILSEN

The Countryman Press
Woodstock, Vermont

AN INVITATION TO THE READER

Over time trails can be rerouted and signs and
landmarks altered. If you find that changes have
occurred on the routes described in this book,
please let us know so that corrections may be
made in future editions. The author and publisher
also welcome other comments and suggestions.
Address all correspondence to:

Editor, 50 Hikes Series
The Countryman Press
P.O. Box 748
Woodstock, VT 05091

Maps by Erin Greb Cartography,
    © The Countryman Press
Book design by Glenn Suokko
Text composition by Eugenie S. Delaney
Interior photographs by the author unless
    otherwise noted

Published by The Countryman Press,
P.O. Box 748, Woodstock, VT 05091
Distributed by W. W. Norton & Company, Inc.,
500 Fifth Avenue, New York, NY 10110

Printed in the United States of America

10 9 8 7 6 5 4 3 2 1

My daughters, Shyloah and Willow, and my granddaughter, Sage, like to hike as much as I do. This guidebook is dedicated to them. May they have long and happy years tramping this grand green earth.

50 Hikes at a Glance

HIKE	REGION	DISTANCE (MILES)
1. Owl's Head Trail and Martha's Mile	Jefferson Dome	Loop: about 7.5.
2. Little Cherry Pond Trail	Jefferson Dome	5.0 r.t.
3. Presidential Rail Trail to Cherry Pond	Jefferson Dome	About 4.0 r.t.
4. Col. Whipple Trail and Ice Ramparts Trail	Jefferson Dome	About 5.5
5. Mud Pond Trail	Jefferson Dome	Less than 1.0 r.t.
6. Starr King Trail to Mt. Waumbek and Beyond	The Kilkenny	6.4 r.t.
7. Kilback–Unknown Ponds Loop	The Kilkenny	11.0
8. Bunnell Notch Trail and Mt. Cabot Trail to Mt. Cabot	The Kilkenny	5.1 o.w.
9. Unknown Pond Trail to The Horn	The Kilkenny	8.2 r.t.
10. Rogers Ledge	The Kilkenny	8.2 r.t.
11. Devil's Hopyard	The Kilkenny	2.4 r.t.
12. Mossy Glen	Androscoggin Flowage	2.0
13. The Ledge Trail Loop	Androscoggin Flowage	3.2 loop
14. Ice Gulch	Androscoggin Flowage	6.5 loop
15. Mt. Success Trail and the DC-3 Crash Site	Androscoggin Flowage	3.0 to summit, 8.0 r.t.
16. Devil's Slide	Nash Stream Forest	Less than 0.5 to cliffs
17. Bald Mountain Notch Loop	Nash Stream Forest	About 8.0 loop
18. Victor Head Cliff	Nash Stream Forest	About 2.5 to cliffs
19. Old Summer Club Trail	Nash Stream Forest	About 8.0 r.t.
20. Percy Peaks Trail	Nash Stream Forest	4.4 r.t.
21. Percy Loop	Nash Stream Forest	2.2 to summit, 5.4 loop
22. Pond Brook Falls	Nash Stream Forest	Less than 0.5 r.t.
23. East Side Trail Loop	Nash Stream Forest	About 5.0 loop
24. Sugarloaf Mountain Trail	Nash Stream Forest	4.4 r.t.
25. Gadwah Notch Trail	Nash Stream Forest	5.5 o.w. to shelter
26. Baldhead Mountain Trail	Nash Stream Forest	About 5.0 r.t.

DIFFICULTY	GOOD FOR KIDS	FEATURES	CAMPING	NORDIC SKIING	SNOWSHOEING	NOTES
3.5		H G V				Magnificent views of Presidential Range
1	★	W F V		★	★	Shallow boreal lake
1	★	H F V W		★	★	Large glacial lake, moose, exceptional bird-watching
1	★	G W F V		★	★	Extensive marsh environment, bird-watching, moose
1	★	W F V		★	★	Handicapped accessible
3		H G W V	★		★	Hike to 4,000-footer
4		H G W F V	★		★	Loop trek to remote glacial tarns, moose
3.5		H G W V	★		★	4,000-footer, overnight at old fire tower watchman's cabin
3.5		G W F V	★		★	Backcountry camping only
2		G W V S		★	★	Cliff environment, stunning views, rock profile
2		G W F		★	★	Ice gorge with rare plant community
1	★	H G W F WF			★	Stream gorge and cool glade
4		G V				Grand view of Mt. Adams
5		G F V WF				Challenging ice gorge environment
3.5		H G F V				Underrated hike to plane wreck
3		G V				Extensive cliff environment
2.5	★ older children	W V S		★	★	Forest trek through mountain notch and Christine Lake
2.5	★ older children	G V S		★ with caution		Cliff environment
3.5		G V				Trek through diverse terrain to bald summit
4		H G W F V				Vast bald summit and blueberry barren
3		G W V	★			Tent platform at Percy Loop Camp
1	★	W WF				Big slide-step falls
1.5	★	H W F V S				Long loop around vast bog
3.5		H G V				Dramatic views from summit ledges
3.0		G W F V	★			Mountain meadows, remote shelter with fine views
3.5		H G W V	★			Unofficial route to Baldhead Shelter

50 Hikes at a Glance

	FEATURES	
o.w. = one-way	H	history
r.t. = round-trip	G	geology
	W	wildlife
DIFFICULTY	F	flora
1 = easiest	V	scenic views
5 = most difficult	S	swimming
	WF	waterfalls

HIKE	REGION	DISTANCE (MILES)
27. Kelsey Notch Trail	Dixville Notch	More than 6.0 r.t.
28. Mt. Gloriette to Dixville Peak	Dixville Notch	About 7.0 r.t.
29. Table Rock Trail	Dixville Notch	About 2.6 r.t.
30. Three Brothers Trail	Dixville Notch	5.0 r.t.
31. Canal Trail to the Lake of Floating Islands	Dixville Notch	About 6.0 r.t.
32. Sangquinary Ridge Trail	Dixville Notch	1.2 o.w.
33. Sanguinary Summit Trail (SST)	Dixville Notch	8.0-plus loop
34. McAllister Road to Weirs Tree Farm	CT River Headwaters	6.6 r.t.
35. Mt. Monadnock Trail	CT River Headwaters	6.0 r.t.
36. Hurlbert Swamp Trail	CT River Headwaters	2.0 r.t.
37. Lake Francis Trail	CT River Headwaters	6.4 r.t.
38. Mt. Prospect Trail	CT River Headwaters	About 1.6 r.t.
39. Mt. Covell Trail	CT River Headwaters	4.4
40. Mt. Magalloway	CT River Headwaters	3.5 loop
41. Indian Stream Canyon	CT River Headwaters	2.2 loop
42. Little Hellgate Falls	Dead Diamond Country	Nearly 3.0 r.t.
43. Garfield Falls	Dead Diamond Country	Less than 1.0
44. Magalloway River Trail	Dead Diamond Country	1.0, all paths
45. Diamond Peaks Trail	Dead Diamond Country	6.2 r.t.
46. Falls in the River Trail	Boundary Mountains	2.0 to Moose Alley
47. Deer Mountain Trail	Boundary Mountains	About 4.5 r.t. to bog
48. Fourth Connecticut Lake Trail	Boundary Mountains	3.0 r.t.
49. Mt. D'Urban to Crown Monument	Boundary Mountains	About 8.0 r.t.
50. The Cohos Trail	Trans–Coos County Path	165 in entirety

DIFFICULTY	GOOD FOR KIDS	FEATURES	CAMPING	NORDIC SKIING	SNOWSHOEING	NOTES
3.5		G W V	★		★ Strenuous	Remote northern route to Baldhead Shelter
3.5		H G W V		★	★	Ski area, wind turbines
2.5	★Older children	H G W V			★ Part of trail	Old trail to knife edge cliff
3.5		H G W V WF				Two falls, ice cave, cliffs
1.5	★	H W V S		★	★	Trail beside hand-dug canal, moose, bears
3.0		H G V WF				Numerous cliffs, small flume
3.0		G W F V	★			Panorama shelter, moose, bears
2.0	★	H W F V		★	★	Farm lanes, fine views, meadows, cellar holes
2.5	★	H V			★	Restored fire tower high over Connecticut River Valley
1	★	W F		★	★	White cedar stands, bog bridges
1.5	★	W F V S	★	★	★	Vast lake views, campground
2.5	★	W V		★	★	Cleared summit with expansive view
2.0	★	W V		★	★	Cleared summit, view over 2,800- acre lake
3.0	★	H W S	★			State-leased cabin, fire tower, cliffs
1	★	G V WF				Rugged gorge in Perry Stream
2.0	★ With caution at falls	G WF				Falls in remote region
1	★	G WF				Falls and dramatic gorge
1	★	W F V		★	★	Wildlife habitat
2.5		H G F V				Cliff environment
1.5	★	G W F V WF			★	Falls, wild river country
3	★ Older children	W F V				Flagged route to high elevation bog, trail to be restored to summit
2.5	★ Older children	H G W F V				Headwaters of Connecticut River
3.0		H G W F V				Trek on international boundary clearings
1 thru 5		H G W F V S WF	★ Some areas	★ Some terrain	★ Some terrain	Long-distance hiking experience in remote country

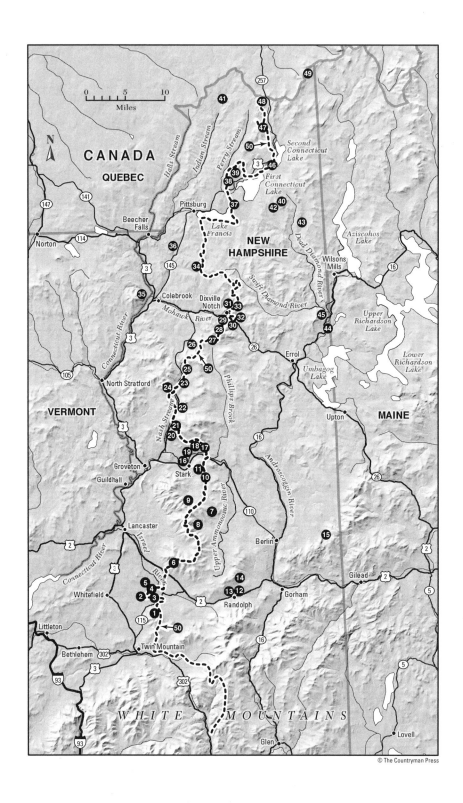

© The Countryman Press

Contents

Acknowledgments

In the early 1970s, a New Hampshire conservation officer by the name of Arthur Muise walked into the Lancaster newspaper office where I was holding down my first real job. Arthur pulled the pipe out of his teeth and began to spin yarns about the backcountry of the Granite State's largest and most remote county: Coos County. His stories were so compelling, I had to run off and go visit those places he was waxing so eloquently about. So in a very real sense, this guidebook has its origins in Arthur's words.

I must thank Lainie Castine, Yvan Guay, Chad Pepau, and Tracy Rexford, people who have helped me build a big web of trails in the Great North Woods where no trails existed. Their sweat and effort is evident throughout this tome.

I have to give credit to the State of New Hampshire's Trail Bureau, Division of Forests and Lands, and the Fish and Game Department for considerable support, for having faith in the idea that there could be within the logging lands in the Granite State's northernmost terrain multiple-use trails that could embrace hikers on foot. The timberland owners, too, went through a seismic shift in policy and philosophy over the four decades I spent moving about in the distant places. Exclusionary policies toward hiking and overnight camping dissipated when it became clear that multiple uses of forests benefited all parties greatly and actually helped keep vast tracts of land open and productive. So a great deal of credit must be bestowed on the timberland owners, for without those grand tracts of land to tramp on, there would be no trails, certainly no new trails, and no need for this guidebook.

Other players gave me a hand up in this process. John Lane, owner of an old labor camp in the Nash Stream Forest, made his camp available free of charge for years to me and trail builders, so we could carry on our work. Will Staats, a state biologist working out of the Lancaster state offices, was instrumental in paving the way for new pathways in very remote country. David Dernbach of the former Trailmaster's youth program helped improve lots of trails listed in this guide. And Luke O'Brien of the NorthWoods Stewardship Center at E. Charleston, Vermont, has done Herculean work with Kingdom Corps crews on trails within northern Coos County.

Steve Barba, former managing partner of the Balsams Grand Resort Hotel in Dixville Notch, has always been a big booster of northern Coos County and its recreational potential. The Tillotson family, through their important regional development granting foundation, the Neil and Louise Tillotson Fund, supported considerable trail development in the region.

Garfield Falls close up

Introduction: Discovering New Hampshire's Great Unknown

The mile-high peaks of New Hampshire's White Mountain National Forest are Mecca for hikers in the eastern United States. For seasoned trekkers, Mounts Washington, Adams, Jefferson, Madison, Monroe, Eisenhower, Lafayette, and Lincoln are household names.

In some sense, though, these peaks and the dozens of 4,000-footers that pepper the forest are a love trap. Hikers lavish their attention on these lofty Appalachian Chain summits, at the expense of a whole host of other mountainous and backcountry features nearby.

That's a shame, for to the north of the White Mountain National Forest stretches a vast timbered terrain bristling with summits and high ridgelines, and cradling waterfalls, canyons, elevated meadows, deep cold lakes, and drop-dead cliff faces. Just across NH (New Hampshire) 2 and NH 115 between the Granite State communities of Lancaster and Gorham, where the bulk of the White Mountain National Forest acreage comes to end, sprawls the sparsely populated realm of central and northern Coos (pronounced *Co-ahss*) County, a million acres of wild country and logging lands that few people know anything about and fewer venture into.

But there is an entire universe of tramper terrain to be explored, new trails to try, and historic old pathways to get acquainted with.

While Presidential Range hikers do move about within the political entity known as Coos County, the big summits rise near its southern tip. To the north, a central spine of lofty wooded peaks runs for 90 miles to the Canadian border and the province of Quebec. On either side of the county flow big rivers: New England's largest—the Connecticut River—to the west, and the Magalloway/Androscoggin river system to the east. Squeezed between these two mighty flows is a long band of upland just 30 miles wide that supports several 4,000-footers, some of the tallest ridgelines in the state outside the national forest, and mile after mile of remote and quiet trails that increasingly appeal to trekkers who no longer want to hike with the crowds.

Only 33,000 people reside in Coos County, and that number is actually declining and has been declining for nearly one hundred years. Half the population clusters around the 5-mile NH 16 as it threads through the communities of Berlin and Gorham. The remaining souls live in tiny villages strung out along NH 3 in the Connecticut River Valley. To this day, most local residents do not hike in the mountains, so chances are excellent you will have this million-acre big-forest environment to yourself.

Just stride across NH 2 and NH 115 to the north and the number of hikers falls away exponentially. Drift north of NH 110 or NH 26 and moose may outnumber the hikers on any given day. In fact, the wildlife is very much a solid reason why trampers come this far north. Hikers want to see wild creatures in their natural environment, be it a moose cow and calf on the trail, a porcupine climbing a tree to put some distance between itself and visitors, a black bear tearing at old logs in search of grubs and ants, or a loon paddling about in a remote cove.

Those who must have bony summits to prowl will not be disappointed; there are bald topknots and open ledges aplenty. Northern Coos County boasts the highest cliff ledge in the state, perhaps the largest blueberry barren above 3,000 feet in elevation, and the best rock profile for 100 miles: the terrific and very big likeness of the head of a beagle dog.

I sat down and wrote this guidebook because I've been tramping about in the wilds of Coos County north of the national forest for nearly 40 years. I don't get tired of it. I began my exploration of this remote terrain after taking a seat on a rock slab on Maine's marvelous Mt. Katahdin. When I leaned back and placed my hands behind me to relax and take in the view, I placed my left hand in a pile of human excrement. I swore then and there that I would no longer hike with the hordes. I made up my mind to trek in peace and quiet and to experience the mountains on their own terms. After these many decades, I feel I have made a wise choice.

But others should experience this vast relatively unexplored terrain for themselves. There is plenty of room and lots of destinations. The majority of outdoors enthusiasts will always be siphoned off by the Whites to the south. Safe to say, northern Coos County should remain a solitary fastness that manages to lure the intrepid tramper with the prospect of fine summits, expansive and beautiful forests, continental silence, abundant wildlife, and an almost spiritual peacefulness.

If one hikes from the town of Jefferson in the south, say, to Pittsburg in the far north and treks along the central elevated spine of the county all the way, there will be no intervening communities to stop in for nearly 90 trail miles. No place to buy a sandwich. No watering hole. No emporium at which to purchase a Band-Aid for that blister on one's left foot.

While some features, such as the critical habitat that makes up the 6,000-plus-acre Pondicherry Wildlife Refuge, are no farther distant by car than the trailheads of the northern Presidential Range peaks, other features, such as the Indian Stream Canyon in northern Pittsburg or Diamond Peaks in the Second College Grant, might take a Massachusetts resident six hours' driving and hiking to reach.

Don't be deterred. A little extra effort or time is all that is needed to slip quietly into the Coos County backcountry, into New Hampshire's great unknown. There are natural wonders aplenty to behold.

THE MOUNTAINS

North of the Presidential Range, only two summits top out above 4,000 feet. But who gives a damn, really. Central and northern Coos are chock-full of fine peaks, some isolated monadnocks, some clustered along 3,500-foot ridges, and some snakelike uplands that run for miles, sometimes more than a dozen.

Some of the mountains in the Great North woods are New England gems. If you have not climbed North Percy Peak, The Horn, or Mt. Magalloway . . . if you have not tiptoed out to the frightening gangplank that is Table Rock . . . then you're just a flatland greenhorn.

THE LAKES

New Hampshire boasts about its Lakes Region, and for good reason. The Granite State's middle latitudes are awash with grand lakes with Native American names, such as Winnipesaukee and Squam, to name just two.

Yet there is yet another lakes region in New Hampshire. The Whites are too tall and steep to support great bodies of water, but the mountains near the Canadian border are spread out and form natural bowls large enough to cradle vast expanses of water. Lake Umbagog on the Maine–New Hampshire border is 8,000 acres large but so shallow you could, figuratively speaking, hold its waters in a teacup.

Then there is the great string of Connecticut Lakes–First, Second, Third, and Fourth–tied to the 1,800-acre man-made reservoir, Lake Francis, which drowned the original town of Pittsburg in the 1930s.

Today, trails approach some of these lakes or swing down to sections of the wild Connecticut River that binds them all together into a watery confabulation.

THE RIVERS

Sports fishermen have long ventured into northern Coos to reach fly-fishing waters so promising, they once attracted President Eisenhower to try his luck in the back of yonder.

The names of the great flowages trip off the tongue up here, so wonderful are the assemblage of letters that forge the names: Magalloway, Connecticut, Androscoggin, Upper Ammonoosuc. Then there are the names given by loggers, who loved the Swift Diamond because its waters would move logs rapidly and rarely bind them up in log jams, but hated the Dead Diamond because its waters ran too damn slow and logs often piled up in the endless oxbow turns along the river's course.

There are a goodly share of great streams and brooks, too–high-volume arteries such as the Halls, Indian, Perry, Nash, Phillips, Clear, and others that profoundly shaped the landscapes in which they flow. Some of these streams and their lesser tributaries can actually be dangerous to cross in times of spring runoff or after heavy storms. Hikers rarely have to watch their step because so many of the stream crossings in this guidebook are bridged. But a few are not. When water is raging in its rocky confines, be wary about where you cross. Sometimes a good bushwhack far uphill is a better choice, when a crossing seems an invitation to be dragged or even drowned.

THE WETLANDS

The Great North Woods region above the Whites harbors a secret. In some sense, this realm could be more notable for its vast wetlands than for its summits. The towns of Whitefield and Jefferson share a huge tract of bog and marshland coveted by the Audubon Society, by the U.S. Fish and Wildlife Service, by New Hampshire Fish and Game Department, and by serious birdwatchers of the Northeast.

The unincorporated township of Odell, high in the Nash Stream Forest, shelters a great bog that was liberated from its watery prison when a big log and stone crib dam failed suddenly during three days of rain in 1969. A stellar example of eastern white cedar swamp stays quiet and out of sight on the Clarksville-Stewartstown line, and the northernmost community of Pittsburg is big enough to house a dozen bog environments, from the high-elevation wetland on Deer Mountain, to the sprawling sink known as Labrador Swamp, south of First Connecticut Lake.

But in the county's northeast corner, water rules and has shaped the landscape in wonderful ways. Small dams at Errol and Pontook Reservoir back up dozens of square miles of moisture. This water world is exceptional habitat for almost all creatures great and small that live here seasonally or all year round.

Above the dammed expanses of water, the Magalloway drains southward out of 17-mile Aziscohos Lake to add its flow to the mix. From the east comes copious discharge from the Rangeley Lake behemoths: Kennebago, Richardson, Mooselookmeguntic, Cupsuptic, and Rangeley itself.

The little town of Errol is the gateway to this wet wonderland, as much a marvel to me in its own right as the high peaks of the Presidential Range are many miles to the south.

THE WILDLIFE

The local fauna of Coos County are all the more reason to come farther north than the Whites. In northern New Hampshire, none of the animals is dangerous. You are not prey for any predator. Black bears are not habituated to human activity and food, so they flee the area when hikers arrive. There has never been a fatal bear attack in Coos County, or elsewhere in the state, of which I'm aware.

Coyotes will avoid you completely. You may hear them but you will likely never see them, even if they are close by. Don't give them a second thought. They are not a threat to you, period!

In reality, moose are the most dangerous creatures, and that's usually only in the fall of the year. Bulls that will pay you no mind in spring and summer may become territorial during the rut: mating season. They can be unpredictable then. Simply give moose a wide berth and there should be no problem. Although I have heard of a few minor injuries due to moose, over 40 years, I know of no one who has been killed.

Mountain lion sightings crop up now and again; however, state biologists believe that there is no resident population of big cats in the state. If there were, the animals would most certainly have located the deer yards, where deer congregate during the winter. But a cousin, the lynx, has made a comeback from the brink of extinction in the state. And a lesser cousin, the bobcat, never lost its footing here.

The most visible of all wildlife are the birds. Coos County's great bogs and marshes are home to unbelievable numbers of species. At Pondicherry Wildlife Refuge, more than 230 different winged creatures have been counted over the span of 10 years, some of them oh so common, some extremely rare.

Because Coos County's forests are smack within the transition zone between northern hardwood and Canadian boreal softwood woodlands, all sorts of species overlap here, giving hikers the opportunity to see creatures they would not otherwise see in the eastern megalopolis cities and communities.

THE HUMAN IMPACT

The history of settlement of the White Mountains region and the vast forested tract, known as the Great North Woods, north to the Canadian border is intimately bound up with the fortunes of woodcutters and paper barons and the tourist trade.

In the White Mountains, powerful timber interests, utilizing clear-cutting methods to literally mine the forests, came to blows with well-heeled gentry who sought to protect God's wilderness providence from resource rape and to ensure the mountains would continue to attract hordes of tourists, who arrived by train each summer and stayed for weeks and sometimes many months in any one of scores of luxury hotels.

In the opening years of the 20th century, conservation interests proved victorious, while standing in the ashes of a dozen major forest fires that had consumed more than 100,000 acres of logging slash left behind by the axmen. The 1911 Weeks Act established the White Mountain National Forest with the stroke of a pen, creating the wooded and mountainous treasure we take for granted today.

North of the national forest, timber companies continued to dominate the economy and the culture. At the little city of Berlin, corporations produced more paper pulp and newsprint per annum than on any place on planet Earth, right up until the dawn of the Great Depression.

To this day, timbering is a major economic driver north of the White Mountain National Forest. But now, recreational interests are beginning to exert more pressure because, frankly, the traditional livelihoods of farming, sawmilling, and papermaking have been reduced by myriad global forces to a shadow of their former selves.

Today, in the winter months, snowmobiling is big business north of the White Mountains. All-terrain vehicle activity interests are now trying to replicate the vast tertiary transportation system that the snowmobilers created in the 1960s and '70s. In the '80s, the White Mountain National Forest managers opened the 20-mile Kilkenny Ridge Trail in the isolated northern Kilkenny region of the forest, to try to take hiking pressure off the Presidential and Franconia Ranges. More recently, the Northern Forest Canoe Trail promoters developed a long-haul paddling trail just beyond the northern edge of the Whites, and the fledgling Cohos Trail Association tied together a score of old trails, moose paths, logging skidder ruts, snowmobile trails, and striking but very remote features into a long-distance hiking trail that snakes out of the Whites and reaches the Canadian border.

Thirty years ago, this guidebook would have been impossible to write. The hiking infrastructure simply was not in place. Yes, there were service lanes to existing or abandoned fire towers on Deer Mountain, Mt. Magalloway, Signal Mountain, Dixville Peaks, Mill Mountain, Sugarloaf, Milan Hill, Mt.

Prospect, Cherry Mountain, and so on. But most of the scores of mountains in the far north simply had no hiking trails built to their summits, and scant information was available about how to get into the remote peaks. What access there was came in the form of deep-rutted logging skidder paths.

That is changing. New trails are being developed. Timber harvesting practices are changing, as well, as new generations of logging machines impact the land less severely and leave less slash behind.

Forest land owners and managers, once fiercely adamant about keeping hikers out of the woods, now recognize that everyone benefits greatly from multiple-use policies that embrace timbering and such traditional uses as hunting, fishing, hiking, and more recently, snowmobiling and wildlife watching.

Nowadays, logging interests, conservation organizations, and state and federal agencies—once strange bedfellows—have developed alliances and new land-use strategies that recognize that the timber companies had managed to keep vast tracts of land open and undeveloped. These timberlands are invaluable as sources of clean water for multitudes of citizens to the south, as carbon sinks to absorb the excesses of our manic fossil-fueled lifestyle, as flood control systems, and as stress relievers for people bottled up in the asphalt and concrete warrens of megalopolis.

Into these forests that the state of New Hampshire now markets as The Great North Woods, citizens of every stripe can now come. One does not have to wear spiked boots, or shoulder an ax or a chainsaw to enter this realm any longer. A fanny pack, a day pack, or a well-stocked backpack will do.

Now, a guidebook called 50 Hikes North of the White Mountains is possible.

Unknown Pond. The Horn

How to Use This Guidebook

The 50 hikes featured in this guide have been organized into a number of sections, such as the Jefferson Dome region or the Boundary Mountains, defined by related geological features and geography.

In Coos County north of the main body of the White Mountain National Forest, there are distinct differences in terrain. Close to the high peaks of the Presidential Range are a series of satellite mountain ranges, two of which harbor 4,000-foot summits. Far away to the north on the Canadian border, the forests are true boreal assemblages that mimic the cold woodlands of interior Canada.

Because of these differences geology and flora, it seemed logical to divide this guide accordingly. This arrangement simplifies the process of picking a trail to hike or feature to visit. It makes it possible to easily plan a trip to take in one, a few, or all of the trails within a given section.

CHOOSING YOUR TREK

How do you choose where to hike in territory you are unfamiliar with? Good question. To help you decide where to set down your hiking boots, review the following nine sections that represent allied and unique geographical environments. Each offers a host of novel features.

JEFFERSON DOME REGION

Hike on the very bottom of a vast glacial lake and explore one of the largest and most critical inland bird refuges in the Northeast.

THE KILKENNY

Tramp to two 4,000-footers and a remote rocky pinnacle known as The Horn. Stay overnight in a rustic summit cabin. Meander in the Devil's Hopyard, a cold ice canyon filled with rare plant communities. Repose beside a high-elevation glacial tarn, and meet Capt. Robert Rogers's 12-foot dog.

ANDROSCOGGIN FLOWAGE

The Crescent Range and the Mahoosucs share a watershed just to the north of the northern Presidential Range peaks and NH 2. The Crescent Range is crisscrossed with historic trails that lead to dramatic outlooks and to wild, wild Ice Gulch, one of the more challenging 5,000 feet of trail in the eastern United States. Not far away to the east rises Mt. Success, a splendid peak that harbors a great cliff face, a broad open summit, and a horror story.

NASH STREAM FOREST

Scramble about in an ecological rebound environment utterly destroyed by a dam breach in 1969. Test your mettle and eat blueberries galore on a literal killer of a mountain called North Percy Peak. Explore acres of high-mountain meadows, chill out at a remote mountaintop lean-to, or relax in a natural (if cold) Jacuzzi named for the devil himself.

DIXVILLE NOTCH

Stand on the edge of a 700-foot cliff, the loftiest near-vertical crag in the eastern United States. Take in waterfalls, a flume, a five-star world-class hotel, geological chaos, and half a dozen additional cliff faces, all within a few miles' radius.

CONNECTICUT RIVER HEADWATERS

Sample wild canyons, new summit trails, a working fire tower, vast lakes, and long vistas into Quebec, Vermont, and Maine. What more do you want? Other than, say, a rendezvous with one of the many moose that likes to hike the trails as much as humans do.

DEAD DIAMOND COUNTRY

Explore the backwater realm of the Magalloway River and tiptoe along the lengthy cliff ledge of Diamond Peaks, a mountain that glaciers literally tore in half. Or go seek out isolated waterfalls that, each year, once took the lives of loggers who tried to free up log jams caught in the cascades.

BOUNDARY MOUNTAINS

Root around where the Connecticut River gets it start. Take in thundering cataracts, trek a smugglers' route, amble along in the international border clearings to remote 3,000-footers, and test your bushwhacking skills on a historic but obliterated pathway.

THE COHOS TRAIL

When a day hike just is not enough, try your luck on the Northeast's newest long-distance trail, the Cohos Trail. Take a week or take two to test out this mountain thoroughfare, a pathway that now rivals the Appalachian Trail in length in New Hampshire, and Vermont's Long Trail, too.

Once you've selected a region to visit, read through the copy about each trail and make your selection. In some areas, it would be a simple matter to tick off two or even three hikes in a single day, as some are short and easy, whereas others are lengthy and, in some cases, strenuous.

JUST A WORD OF CAUTIONARY ADVICE

Before you set out for the wilds of New Hampshire north of the White Mountains, take a moment to consider what you are about to undertake. No journey is without risk. Knowing what the risks are allows you to prepare accordingly, so you are not thrust into an awkward situation, or worse, while in the backcountry.

Hikers in the White Mountain National Forest are usually never very far removed from other fellow humans tramping the scores of trails in the region. On any given trail in the summer and fall, it is customary to meet others engaged in the same activity. In the case of injury or other medical emergency or a wrong turn, help is usually not too far away.

That is not the case on many of the trails north of the White Mountains. Some pathways and features are very isolated; it is uncommon to meet others on the trails. Therefore, you have to be prepared for any eventuality. It is wise to hike with extra food and water, a warm coverall in the pack, a hat, gloves, and, at the very least, a rain poncho. A foil space blanket and a first-aid packet should be in the backpack. Carrying a waterproof bottle filled with matches could be a lifesaver.

In the unlikely event that you run into trouble enough to require aid, you may be forced to perform self-rescue. A broken leg or badly sprained ankle may require you to fashion a pole crutch from a stout branch. Knowing that, it may be wise to carry a small folding Fiskars saw so you can cut wood. A deep cut or puncture wound may require a tourniquet to staunch the flow of blood. Never fail to pack a long Ace bandage that can be used to stabilize a knee or ankle and can be used as a tourniquet.

While emergency situations are very rare

occurrences, they do happen every year, and the farther you are away from help in northernmost New Hampshire, the more likely it is you may have to resort to unusual or extreme measures to reach civilization.

Unfortunately, hypothermia is the most common problem that people experience in the far north. Coos County is not Boston or New York in terms of climate and ambient temperature. Some locations in the county can be 10 to 20 degrees Fahrenheit colder than along the Atlantic seaboard, particularly in the spring and fall.

Being prepared for chilly temperatures and cold rain and high winds even in summer is critical to enjoying your hike. If you become severely chilled, you'll begin to become disoriented. That's a recipe for disaster.

So plan well, plan ahead, and pack a warm set of clothes plus that hat and gloves and some sort of rain gear. Pack extra calories, too, and you should feel confident that you can handle most anything that the great Coos forests can throw at you.

Oh, and one last thing. Be sure not to rely on a cell phone. On the majority of trails featured in this tome, you will be far out of range of cell phone service.

GETTING TO COOS COUNTY

Lastly, it's not enough to want to hike in New Hampshire's great unknown; you have to get there by car, by river, by airplane, or by foot.

No interstate highways reach Coos County, but both I-93 and I-91 come fairly close. I-93 out of Boston reaches NH 3 north just above Franconia Notch and NH 116 at Littleton. The southern Coos line is less than 10 miles away, regardless of which exit you take.

I-91 reaches St. Johnsbury, Vermont, and US 2. US 2 swings east and reaches Lancaster, New Hampshire, within half an hour. I-91 also rendezvouses with I-93 south to

Littleton. So both interstates drop you fairly close to the southern tier of your destination.

Other avenues from Vermont and points west include VT 105 to North Stratford on the Connecticut River; or VT 114 along the border to the twin towns of Canaan, Vermont, and West Stewartstown, New Hampshire.

From Maine, westbounders can reach Coos County via US 302 out of Portland through Crawford Notch; US 2 to Gorham; NH 26 to Errol, Dixville Notch, and Colebrook; or even NH 16 out of the northern woodlands

Canadian trekkers can reach the northernmost border crossing at Pittsburg, below the tiny Eastern Townships village of Chartierville, by traveling QK 257. It becomes NH 3 on the U.S. side. Those who orbit around Montreal would be served by traveling south on QK 55 to the Rock Island–Derby Line crossing and picking up VT105 eastbound from the Newport area. Quebec City region residents might want to go southbound to the Coburn Gore border crossing south of Lac-Mégantic and roll onto US 27 to NH 16 westbound.

Those on the New Hampshire coast or the North Shore of greater Boston might want to motor north on NH 16 to North Conway and then swing into Coos County through Pinkham Notch, or split off on NH 302 through Crawford Notch and cross the county line into the town of Carroll.

NH 3 and NH 16 reach far into Coos County; the former runs the entire length of it. Just across the Connecticut River, on the Vermont side, lies VT 102. It reaches the border at Beecher Falls and is, by far, a more scenic drive than NH 3. Whenever I motor north along the Connecticut River, I take VT 102, which diverges from US 2 at the Rogers Rangers bridge just west of Lancaster. VT 102 has some hair-raising turns in it, but the views to the east into Coos

County over much of the length of the drive are delightful.

I was not being facetious when I wrote that you can come by boat. You can. The Northern Forest Canoe Trail crosses Coos County, utilizing the Connecticut River, the Upper Ammonoosuc River through the beautiful small village of Stark, and, after quite a portage, the Androscoggin River.

You can fly in, as well. Whitefield and Milan both boast a paved runway with instrumentation capability and lighting. Lancaster and Colebrook harbor grass strips, as does Errol and even the Second College Grant. Groveton keeps up a paved strip with no amenities.

You can hike into Coos County, too, either on the famed Appalachian Trail or the new county-long Cohos Trail. Each is nearly equal in length within New Hampshire and each is plenty challenging.

THE LAST WORD

After tramping all over the White Mountains and The Great North Woods for decades, I have become a devoted and vocal fan of the great forested terrain north of the Whites. By the time you experience a few of the hikes spelled out in this guidebook, I feel certain that the magic of this isolated realm will seep into your pores and invigorate your nervous system just as it has mine.

There are other hikes I could have added, but I stuck rigorously to within the borders of Coos County, with the exception of Vermont's Mt. Monadnock, which looks directly down on the trading community of Colebrook, just over on the Granite State side of the Connecticut River.

I could have added a few good bushwhacks I know, but the few finer ones that are in this book are either well marked or are no mystery at all to hike.

And I could have added a few more farm lane treks, but the one I chose to Weir Tree Farm simply can't be topped in the North Country.

So I leave you to your hiking boots and backpack. Don't take a White Mountain guide with you on this trip. Take this tome instead. Get out of your comfort zone. Get into some new and remote terrain. Slip into New Hampshire's far north above the Whites and "get lost," as I like to say. You may come out wild-eyed crazy about New Hampshire's great unknown, just as I am.

Now, what could be better than that, eh?

I. The Jefferson Dome

Owl's Head   JOHN COMPTON

"Jefferson Dome" is a geological term used here to encompass hikes in the Dartmouth Range and the critical wild habitat known as the Pondicherry Wildlife Refuge. The term denotes heavy crustal basement rock strata that provide the foundation for the remarkable features in the region, including the famed Presidential Range, and the Crescent, Pliny, Pilot, and Dartmouth Ranges, as well. At the heart of the Jefferson Dome terrain is a sprawling, dead-flat lowland that was once the basin of a vast glacial lake known as Lake Coos or Lake Israel, depending upon whom you talk to. That great lake drained away completely probably within one to two thousand years of the retreat of the continental ice sheet from the region, about 12,000 years ago.

When you come to hike in this region, particularly within the 6,000-plus-acre Pondicherry Wildlife Refuge, you are quite literally walking on the floor sediments of an extinct lake, a few shallow remnants of which are still with us.

1.

Owl's Head Trail and Martha's Mile

Location: Jefferson, NH

Distance: 2.2 miles to the Owl's Head ledges and 0.8 mile to Mt. Martha summit; about 7.5 miles if continuing to the Cherry Mountain Trail and backtracking NH 115 to your vehicle.

Difficulty: Moderate to strenuous

Trailhead: 44°21.35'50'N, 71°29'11.80'W

GETTING THERE

Roll north on NH 3 from Twin Mountain or south from Whitefield to the junction with NH 115. Turn east onto NH 115 and travel about 3 miles northeastward, passing over a broad height of land and then descending a long gradual hill until the trailhead parking lot of the Owl's Head Trail comes into view on the right. If traveling southwestward on NH 115 from US 2 between Jefferson and Randolph, pass the junction of NH 115A and travel one more mile until the highway begins to pitch upward at a long incline. Look for the Owl's Head Trail parking lot on the left.

The parking lot is fronted by a green place-name sign that explains the circumstances of the Cherry Mountain landslide of the late 1800s that killed one person. See that metal sign posted by the State of New Hampshire and you know you have landed in the right spot.

GETTING TO THE POINT

A storied footpath that began its life all at once in a torrent of sliding rock, mud, and forest debris, Owl's Head Trail is the child of tragedy. When the so-called Cherry Mountain Slide buried a farm at the foot of the Owl's Head peak in the 1880s and killed a farmhand, it left a distinct gash in the flank of the mountain, a depression that can be seen running the length of the mountain when the sun is low on the horizon. Beside that depression rises the wonderful Owl's Head Trail—a path well cared for by the Randolph Mountain Club—and makes for a

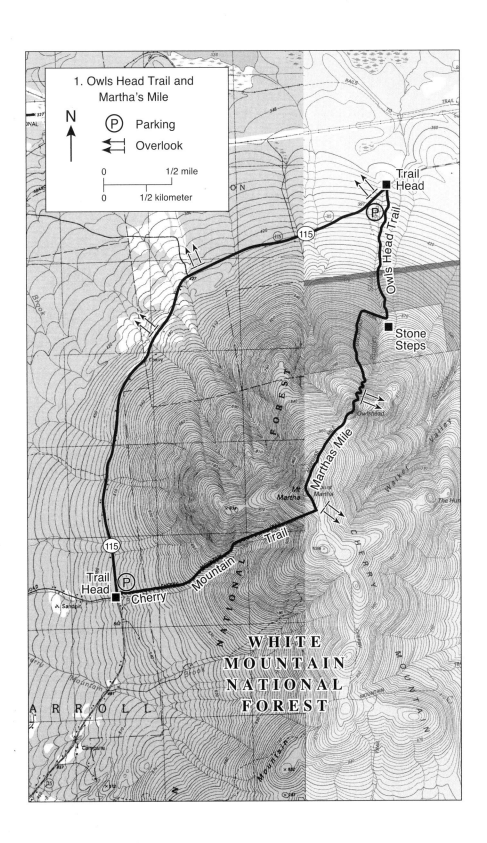

1. Owls Head Trail and
   Martha's Mile

N

Ⓟ Parking

Overlook

0 ——— 1/2 mile
0 ——— 1/2 kilometer

Trail Head

Owls Head Trail

Stone Steps

Marthas Mile

Mt Martha

Mountain   Trail

115

115

Trail Head

Cherry

Sandpit

WHITE
MOUNTAIN
NATIONAL
FOREST

ARROLL

Owl's Head super view   JOHN COMPTON

series of exposed summit ledges that face due east toward the towering west wall of the Presidential Range. The view is a show-stopper, one of the finest that can be had in the mountains.

The Owl's Head Trail and the short, high-elevation link to nearby Mt. Martha, called Martha's Mile, are the northernmost extensions of a through trail that runs up and over the entire ridge that supports the Owl's Head and Mt. Martha summits, elevated real estate known locally as Cherry Mountain. While the Cherry Mountain Trail swings up to the ridgeline from two points on either side of the mountain, the Owl's Head Trail and Martha's Mile reach the finest views. Both are true woods trails, whereas the long eastern arm of the Cherry Mountain Trail is an old jeep lane cut to reach the long-dismantled Cherry Mountain fire tower. All that remain today of the tower are four concrete pylons.

At the Owl's Head Trail parking lot, the path exits down a little slope and crosses a rivulet. In 2009, the trail was closed due to a landowner dispute. For the second time in a decade, the trail had to be rerouted. A suitable way was found, thanks to a concerned local property owner and to volunteers with the Randolph Mountain Club and the Cohos Trail Association. A 900-foot bypass was cut in short order in the fall of 2010 and the entire trail to the summit reopened.

The new stretch is a considerably better one than the older bypass, as it is dry underfoot all the way to its reconnection with the old route on the flank of the mountain. Strike off on gently rising terrain, running southwesterly to a point where the path turns south and begins to gain elevation. New blazing marks the way in mixed hardwood. The path intersects with the original trail, crosses a gully, and climbs a series of well-built stone stairs. Shortly, the trail crosses directly over a former logging road. Now the trail pitches up at a moderately steep angle and stays at that pitch for most of the remainder of the climb.

Rising quickly on trail that is a direct route up the mountain, you will be flanked by young growth filling in a decade-old logging cut on the right and by mature forest on the left. If you know what to look for, you may be able to make out the course of the Cherry Mountain Slide. In fact, the trail once crossed the route of the slide, but the Randolph Mountain Club sealed off the original pathway years ago because the soils were so unstable.

After a somewhat tedious and uneventful climb up the mountain's midsection, the trail reaches the site where it once crossed into the slide terrain. Now the path bends a hard right into a series of short switchbacks. In this area, the forest converts rather quickly from mixed hardwood to boreal species—spruce, fir, and yellow birch.

The few switchbacks make the going more interesting, but you will get through them in short order. The climb begins to moderate as the pointed, wooded summit nears. The path crosses directly over the true summit, but the real destination here is a series of bony ledges just ahead and to the left. The trees part, raw granite takes over underfoot, and a truly grand view opens to the east. Pace out onto the Owl's Head ledges to take in the sweeping vista.

Before you looms the entire western wall of the Presidential Range. With a little maneuvering, you can see far to the south along the serpentine spine of the Southern Presidentials to a pronounced gash in the terrain, that of Crawford Notch. But all you have to do to take in the real prize is have a seat on the rock and count the major Northern Presidential summits—Madison, Adams, Jefferson, Clay, Washington—dead ahead to the east. Seasoned trampers in the White Mountains can count off their favorite vistas on the fingers of two hands. The view from Owl's Head will be among the count, certainly.

The Owl's Head ledges are a fine spot to have a snack or lunch. I've camped here (note: no water nearby) in the past so that I could take in the sunrise over the Presidential Range. If you are curious about what the western horizon looks like, just walk a few paces west of the ledges and part the bows of the spruce and fir. With little effort you can look down on Cherry Pond and Little Cherry Pond in the Pondicherry Wildlife Refuge and discern the straight strip that is the Whitefield Regional Airport. In the distance, the Green Mountains make an appearance.

Many people who come this way take in the view from the ledges and then retreat down the mountain to the parking lot. But there is a rather easy $8/10$ mile of pathway yet to go, to reach the taller summit of Mt. Martha.

Martha's Mile is a delightful little thoroughfare that begins with a little drop and a jog off the very end of the ledges. Sit on your can, use your hands to lower your feet to the trail, and descend in a narrow passage between a rock outcropping and forest growth. Once you're beyond the rock, the way becomes a pleasant woods walk that descends a few hundred vertical feet to a col between the summits. At the bottom of the saddle, the forest is well stocked with yellow birch of some girth but modest height. This is a cold environment much of the year; trees grow slowly here and streamers of moss can get purchase on the branches and trunks. It is also dead quiet in the depression. With Owl's Head summit between you and NH 115 now, no traffic sound reaches the col.

Pull out of the saddle and begin a climb at a modest angle toward the summit of Mt. Martha. Just before the summit, a gap opens in the trees and the eastern view is reprised. In a minute, you'll reach a grassy clearing where four concrete pylons stand, poured and set to anchor the tall Cherry Mountain fire tower that stood here until it was dismantled in the 1980s.

South of the clearing, follow a herd path through a few spruce and fir to a scrubby opening where the southern horizon expands—the very reason to come this far. Now you can see unobstructedly far to the south to the Franconia Range, commanded by mile-high Mt. Lafayette and its 5,000-foot attendants, Lincoln and Haystack. For most trekkers' purposes, the hike ends here. Most day hikers who reach Mt. Martha's summit simply retrace their steps back to their car. But one more option is open to the intrepid soul.

If you don't mind another 4-plus miles of walking on woods trail and highway shoulder, the trek can be prolonged by using the highway to create a loop hike. If you think nothing of ticking off 10 miles in a day, then dodge south down the old fire tower access lane, a short spurt to the junction with the Cherry Mountain Trail, that path coming up from a parking lot in the valley to the west. Turn right, downhill, and begin a rather steep descent into the valley. Within an hour, the Cherry Mountain Trail reaches a parking lot situated on a knoll just above NH 115 and across the street from Lennon Road. Stride down to the highway and turn northeast, to the right.

Now the way back to your vehicle is a road walk, but it is a fine one because the vista to the west is expansive and a delight once you crest the highest point on the highway. The view stretches far northward up the Connecticut River Valley, as far as the town of Stratford, capped off by the massive summit of aptly named Goback Mountain.

Before your legs give out, you are back at the auto and every footfall has been on fresh terrain.

2.

Little Cherry Pond Trail

Location: Jefferson, NH

Distance: 5 miles

Difficulty: Easy

Trailhead: 44°21'32.49'N, 71°32'19.11'W

GETTING THERE

There are numerous ways to access the Pondicherry Wildlife Refuge, but for this hike into Little Cherry Pond, travel along NH 115, which links NH 3 on the south end at Twin Mountain to US 2 on the northeastern terminus in Jefferson Township. The trailhead parking lot is located on Airport Road, just to the southeast and across the road from a wood chip–fired biomass electric power plant. To locate Airport Road on the west side of NH 115, travel in either direction and reach the broad height of land on the highway, rising considerably closer to Twin Mountain and NH 3 than to US 2. Airport Road is just to the north of the highest point of elevation. If northeast bound, turn left off NH 115; if southbound, turn right.

On Airport Road now, travel downhill a long mile, running through stands of mixed hardwoods and softwoods on both sides of the lane. Watch on the right for an indistinct track that punches a short distance into a good-size parking area. Turn right, cross over a branch brook of the Johns River, and pull into the lot. A large, well-appointed sign kiosk stands at the head of the lot. If you miss the turn, the power plant will rear up within a few dozen yards.

A WILD PLACE UNSPOILED

At Pondicherry Wildlife Refuge, 100-acre Cherry Pond gets all the attention. But those who venture this way only to partake of the large shallow lake miss the refuge's smaller cousin, Little Cherry Pond, truly one of the wildest, least disturbed, and yet critical

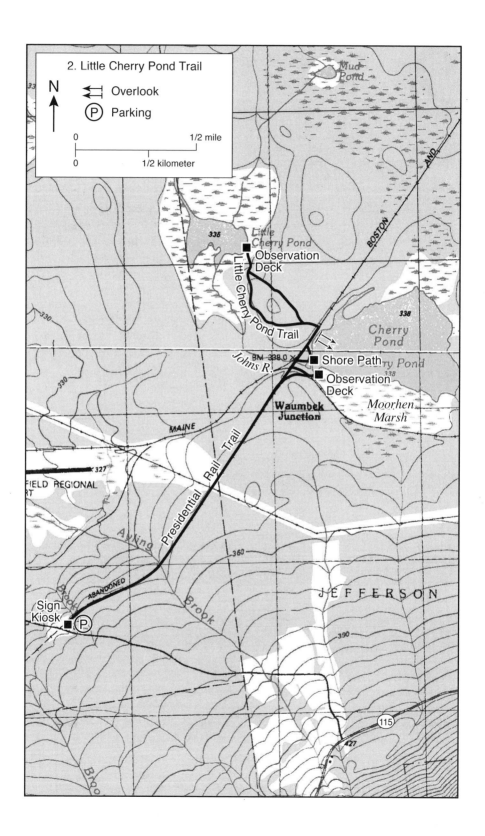

2. Little Cherry Pond Trail

N

⇇ Overlook

Ⓟ Parking

0   1/2 mile

0   1/2 kilometer

Mud Pond

Little Cherry Pond

Observation Deck

Little Cherry Pond Trail

BOSTON AND

335

330

330

Cherry Pond

338

BM 338.0

Johns R.

Shore Path

Observation Deck

338

Waumbek Junction

Moorhen Marsh

MAINE

327

Presidential Rail Trail

ABANDONED

FIELD REGIONAL RT

Ayling

Brook

360

JEFFERSON

Sign Kiosk

Ⓟ

Brook

Brook

390

115

427

wildlife habitats in all of New Hampshire. Several other hikes into the refuge are highlighted in this guidebook, each originating at different points. But don't fail to trek the Little Cherry Pond Trail to a primordial environment that seems like something out of the dawn of creation.

At the parking lot just off Airport Road, familiarize yourself with the copious amounts of information posted on the big sign kiosk established by the Silvio O. Conte National Fish and Wildlife Refuge division that has broad jurisdiction over wild lands the length of the Connecticut River Valley. The Pondicherry Wildlife Refuge, within that division, is one of the more exemplary wetland habitats for migrating and nesting birds, mammals large and small, and a few species of hearty reptiles and amphibians. Its 6,000-plus acres are also home to large stands of black spruce, some of them never cut, which can stand the bitter winter temperatures of this cold boreal sink and tolerate a bit of wet feet, as well.

Many dozens of acres surrounding the great ponds in the refuge are owned and protected by the Audubon Society of New Hampshire. The New Hampshire Fish and Game Department has a stake in the exceptional habitat, as well.

Twenty-five-acre Little Cherry Pond, like its much larger sister lake, is but a shallow remnant of what was once great Lake Israel, a glacial lake that inundated the region for perhaps several thousand years and was held in place by the Pliny, Crescent, Presidential, and Dartmouth Ranges on three sides and glacial ice and debris on its western edge. Lake Israel rose and fell repeatedly, its depth subject to the height of ice and rubble dams. The dams never failed catastrophically, so there is no carved canyon or scoured notch. Over millennia, water quietly drained away as simple erosion played its

hand. Once the waters of Lake Israel receded, the great valley that was left behind lay exceedingly flat in the mountainous landscape, a product of thousands of years of suspended sediments settling out of the water column and forming a remarkably uniform lake bottom. Although the ponds still remain, they are extremely shallow, barely dimples in the terrain.

Once you've read your fill at the sign kiosk, strike off northeastward on a wide and perfectly flat trail that was once a Maine Central Railroad mainline that supported steam locomotives pulling freight and passenger trains. The rail trail doubles as a snowmobile route in the winter. It affords excellent and dry footing for 1½ miles, even though it stretches through lands that are in places saturated with moisture. Dark spruce and fir predominate at first, but give way to a degree to deciduous trees and brush as the rail line rounds a bend and becomes arrow straight. You'll glimpse peaks of the Pliny and Crescent Ranges at a power-line right of way. East of the power line, the trail ever so gradually declines in elevation as it approaches Cherry Pond and the extensive wetlands that surround it.

You'll come to a trail junction. On the right, another wide path bends away and makes for the vicinity of the south shore of Cherry Pond. Just ⅒ mile to the right is a structure called the Tucker Richards viewing platform. The route toward Little Cherry Pond continues straight ahead, but the viewing platform is a must-see feature, as it affords excellent views across the 100-acre lake to three mountain ranges, including the summits of Madison, Adams, and Jefferson. Swing through the turn and the platform comes into view directly. A well-designed and expertly built structure, it can accommodate many people on a deck perched 7 feet above wetlands.

Cherry Pond spring

Leaving the platform, turn right and pick up a short woods path known as the Waumbek Link, going westward, taking care not to turn an ankle on old steel rails that were never pulled up and sold for scrap. In two minutes, you'll be at Waumbek Junction, where a number of different rail lines once crossed one another in the span of just a dozen yards.

At the junction, turn right, northeastward again, and immediately reach an active rail line and an old rail trestle over the headwater outlet of the Johns River. The bridge affords a nice view to the east, and a glimpse at beaver flowage to the west. Once across the span, look for the entrance to the Shore Path on the right. The Shore Path is a short jog east away from the tracks down toward the shore. The trail forms a triangle. At the peak of the triangle, a spur cuts away to the left and swings out to an overlook where the Johns River gets its start.

Keep the shoreline over your right shoulder and pace off the last yards of the Shore Path. It empties out beside a large stone supporting a bronze plaque that boasts that the vast wetland environment is a national natural landmark.

Walk a few yards along the tracks to the northeast, and a grand view opens over the Cherry Pond to the Presidential Range. There is no view quiet like it in the state that has the loftiest peaks in the Northeast. Close to the shoreline float mats of sphagnum and bog vegetation. Waterfowl patrol farther out in the lake. And above it all, 4,000 and 5,000 vertical feet into the clouds, looms the great serrated ridge that carries the highest summits anywhere in the eastern United States, save a few in the Great Smokies.

No one will complain if you tarry for quite a while, but there is a good deal more exploring to do. Walk the tracks until the view begins to recede a bit. Look for a turnout on the right that slips into the woods, rises a few feet onto a narrow berm, yet stays close to the shore. This trail is the Rampart Path, a curious raised footway that was formed by lake ice that bulldozed lake sediments and debris over thousands of years into a low, snaking wall of fill.

Stay with the Rampart Path for just a minute or two, until another trail junction appears. Drop down off the Rampart Path to the left into a little depression and rebound out to the railroad tracks. Cross the planks between the rails and stride into the woods. Now you are on a dedicated forest path whose sole goal is to reach Little Cherry Pond.

Stride westward through cool spruce and fir on a trail that soon divides into two separate corridors. On the way to Little Cherry Pond, swing left at an arrow sign at the first junction. Hike in level terrain for $3/10$ mile to the point where the separate paths rejoin just as the dry environment gives way for good to swamp. The long stretches of puncheon span are a must for moving across the wet terrain.

Before 600 feet of bog bridging was constructed into the bog lands, it was nearly impossible to approach Little Cherry Pond. But 3-inch double timbers spiked down to burly log rounds provide a fine thoroughfare through the bog that surrounds open water. Leave the dark canopy of the boreal forest, step onto the first set of planks, and pace out into a flood of sunlight. This light is made possible because trees have great difficulty getting established in the wet, and they topple over when their weight outstrips the ability of shallow roots to hold the trunks and crowns upright.

Scores of double sets of planks end at a small viewing platform at the edge of the pond. The bright watery expanse is framed by a distant shoreline bristling with dark spires of black spruce. Waterfowl cruise in no more than 3 feet of water. Canadian geese occasionally honk across the expanse.

The platform is the only stable footing anywhere around the circumference of the pond. You will be the only human presence, if you come alone. While bigger Cherry Pond boasts many vantage points and more foot traffic, Little Cherry Pond is isolated and seems as if from another time. Once prehistoric Lake Israel drained away thousands of years ago and vegetation got a footing in the land, Little Cherry Pond evolved into a lake that probably appears much today as it did in the deep past. Visiting this outpost seems much like time travel.

Upon leaving this netherworld, you need not retrace every step. On the way out, at the first trail junction, pull left onto the east leg of the divided trail, a route that boasts a string of bog bridges twice as long as those on the way in. The paths converge again in $1/3$ mile and reach the rail crossing a few minutes later. Before turning southwest and returning to your car, look northward along the tracks to the distant ridgeline that holds the summit of Mt. Waumbek. These days, the tracks are virtually never used and large mammals often use the right of way to move about. Over the years, I have watched black bears and moose go about their business in the distance, oblivious of the human presence.

3.

Presidential Rail Trail to Cherry Pond

Location: Pondicherry Wildlife Refuge, Jefferson, NH

Distance: About 4 miles round-trip from the trailhead parking lot to the Pondicherry Wildlife Refuge observation deck at 200-acre Cherry Pond

Difficulty: Easy; level virtually the entire way

Trailhead: 44°22'08.43'N, 71°28'27.38'W

GETTING THERE

If traveling north on NH 3 from Twin Mountain or south from Whitefield to the junction with NH 115, turn east onto NH 115 and drive for 5 minutes to the junction with NH 115A. Turn northwestward on NH 115A and descend 0.25 mile. Cross under a power line over the road and watch for an informal pullout on the left. To the west of the pullout is a bar gate that, when closed, blocks access to vehicles on the old and long-abandoned Boston and Maine Railroad line.

If traveling on US 2 eastbound from Lancaster, reach NH 115A on the right in the center of Jefferson Village. Turn right and descend into the valley. Cross the Israel River and pass a dairy farm, a cemetery, and a home that is a refurbished old railroad passenger car. With Owl's Head Mountain looming overhead, look for the pullout on the right a few hundred feet prior to where the power line crosses the highway.

If coming along US 2 westbound from Gorham and NH 16, pick up NH 115 southbound and drive several miles until NH 115A appears on the right. Turn northbound, pass under the power line, and look for the pullout on the left.

BIRD LAND

Have an affinity for our avian friends, the birds? Yes? You've come to the right place. Few inland wildlife enclaves anywhere along the northern tier of the United States boast more bird species sightings than Pondicherry Wildlife Refuge, a U.S. Fish and Wildlife Service conservation holding of over 6,000

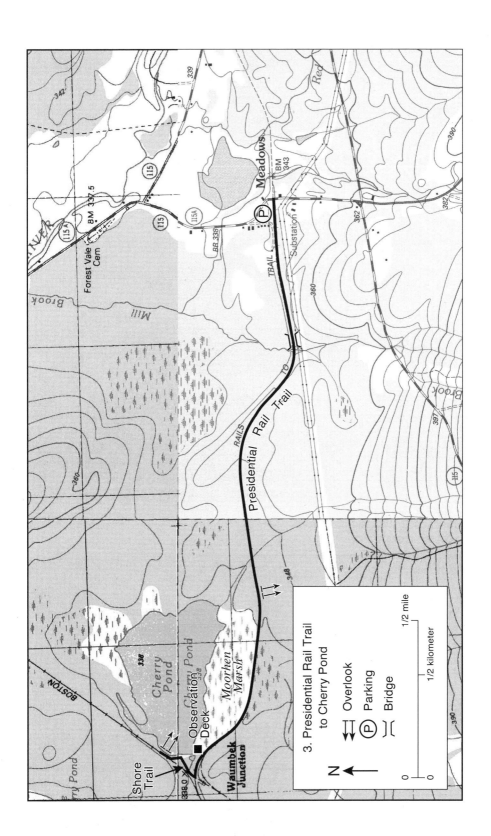

N

3. Presidential Rail Trail
to Cherry Pond

Overlook
Ⓟ Parking
)(Bridge

0   1/2 kilometer
0   1/2 mile

Cherry Pond

Observation Pond
Deck

Moorhen Marsh

Shore
Trail

Waumbek Junction

BOSTON

338

338.0

348

Presidential   Rail   Trail

RAILS

TO

TRAIL

Substation

Meadows

BM 343

BM 337.5

Forest Vale Cem

BR 338

115

115A

115

115A

115

Ⓟ

360

362

382

390

397

342

339

Red

Brook

Brook

Mill

115

RIVER

Cherry Pond viewing platform

acres that straddles a boundary between the communities of Jefferson and Whitefield, New Hampshire.

And while birdwatchers will take delight in the sheer number of different Aves, hikers will appreciate the setting, a vast low wetland sprawling under the 5,000-foot ramparts of the northern Presidential Range and the feminine form of the Dartmouth Range's Cherry Mountain massif. And they'll appreciate the level Boston and Maine rail-bed trail, known as the Presidential Rail Trail, because

it wanders through great marshes framed with distant mountain ranges.

Leave your vehicle within the wide pull-out next to NH 115A and strike westward on the dead-straight rail trail. Pass a bar gate and walk on perfectly level and fine footing into a tree-lined corridor that, during the winter, is a busy snowmobile trail. Pass a few residences on the right and then leave civilization behind for good.

Pace effortlessly along, making for a train trestle far in the distance. The railroad bridge was built high over Slide Brook, draining down from the slopes of Owl's Head peak. Once on the wide trestle, stop and take in the view both to the south and to the north. Southward, Owl's Head looms, its exceptionally pointy summit cutting a striking profile. On the other side of the bridge, the view is across a boggy lowland and out to the Pliny and Pilot Ranges, well off in the distance.

Leave the trestle behind and enter a long, lazy S-curve flanked by spruce and fir trees. At first bend to the right, go straight for a second, then swing to the left. As the curves lose their shape and the rail bed resumes its course westward, the route enters a broad marshland environment and runs dead straight for ½ mile. The railway path enters the first of two shallow expanses of flat water festooned with cattails and other water-loving plants. This is Moorhen Marsh, named for the not-so-common waterfowl that frequents the area and can often be seen, particularly if you think to bring binoculars.

The expansive marshes clear the view in all directions, and tall mountains stand at all points of the compass except due west. The Presidential Range fills up the eastern sky. Owl's Head and Mt. Martha wall off the south; and the Kilkenny Ranges, a lick of the Crescent Range, and even the Goback Range (informal), far away in Stratford Township, seal off the heavy Coos forests to the north.

No sooner does the first marsh narrow down to nothing than a second one materializes, doubling the pleasure afforded by being able to move freely through such a watery world courtesy of the old rail bed. The second marsh, too, peters out. Forest encroaches on the left but low bog plants and shrub continue to hold sway on the right because the footing off the track bed is far too wet and big Cherry Pond has begun to make an appearance through low growth.

The rail bed begins to bend slowly to the left, but a narrow path shows itself directly ahead, a trail named the Waumbek Link. Take that new route straight forward and find that old steel rails and buried rail ties are now underfoot. They had never been torn out. In a minute, a structure appears on the right. Leave the path now and stride out onto a wide catwalk to a broad deck with railings. This structure, erected by the U.S. Fish and Wildlife Service, is an observation deck of sizable dimension, perched on the southwestern corner of 200-acre Cherry Pond, a big oval but very shallow lake. It is really a tiny remnant of glacial Lake Coos, a once frightfully cold body of water that flooded many square miles of terrain here to a depth of as much as 100 feet, as late as 12,000 years ago.

The deck is the terminus point of your day-trip trek down the Presidential Rail Trail. If you are a serious birder, then you may know that more than one hundred species of Aves are carrying out their lives in the environment close by. In reality, over a 10-year span, more than 230 species have been identified in this place, including some extremely rare creatures.

If your intent was to hike all along, don't pass up the opportunity to see some of the many winged beings that inhabit Pondicherry Wildlife Refuge. Don't fail to bring binoculars. You will not only be rewarded if you do, but you will likely stay much longer in this unique and truly important wildlife reserve.

This hike is readily doable in all seasons. The rail bed is a well-groomed snowmobile trail in winter and supports hiking boots, snowshoes, and cross-country skis full well. In fact, winter is among the best seasons to approach Cherry Pond, because its vast frozen surface can be explored easily under the watchful eye of the Northeast's tallest mountain range on the eastern horizon.

4.

Colonel Whipple Trail and Ice Ramparts Trail

Location: Jefferson, NH

Distance: 6-mile loop hike

Difficulty: Easy

Trailhead: 44°23'38.52'N, 71°29'24.35'W

GETTING THERE

Locate NH 116, between Whitefield and Jefferson. Travel 3 miles southwest of Jefferson Village and watch for Whipple Road on the left. From Whitefield, drive 5 miles, cross a railroad track, and look to the right a little beyond the tracks for Whipple Road.

Travel eastbound for about 0.75 mile on Whipple Road. Watch on right for a minor turnout. There is a bar gate at the rear of the pullout. In the future, this may actually become a formal parking lot for a few cars. At this time, there is a grade stake with yellow paint on top at the pullout junction.

ICE BUILDS A TRAIL

The building of a trail is a hallmark of humankind. Or is it? Within the U.S. Fish and Wildlife Service's Pondicherry Wildlife Refuge snakes an unusual pathway atop a narrow and extremely uncommon geological feature that hugs the western marshy shore of 200-acre Cherry Pond. Known by the less than gracious moniker "ice push rampart," it provides the foundation for a fine trek in country that was, 12,000 years ago, the sediment-rich bottom of glacial Lake Coos.

The ice push rampart is reached via the Colonel Whipple Trail, a path originally laid out at the turn of the century by the Cohos Trail Association along logging skidways and game trails through low and sometimes wet country that had been repeatedly cut over. Pull off the south side of Whipple Road at a small parking spot about halfway along between NH 116 and NH 115A. At the head of the lot is a metal bar gate. Don your day

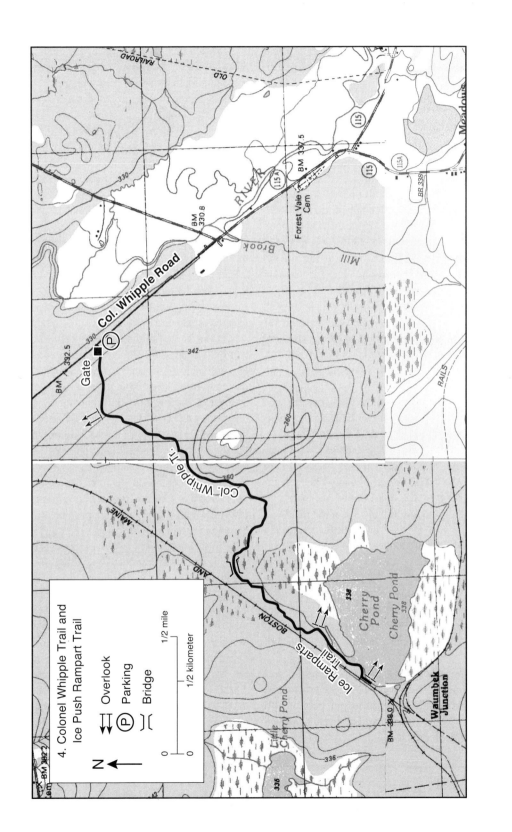

4. Colonel Whipple Trail and
Ice Push Rampart Trail

↓↓ Overlook
Ⓟ Parking
)(Bridge

N ←

0   1/2 mile
0   1/2 kilometer

pack, put on a cap or broad-brimmed hat, lather up with bug dope, and set off southwest by the gate on a loop trek that will bring you back to this point three or four hours hence.

Trek on a grassy, filled tote lane that last saw wheeled vehicles more than a decade ago. You'll be moving through small sunny openings and a narrow, rutted, dark tunnel surrounded by poor forest growth, until the trail bends due south on the edge of a clearing that was once a log yard. The trail rises very gradually in elevation to a low height of land, where it levels out and the terrain opens up considerably. Now the track is drier, more pleasant, and green underfoot. Because the growth is young and low in this region, it provides copious browse for moose and deer. Moose sightings are very common in this domain. I've caught a glimpse of two black bears in the openings over the years, as well.

Pass through another wide, old log yard opening and drift into a narrow track where granite stones project up through the soils, making the going a little rougher. Drop slowly a dozen vertical feet and then rebound to the top of a flat dome, what seems like the highest point on the trail. A view opens to blue Owl's Head and Mt. Martha in the distance, and a hint of the Franconia Range peaks shows through the tree line.

Watch for yellow paint and blaze stakes that point the way to a turn to the right, toward the southwest. Drop off the rounded knoll and enter a skidway path hemmed in by raspberry cane, which grows in profusion in patches that border the trail. Underfoot are the rotted and fragmented remains of branches stripped from trees logged and dragged through this area by giant motorized logging skidders that pulled out poor growth for the pulp industry and biomass electrical energy production.

Now the path seems more and more like a true foot trail. After the turn to the southwest, the route begins to meander, undulating back and forth through low forest growth that is often stunted in appearance because it is so heavily browsed year after year by moose. After a dozen turns, the trail reaches a branch stream slipping through moist terrain, crosses on a double log span, enters a dark and very tightly growing spruce grove, turns right, and begins to drift uphill. Cross a height of land in taller, healthier spruce, and drop quickly into a separate moist environment. Now the path becomes a trek on a long puncheon span of planks and hewn logs. Halfway along the bridging, the trail turns abruptly left and crosses chainsaw-cleaved logs.

On the far side of the span, the trail rises into dry terrain lined with mixed hardwoods and drifts toward the right of way of an abandoned railroad track, then turns away from it. Pass a narrow boundary line clearing flagged by a U.S. Fish and Wildlife Service boundary marker. The forest begins to lighten ahead as the path approaches the marshes lining the western shore of Cherry Pond. But rather than lead into wetlands, the path rises 5 or 6 vertical feet onto a very narrow little ridge and turns to parallel the marshes stretching away below.

After 20 or 30 feet, stop for a minute to examine what is at your feet. The ground you are standing on—the ice push rampart—is no more than a few feet wide but more than ¼ mile in length. All the way, on the path atop the rampart, you may stride half a dozen feet or more above the surrounding landscape.

How did such an odd feature come to be? It's a head scratcher. Perhaps it was created by man, for some odd reason? But humans had nothing to do with it. The ice push rampart was built by the lake to the east, Cherry Pond, when it was a bit deeper and

Winter, Cherry Pond

larger than it is today. Thousands of years ago, during the bitter winters a few millennia after the glaciers had retreated from New England, lake ice formed each autumn and expanded in all directions. The ice literally bulldozed the lake-bottom sediments to the west, moving out tons and tons of soil year after year to the very margins of the pond. Here, at the terminal point, the soils built up slowly, accumulating bit by bit until the lake ice created a narrow wall of sediment.

As the world warmed and the lake contracted in size and depth, the bulldozing process ended and the ice push rampart was left high and dry, fronted by marshes and expanses of very shallow open water. The marshlands are home to scores of species of birds. If you plan to come this way, arm yourself with a good pair of binoculars and a good birding guidebook. There are few places anywhere in the Northeast where so

many different avian species congregate.

The ice push rampart forms a natural trail and it's all yours to ramble on. As you go, you will have the northern Presidential Range peaks over your left shoulder and pointy Owl's Head ahead. Occasionally, Mt. Lafayette, towering within the Franconia Range, shows itself to the south.

About ¼ mile along the rampart, the trail splits. Turn 90 degrees to the right, drop off the rampart into a trough, then rebound out to a railroad line, its rails rusting to uselessness and railroad ties rotting away slowly.

At the rails, you'll be at a junction. Directly ahead is the trail to Little Cherry Pond. Rather than cross the tracks, turn left and pace beside them for 100 yards, until the forest gives way to a grand expanse of open water and sky. For two hundred years, people have made their way here by foot, on horseback, and even aboard trains to see one of the more spectacular vistas that can be had of the Northeast's tallest mountains.

Ten miles to the east, well beyond the full 200-acre dimension of Cherry Pond, stand Mounts Madison, Adams, Jefferson, Clay and Washington. No other body of water in the North Country provides such an unimpeded view of these massive peaks, mountains that, if dropped down on the mile-high plateau at Denver, would be perfectly at home in the Rockies.

The shallow lake huddled beneath the peaks is home to loons and their young in summer; moorhens, too. Ducks cruise at their ease. An osprey nest tower stands on the eastern shore and is occupied. Hawks and harriers circle and glide. Snipes whoop in the heavens, while bitterns and green herons haunt the reeds and rushes.

Take your load off at lakeside. This is a fine spot to have a snack or lunch in the company of the wild things.

When it's time to pack up and go, you may retrace your steps, or turn toward the north and follow the railroad tracks for 1 ½ miles through forest, flowage, and wetlands with the Pliny and Pilot Range peaks looming ahead until you reach the crossing at NH 116. Although a train hasn't been along these rails for years, and the line is deteriorating, the tracks are still designated as active.

If you decide to make the hike a loop trek, walking the tracks and reaching the highway, turn right (northeast) along NH 116 and, in a few hundred feet, take the first right turn onto Whipple Road. Walk the dirt lane less than ½ mile back to your car. You've completed an easy, nearly 5-mile loop trek without duplicating so much as a few dozen steps.

Three decades ago, when the speed limit along the tracks was 10 miles per hour because the rail bed was in such terrible condition but still in daily use, I once ran along with a haggard freight train, grabbed the ladder on the last car, climbed up, and took a ride down to the village of Whitefield a few miles away. I thoroughly enjoyed the ride away from Cherry Pond and I even fancy doing it again sometime. But the trains don't run anymore, and I'm not quite as foolish as I was then.

5.

Mud Pond Trail

Location: Jefferson, NH

Distance: A short, 10-minute trek to a rare boreal bog environment

Difficulty: Easy, on a handicapped-accessible path and well-built boardwalk; an excellent walk for families with small children

Trailhead: 44°23'44.15'N, 71°30'50.44'W

GETTING THERE

The trailhead of the Mud Pond Trail is located 300 feet east of NH 116, about 100 feet southwest of Hazelnut Drive. When traveling northeast from the NH 3 junction at Whitefield Village, travel about 4 miles to the Whitefield-Jefferson town line. Look for the trailhead entrance about 1 mile inward from the town line. In the woods by the road margin, watch for wildlife refuge signs featuring a flying waterfowl image. The trailhead lane will be on your right.

When traveling southwest from the junction of US 2 at Jefferson Village toward Whitefield, cross the old B&M railroad crossing a bit less than 3 miles from the junction. Cross the tracks and go another 0.25 mile. Hazelnut Drive will appear on the left. The trailhead is just beyond, also on the left. Pull in and drive 300 feet to a parking lot fronted by a large sign kiosk.

AN ANCIENT LANDSCAPE REVEALED

In my 30 years of exploring the environs that now make up the Pondicherry Wildlife Refuge straddling the town lines of Jefferson and Whitefield, not once did I find my way into a beautiful but lonely boreal bog with a common but unceremonious name: Mud Pond. Although the low wetland resided less than ½ mile from NH 116, there was no access and the approach was a nightmare of unstable fir and spruce stands with shallow roots growing in perpetually moist soils.

Recently, the U.S. Fish and Wildlife Service began work developing a 5-foot-wide path designed to allow access to Mud Pond

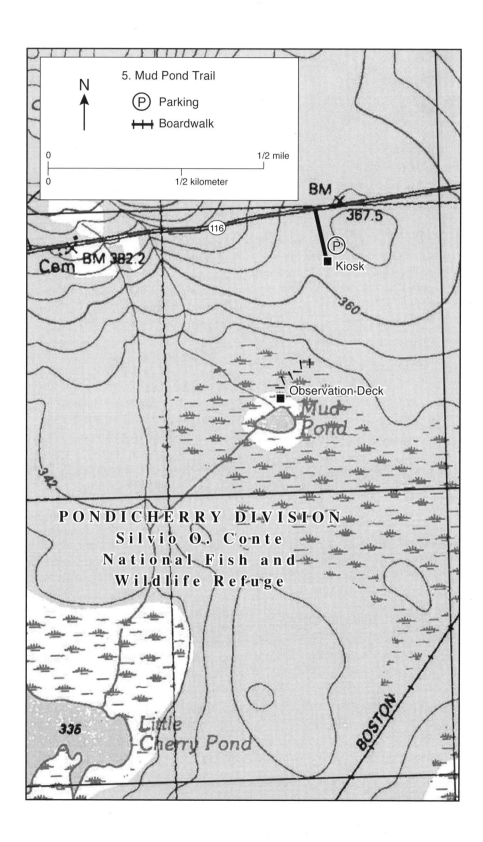

5. Mud Pond Trail

Ⓟ Parking

├┼┤ Boardwalk

N

0   1/2 mile

0   1/2 kilometer

BM

367.5

Ⓟ

Kiosk

360

Cem   BM 382.2

116

Observation Deck

Mud
Pond

342

PONDICHERRY DIVISION
Silvio O. Conte
National Fish and
Wildlife Refuge

BOSTON

336   Little
Cherry Pond

Boardwalk end

to all members to the public, including the handicapped. Today, after just two years of on-the-ground construction effort, the new Mud Pond Trail is open and boasts a set of physical features that are a delight to encounter.

The trailhead just off NH 116 begins at a large parking lot paved with crushed stone. A few steps east of the lot stands a large, multisided kiosk posted with copious information about the Silvio O. Conte National Fish and Wildlife Refuge, which stretches the length of the Connecticut River watershed from the Canadian border to Long Island Sound, about the Pondicherry Division refuge, and about the flora and fauna indigenous to the 5,662-acre protected lands.

Leave the kiosk eastward, striding on a pathway of tamped crushed gravel confined by narrow boards kept in place by 4x4-inch buried posts. The treadway is very stable, suitable enough to support battery-powered handicapped scooters and perhaps even wheelchairs.

The path runs fairly straight on level or very gently sloping ground for 1,000 feet, following to the left an old logging lane. The old road has been seeded in an effort to encourage native plants to gain a hold and soften the scar in the landscape. The path runs along the margin of mixed forest, when it bends left away from the old logging thoroughfare and swings into darker boreal forest growth.

As the trail swings left, it begins to drop gradually in elevation. The decline is of no concern to those on foot, but to anyone in a wheelchair or electric scooter, the descent is a major obstacle. The problem has been overcome by a series of graceful S-curves and four ingenious and abrupt 180-degree switchbacks with level staging points, where those aboard these personal vehicles can stop, reorient themselves, adjust their conveyances, and continue downhill.

Once through the maze of switchbacks, the path reaches dead-level moist terrain populated primarily by spruce and fir. The infirm soils presented an impediment to all manner of travel, but that hurtle has been overcome by the construction of a long and winding boardwalk complete with safety railings and pullouts, and even a bench or two.

Tramping along on the boardwalk is a pleasure, given that on all sides is spongy terrain pocked with downed logs and limbs at every turn. The design is organic, almost playful, the structure wriggling through the cool boreal thicket as if it was built for an amusement park. But it's all business.

The boardwalk jogs left suddenly and begins to make for a brightening horizon. The soils grow progressively moist. Trees become progressively anemic and give way to scrub shrub and sedges.

The boardwalk arcs gracefully one last time and ends at a 200-square-foot viewing platform fitted with benches near the shores of a shallow pond of maybe 5 acres. Surrounding the body of water is an extensive boreal bog many times larger in dimension than the pond. Sunlight pours into the opening, providing energy for a host of rare plants that grow in the nutrient-poor and acidic bog environment.

The observation deck offers birdwatchers an opportunity to stay out in a true boreal bog for an extended period. If you have brought binoculars, you may chance to see true boreal species, such as the black-backed woodpecker and the brown-capped chickadee, and a host of other birds, as they forage. Since records have been kept, 236 avian species have been identified as living in or migrating through the Pondicherry Wildlife Refuge, 131 of which are known to nest in the area's forests and wetlands.

When I visited, the bog shimmered blue and motley green in brilliant sunshine. Great white cumulus clouds loomed on the horizon. The air was almost hot, a rarity in these parts. In the stillness and the heat, the bog was silent except for the occasional buzz of a fly. Resident moose, deer, and black bears had settled down in some shady glade to quietly wait out the heat of midday. I had the bog to myself.

Although the hike in is a short one without challenges, I've been back several times so that I may get a good dose of true boreal wetland wilderness, an environment so different from what most citizens of the Northeast are accustomed to. The smell of fir and black spruce on a hot day is intoxicating. The dense growth is decidedly cool, even in the heat.

When in the region, put this little trail on your agenda, and mix it in with one or two other hikes. I can't imagine anyone being disappointed by the short jaunt out to Mud Pond.

II. The Kilkenny

Kilkenny moss

The White Mountain National Forest is not one contiguous mass of mountain terrain and cold stream drainages. It is actually divided into two separate entities. The main body encompasses all the great ranges and wilderness tracts that most are well familiar with, including the Presidential Range, the Franconia Range, the Carter-Moriahs, the Pemigewasset Wilderness, and so forth.

But there is another northern domain of wild country, one completely separate from the far bigger southern whole, walled off by US 2 and NH 115. This netherworld, known as The Kilkenny, comprises more than 100,000 acres of isolated wilderness that, until recently, received very little hiking traffic, except perhaps those seeking to climb the two 4,000-footers in the realm, Mt. Cabot and Mt. Waumbek.

This was nothing but logging country, until the great fires of 1903 burned over much of the region and left it badly scarred for decades. But the white birch reclaimed the land and other species eventually gained a foothold. Today, The Kilkenny is gaining in popularity as trekkers seek untrammeled places away from the crowds that congregate on the high peaks of the Presidentials and the Franconias.

6.

Starr King Trail to Mt. Waumbek and Beyond

Location:Jefferson, NH

Distance: 6.4 miles

Difficulty: Moderate to moderately steep in a few stretches

Trailhead: 44°25'13.14'N, 71°27'43.67'W

GETTING THERE

Just east of the small village of Jefferson on US 2, a post that bears a standard international hiking symbol stands on the north side of the highway at the head of a private drive. The lane intersects the road atop a little knoll 600 from the Jefferson Village Store. If traveling east from Lancaster, turn left onto the lane; if traveling west from Gorham, turn right. Swing uphill and stay to the left at all other drives you encounter. Pass a few large summer homes and reach the parking lot at the trailhead just a minute's drive north of the highway.

A MOUNTAIN OF FAME

Starr King: Now, that's a name. Not a Hollywood moniker, no; it once belonged to a Unitarian minister who left a substantial stamp on mountain histories on both sides of the continent. Anyone who is steeped in the history and lore of New England's mountains knows the name Thomas Starr King, author of the first major work about the great peaks of northern New Hampshire: *The White Hills.* Californians know the name, as well, so influential was he on the politics of that state in the years following the Civil War. And those who climb in Yosemite National Park may have climbed the fine double-domed peak named in his honor.

To the north, above the hamlet of Jefferson, stand two major Pliny Range twin peaks connected by a near-level, high-elevation ridge. Both are intimately linked in the minds of hikers, for rarely will trekkers climb one without summiting the other. Both Mt. Starr

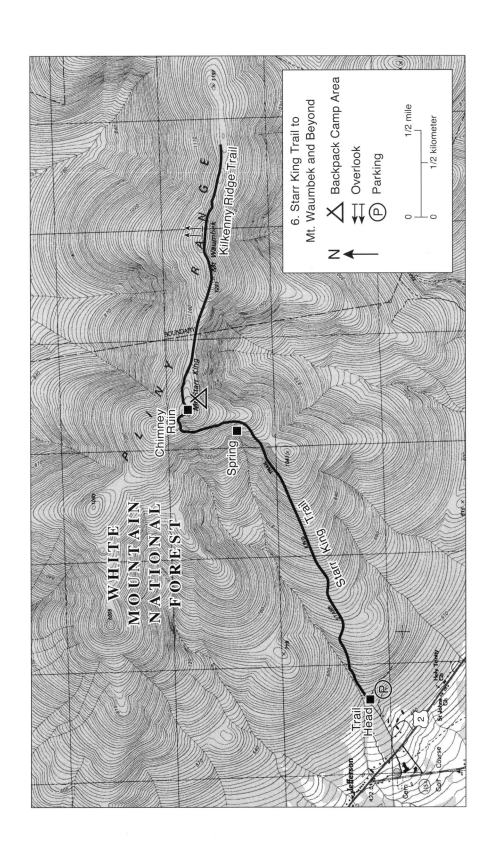

6. Starr King Trail to
Mt. Waumbek and Beyond

△ Backpack Camp Area
⇊ Overlook
Ⓟ Parking

0 _____ 1/2 mile
0 _____ 1/2 kilometer

N ←

WHITE
MOUNTAIN
NATIONAL
FOREST

P L I N Y

R A N G E

BOUNDARY

Mt. Waumbek

Kilkenny Ridge Trail

Mt. Starr King

Chimney Ruin

Spring

Starr King Trail

Trail Head

Ⓟ

Jefferson

Golf Course

2

Starr King chimney

King and Mt. Waumbek are chained together by the Starr King Trail, a fine pathway maintained by the venerable Randolph Mountain Club. Starr King, at a 3,913-foot elevation, is the lower of the two peaks, but really the more interesting of the two. Mt. Waumbek, at 4,005 feet and a short mile farther on, is a must-hike for those who wish to attain all the White Mountain summits over 4,000 feet in elevation. The shortest route by far to reach Mt. Waumbek's tall, stone-pile summit cairn is via the Starr King Trail.

The Starr King Trail has a long history that has its origins in the construction of the very large and fine Waumbek Hotel, undertaken in 1860 after Thomas Starr King persuaded wealthy summer visitors to the region that the grand vista of the Presidential Range to the east should be exploited by the development of a grand resort hotel. Starr King was right. The guests, he said, would come in great numbers. And they did. By the turn of the 20th century, a vast, rambling establishment had become the centerpiece of the community. One of the larger tourist hotels ever to be constructed in the mountains, it even boasted 11 "grand cottages" on the hills above. Six of these guest accommodations, now second homes, still stand. But the hotel is gone, much of it burning down in the twenties. The surviving annex was dismantled a generation ago.

With tall, wooded peaks hovering just north of the great hotel complex, access to the summits became a priority. Many mountains in the region already boasted bridle trails and others were being planned and cut. Although there are few references today to the original trail, it was first built to allow the passage of riders on horseback.

At the trailhead is ample parking for half a dozen vehicles. At the head of the lot, the trail moves uphill immediately on the shoulder of an old logging road, perhaps laid out atop the original bridle path. The trail climbs with the old way a short distance and then leaves it. A curious circular stone structure appears on the right, the sole evidence of horse traffic. The low stone edifice is a trough that held water piped in from a spring in the forests above. Horses were watered here before and after climbing the mountain.

Pass the large stone doughnut and the route becomes steeper, more stony, but rarely difficult. Much of the way, the path underfoot is in fine condition, well maintained by the Randolph Mountain Club. Whereas most trails in the region follow streams and cross numerous branch brooks, the Starr King Trail never does. It runs uphill on the apex of a wide ridge and all water sources save one get their start in the forests below.

The climb is pleasant in mixed hardwoods for nearly two-thirds of the way toward Mt. Waumbek. Pass through a large patch of blown-down trees that fell nearly a decade ago. Once you're beyond that point, the forest begins its customary shift to a birch and spruce woodlands. As the softwoods begin to dominate the growth, the trail passes just to the right and above a water source marked by a small sign. This spring is almost always reliable and the water is excellent. For those who are bound much farther north to the three Weeks peaks, Mt. Terrace, and Mt. Cabot, this spring provides the last reliable water for many miles. It is advisable to top off water bottles here.

The footpath now enters the domain of spruce and fir. The way is bonier underfoot and the softwoods tighten the way a little. The route becomes more steadily steep, but the push to the summit is never really taxing.

Most of the trek has been to the northeast. After the spring, the trail bends to the north and makes for the summit ridge. Approaching that ridge, the path suddenly veers east and reaches its highest elevation a short distance from the true summit. Walk on level footing to exposed ledges that provide good but somewhat restricted views to the south to the Franconia Range and easterly toward the Presidential Range.

You will not be alone here. Inevitably, the resident robbers will come pay you a call. Known as whiskey jacks to the regional residents, Canada jays often sweep in from all directions. Atop Starr King, hikers for many decades have been luring the rather tame birds to snatch a morsel of food either from the ground at their feet, from a hat brim, or from their fingertips. The jays have learned that humans are a meal ticket. They will not disappoint. They are actually quite brazen and will hang out with you as long as they think you might provide a free lunch.

Step down off a rock slab and enter an improbable grassy opening that was once a lawnlike environment. It once surrounded a large summit cabin that received visitors arriving by horseback. A crumbled chimney and a few foundation stones are all that remain of the building. People can't resist having their pictures taken beside it.

The trail to Mt. Waumbek runs alongside the chimney and leaves the grassy opening. To the right just beyond the clearing, a dozen unofficial tent sites hide in the trees, testifying to the popularity of this summit.

The trail now enters a wide and nearly level col between Mounts Starr King and Waumbek. Ferns carpet the forest, growing well beneath trees that are fairly evenly spaced, like a glade. The going is very pleasing. In high summer, the smell of the forest is a delight.

Descend ever so gradually to the lowest point in the ridge and then rebound more quickly on the west flank of Mt. Waumbek's unassuming summit. Gain perhaps less than 200 vertical feet and round out on a flat ridgeline with no distinct topknot. Walk on the level up to a 5-foot-tall cairn expertly compiled of small stones, which marks the very summit of Mt. Waumbek.

At the summit cairn, there are no views unless you paw your way through thick grow to the east (I don't recommend it). The summit seems quite disappointing, but most people who come this far make the mistake of turning around and heading back down without moving farther to the east along the long, level elevated ridge that is the hallmark of the mountain.

At the summit cairn, the Starr King Trail ends and the Kilkenny Ridge Trail, or KRT, begins. The new trail snakes more than 20 miles through the Pliny and Pilot and ranges all the way to the town of Stark near NH 110. Continue east into a remote realm where the Kilkenny Ridge Trail is the only game in town.

Cross a shallow knoll; soon a blowdown swath on the left will permit a good view to the north and northeast. The other 4,000-footer in the realm, Mt. Cabot, is clearly visible, as is its broad talus slope. The entire form of Mt. Terrace is in view, including the naked slide on its southeast flank. And the most easterly peak visible is a half–bowling ball: Mt. Weeks.

For those with a love of isolation and real solitude, breezy ridge running for several miles on near level terrain, and open, low canopy forests with hints of expansive views through blowdown patches, Mt. Waumbek is your Valhalla. You can have much of the mountain to yourself much of the day if you just move beyond that summit cairn. Waumbek's great lengthy eastern ridge is the real goal of the hike, but most trekkers assume the best is behind them at Mt. Starr King. Don't turn around; keep tramping eastbound for half an hour until the trail dips and takes a tight turn to the left. Call it quits there and then, and only then, make the long trek back to your car.

7.

Kilback–Unknown Ponds Loop

Location: Kilkenny, NH

Distance: 11-mile loop hike; 5 to 7 hours. Please note, the hatchery gate is often closed after 4 PM.

Difficulty: Moderate but steep in a few short stretches; moderately steep over 1 mile of the Kilkenny Ridge Trail

Trailhead: 44°30'24.87'N, 71°20'16.30'W

GETTING THERE

Travel on NH 110 between Berlin and Groveton. About 10 miles west of the small former paper mill city of Berlin, you'll reach York Pond Road on the left. Nearly 20 miles east of Groveton Village, watch for York Pond Road on the right. An international hiking sign is posted at the junction, as is a sign for the Berlin Fish Hatchery.

Swing downhill for nearly 4 miles on York Pond Road, until the buildings of the Berlin Fish Hatchery hove into view. There is a bridge over Cold Brook within the hatchery compound. A sign that directs hikers to either the Mill Brook Trail (right) or the Unknown Pond Trail and York Pond Trail (straight ahead) is posted just before the little bridge. Turn right; do not cross the bridge. Drive gradually uphill to several large buildings. To the left of the main building, stands a large trail sign kiosk. Pull up beside it and park.

LIQUID GEMS GLACIERS LEAVE BEHIND

At the trailhead parking spot beside the main building at the Berlin Fish Hatchery stands a solid sign kiosk. Read the broadsheets, then turn right, uphill, and walk on open lawn and gravel to a small water control structure at the head of a little man-made pond. Circle the pond to the right and pick up the trail head at the eastern bank. The path cuts uphill in to the forest on a gentle grade with good footing. The sound of rushing water from Cold Brook fills the air, and that pleasant background noise will stay with you for 2 miles.

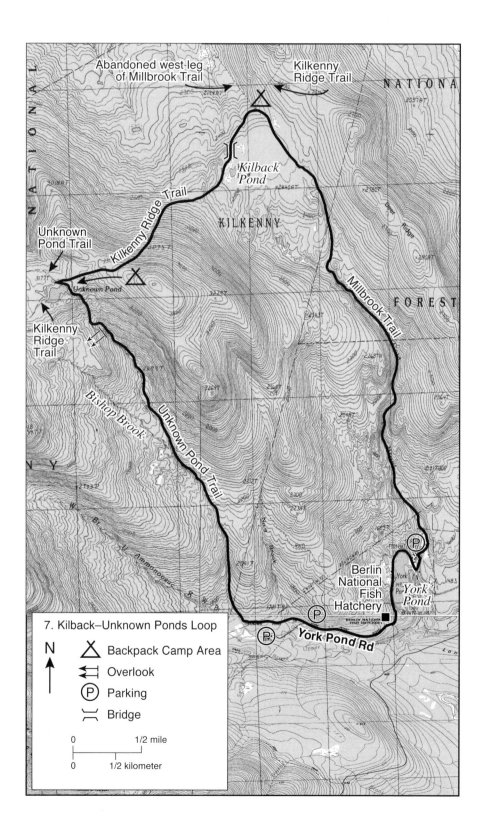

Abandoned west leg
of Millbrook Trail

Kilkenny
Ridge Trail

NATIONA

Kilkenny Ridge Trail

Kilback
Pond

KILKENNY

Unknown
Pond Trail

Unknown Pond

Millbrook Trail

FOREST

Kilkenny
Ridge
Trail

Bishop Brook

Unknown Pond Trail

Berlin
National
Fish
Hatchery

York
Pond

York Pond Rd

7. Kilback–Unknown Ponds Loop

N

△ Backpack Camp Area

⇄ Overlook

Ⓟ Parking

⊐⊏ Bridge

0   1/2 mile

0   1/2 kilometer

For a trail that sees little formal maintenance, most of the 3.6 miles of the path to the junction with the Kilkenny Ridge Trail are in quite good shape. Other trails in the area receive quite a bit more traffic and therefore more wear. Whereas the Unknown Pond Trail reaches the beautiful glacial tarn of the same name under the shadow of The Horn, and the Bunnell Notch Trail puts hikers on a direct route to 4,170-foot Mt. Cabot, the Mill Brook Trail ends at a lonesome junction $2\frac{1}{10}$ miles from Unknown Pond and $\frac{6}{10}$ mile from Rogers Ledge. Although many trampers use the Mill Brook Trail to reach Rogers Ledge, much traffic is siphoned off by the Kilkenny Ridge Trail, leaving from South Pond Recreation Area and deadheading south to the great cliff face.

But the Mill Brook Trail is a perfect first leg of an 11-mile loop hike that takes you to remote Kilback Pond, situated beneath the long and lofty Unknown Pond Ridge (informal name); traverses an extensive white birch glade where severe die-back is evident; swings beside renowned Unknown Pond with its excellent view of The Horn; and drops into a high-elevation meadow that offers a show-stopping view of the 5,000-foot summits of Mounts Madison, Adams, and Jefferson poking up high over the blue north wall of the Crescent Range.

Over the first mile of the Mill Brook Trail, ascend very gradually on fine surface through mixed hardwoods and infrequent softwoods. The trail is dry in this section; it crosses but one small rivulet but stays close to Cold Brook. There are virtually no turns in this section, as the route runs remarkably straight. Anyone can make good time here.

Things change abruptly after the first mile. The gently rising trail plateaus and flattens for about ½ mile. In this section and old logging cut, extremely slow regeneration, and moist soils have conspired to create a narrow, meadowlike environment where grasses are the predominant plant species. In dry weather, this section is not difficult. But during a wet summer, moving through this area can take some finessing if one is to emerge on the far side with dry boots.

Moist soils have become mud patches. In some locations, long-ago trail crews placed stepping stones to alleviate the problem and built a few puncheon spans that have deteriorated to remnants. There are not nearly enough stones to pave the way, so picking a route becomes a primary concern. Forward momentum slows considerably, yet still the trail runs straight toward a low ridge, the presence of which finally begins to exert itself.

The path pitches up out of the wet abruptly, rises moderately for a moment, then begins a gentle uphill glide once again. The way becomes a little rockier underfoot as elevation increases and birch trees begin to overtake the landscape. The birches are a by-product of severe fires that raked these Kilkenny peaks more than a century ago; they were among the first colonizers and grew in great beautiful glades. But these trees are in trouble now, as we shall see in dramatic fashion several more miles up the line.

The angle of the path increases again and mounts a shallow ridgeline, the first of two over the next mile. Easily overtake the first pitch, cross the height of land, and descend between the two ridges. A small stream crosses the trail, draining a pocket bog to the right.

Rebound out of the saddle on a little steeper terrain, but the going is never difficult. Cross the second height of land, quite a bit higher that the first, and level out. The trail flattens for ¼ mile, crossing a narrow seep at a badly rotting bog bridge that still offers enough footing to allow passage without your getting wet.

Birch Glade above Unknown Pond   WILL LEAVITT

The footway crosses the whole of the flat-top ridgeline and beings a gradual descent. Now for the first time, the trail swings to and fro as it defends toward the valley of Mill Brook, which drains toward Stark Township to the north.

The forest on the north side of the ridge changes to a fir and spruce woodlands. The way becomes darker as much less sunlight reaches the forest floor, and will fall gradually in elevation for ½ mile, when the trail suddenly ends at a T-junction. A decade ago, this junction was a crossroads, but the north leg of the Mill Brook Trail is now closed for good. Veteran trampers can still follow the old route north to Mill Brook Road several miles away, but few attempt the trek any longer.

At the junction with the 20-plus-mile Kilkenny Ridge Trail is a solid White Mountain National Forest sign. It signals that Rogers Ledge is ⁶⁄₁₀ mile away to the north (right) and the Rogers Ledge campsite is just a few minutes away in that direction as well. In the opposite direction, Unknown Pond reposes 2¹⁄₁₀ miles distant.

Strike left (southbound) at the junction with the Kilkenny Ridge Trail. Immediately, the route changes character. Climb a short, steep pitch fitted with deteriorating log steps. Cross a height of land and walk into a fairy-land fir forest. The limbless and smooth bark on the trucks of the trees creates an altogether uniform look. The canopy above is so dense that only a low carpet of bright yellow-green mosses grows among the trunks. The effect is almost joyous, something out of a children's book.

Beyond the fir grove, the horizon brightens and the trees give way to a shallow fen known as Kilback Pond, a lonely watery outpost tucked under Unknown Pond Ridge. A

The Kilkenny

series of two separate bog bridge clusters allows passage along the margins of this glacial sink and unimpeded views. The second set of puncheon spans were built on log cribs that have become waterlogged and have sunk into the muck of the pond. The saturated wood has pulled the walking surfaces below water at two points. At low water this doesn't pose a much of a problem, but during periods of high water, it may be easier to cross the divide by walking atop the beaver dam just 25 feet downstream.

Just beyond the pond, look to the north at one of several openings through the trees. A broad cliff face is visible 2 miles off. The craggy feature is Rogers Ledge, an outcropping that permits sweeping views of the whole northern half of the Kilkenny region.

Now the recent easy terrain gives way to tougher going. A few hundred yards south of Kilback Pond, scale a short but very steep pitch. Crest a knob, level out for a moment, then begin a 4,000-foot pull up the northwest flank off Unknown Pond Ridge, a moderately steep incline the entire way, for an elevation gain of about 800 feet.

On the way uphill, the forest is almost completely given over to white birch trees. Thirty years ago, this grove was magnificent, but no more. Although hundreds if not thousands of birches crowd the slopes, most are in advanced stages of decline. Many are dead. Hundreds have lost all their small branches in the crowns and are raining down chunks of main leaders that, during windy days, can be heard falling with a thud once in a while.

Climate change, industrial pollution stress, and old age are conspiring to remove the majestic trees from the environment. They are, to some extent, canaries in a coal mine up here. They tell a troubling story about what is in store in the future for the forests as we know them now.

The long pull out of the Kilback Pond basin ends on a plateau of almost perfectly level ground. Catch your breath. Let your legs swing easily for a few minutes and then begin a gradual descent of nearly ½ mile into the pocket of Unknown Pond. The downhill stretch ends at an elongated, complex junction, where trails branch in all directions and a side spur runs uphill to an organized campsite with a composting latrine.

At the junction, the Kilkenny Ridge Trail runs straight ahead intertwined for a minute with the Unknown Pond Trail's western leg. The eastern stretch of the Unknown Pond Trail, the third leg of this loop hike, cuts left abruptly along but above the eastern shore of the pond. A spur immediately off to the left runs uphill to the campsites. Opposite that spur is a path directly down to the water.

Drop down to the shore of Unknown Pond. The glacial tarn is a shallow body of water cradled in a saddle between elevations. The bowl was formed by a massive ice block remnant of the receding continental ice sheet. The ice mountain was left behind as the ice sheet retreated into Canada 12,000 years ago. That icy feral pup melted ever so slowly but depressed the terrain sufficiently to form the watery expanse we see today.

Unknown Pond is one of the more isolated bodies of water in New Hampshire. Although Mill Brook Road, in Stark, comes within 2 miles of it, that road is rarely traveled. Years ago, few people ever ventured into this domain. But the Kilkenny Ridge Trail changed that when it was built in the 1980s, and the explosive growth of hiking enthusiasm has brought fresh faces to the region, those looking for backcountry experiences where few people disturb the quiet.

Unknown Pond is a moose haunt. The creatures often move along the trails to browse and get a drink. In late summer and fall, moose often show up in the campsites,

Hikers on KRT   WILL LEAVITT

disturbing people in their slumber with the clomping of heavy, cloven hooves on the soils.

From the shore of the pond rises the majestic cone of The Horn. The peak stands 1,000 feet above the waters. Its shape is that of a classic Appalachian summit. It is a thing of beauty. Visitors can't resist photographing the scene.

At midsummer, water lilies and other aquatic plants thrive along the margins of the pond. In the fall, The Horn lights up with a coat of bright maple leaf red set against the black waters.

Leave Unknown Pond by taking the left turn (south) at the junction for a 3.3-mile trek to York Pond Road. Pass by and above the pond and its bog backwater. Begin a moderately steep decline through an open birch glade. Enter a domain of fern and low understory plants that now bask in full sunlight, as the birches above are just skeletons. The die-off has opened a sweeping view to the south and west. Over the right shoulder, the big cone of The Horn rises. Ahead, the purple north flanks of the Crescent Range at Randolph Township wall off the southern horizon. But high above the Crescent Range stand three blue unmistakable summits, the northernmost high peaks of the Presidential Range.

The open terrain, sunny south face, twisted birches, and lofty distant peaks conspire to create a majestic realm. After you've walked under forest canopy for three or four hours, the sun-filled break is most welcome and the vista a pleasure.

The rapid decline drops you out of the view in 10 minutes. Cross two branch streams flowing toward Bishop Brook. Soon the trail intersects the main stream and runs with it toward the valley, staying above the eastern bank for the first mile. The way moderates and assumes a modest but bonier pitch. The farther down, the more you'll encounter moisture. Several spots along the route are soupy and some care is necessary to bypass the worst of it.

The rocks in the pathway soon play out and the way becomes one of soils and sandy gravels. The pace picks up and you can cover now ground quickly. Below the first mile from the pond, the trail suddenly swings to the stream and crosses it in an area of good footing. The path stays with the far bank for ½ mile, crosses a fat freshet, and then swings back across Bishop Brook. This crossing is far trickier than the upper one because the rocks are rounded, covered with mosses, very slick, and in high water, difficult to gain a good foothold on.

Back on the eastern bank, the route becomes progressively flatter, and after a second mile, nearly levels into a woods walk on an excellent surface.

After running straight for a while, the trail swings into a wide bend to the left and runs atop fill that was deposited to create a level grade for a logging railroad. The path rides the shallow berm for maybe 5 minutes, rising no more than a dozen vertical feet in that time.

The route abruptly leaves the old rail bed to the right, masks a long, lazy S-curve, and pops out onto a gravel parking lot where a large sign kiosk stands. The lot is really a junction point for this and other trails in the region. An excellent map on the kiosk gives hikers a good idea what's in store for them in the region.

Walk out to York Pond Road. Turn left (northeast) and begin a 2-mile road walk back to the Berlin Fish Hatchery and your vehicle. The road trek would be dull if it were not for the hatchery complexes that line the route. Half a mile along, a large series of rectangular concrete trout-holding races nestles in the terrain. A walk up to it reveals thousands upon thousands of fish, all being reared for transport to New Hampshire's lakes and streams in the region.

Blue herons love this complex. Although netting keeps the birds from fishing at most points, they have exploited a few weak points in the deterrent system and sometimes get a free meal. Often, several of the big birds can be seen about the complex.

Farther along, round a large pond and enter the Berlin Fish Hatchery's main complex from the opposite direction from which you first arrived. Cross the little bridge and turn left back toward your vehicle. Inspect the fish-holding tanks along the way, a few filled to brimming with trout, as well.

Upon returning to your vehicle, you will have finished an 11-mile circuit without undergoing too much stress and strain. If you're in good condition and used to long overland treks, you can make the journey in a little under 5 hours. If you like to languish pondside and take a leisurely lunch, figure on 7 hours, provided you start your trek at 8 to 8:30 AM. The hatchery personnel close the gate to the facility at 4 PM. If you don't motor beyond the gate by the appointed closing time, you might spend the night in the backcountry of The Kilkenny.

Come to think of it, that's not such a bad fate.

8.

Bunnell Notch Trail and Mt. Cabot Trail to Mt. Cabot

Location: Kilkenny unincorporated township, NH

Distance: 5.1 miles from York Pond Road to Mt. Cabot Summit, one-way

Difficulty: Lengthy but moderate most of the way, with a few moderately steep pitches

Trailhead: 44°29'48.00'N, 71°21'29.98'W

GETTING THERE

Travel 10 miles west of Berlin, or some 15 miles east of Groveton, along NH 110 and turn south down York Pond Road toward the Berlin Fish Hatchery, 4 miles away in the valley below. Go through the hatchery complex and an access gate to trailheads a mile beyond. The gate is usually closed and locked at 4 PM, so time your exit accordingly.

A parking lot sits to the right just off the road and a few feet uphill. A sign kiosk stands at the head of the lot. If the lot is full, continue straight ahead a few hundred feet to where concrete fish sluices stand in the landscape. Park across the road, parallel to traffic. The trailhead to the Bunnell Notch Trail is across the lane from the concrete structures.

CLIMB 4,000 FEET FOR A ROOM WITH A VIEW

Reaching the summit of 4,170-foot Mt. Cabot and the old fire tower watchman's cabin ¼ mile south of the peak's highest point got a bit harder some years ago. Where once hikers could ascend the historic Mt. Cabot Trail from Lancaster, that route was lost due to paint-bucket vandalism and a landowner's reluctance to permit more people to cross his land. Now, trekkers must attempt the climb from a trailhead near the Berlin Fish Hatchery in the forested back acreage of the city of Berlin (pronounced *BURR-lyn*). The trek is a good deal longer than the original route, but who's complaining? A round-trip can still be accomplished in a day, or you can choose to stay overnight

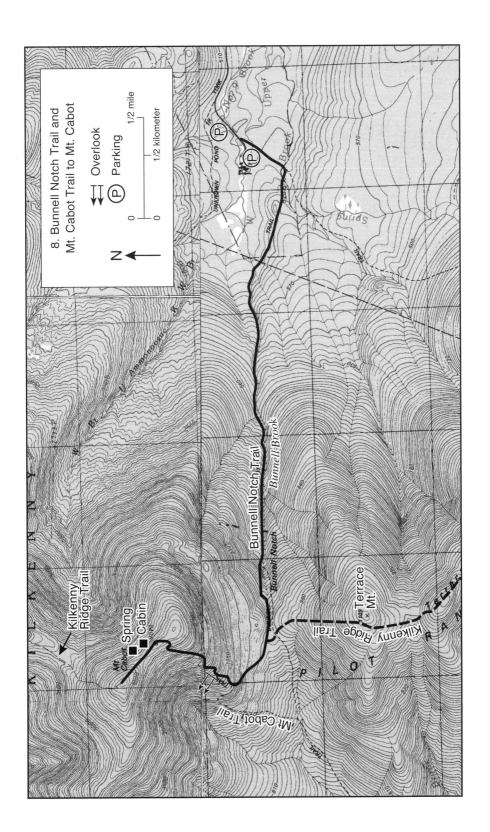

8. Bunnell Notch Trail and
Mt. Cabot Trail to Mt. Cabot

N

Overlook
Ⓟ Parking

0 _____ 1/2 mile
0 _____ 1/2 kilometer

K I L K E N N Y

Kilkenny Ridge Trail

Mt. Cabot
Spring Cabin

Mt. Cabot Trail

Bunnell Notch Trail

Bunnell Brook

Bunnell Notch

Kilkenny Ridge Trail

Terrace
Mt.

P I L O T   R A N G E

Upper Ammonoosuc R.

W. Br. U. Ammonoosuc R.

UNKNOWN POND

Upper Black Brook

Spring

Mt. Cabot Summit   JOHN COMPTON

in the small bunkroom of the old watchman's cabin, a structure managed by Forest Service personnel with the White Mountain National Forest.

Don your pack beside Berlin Fish Hatchery concrete water races in the company of hungry trout on York Pond Road, just south of the Unknown Pond Trail trailhead parking lot. Strike off down the York Pond Trail across the road from the fish races, trekking on perfectly level ground that was a logging lane years ago. Stay on the level in narrow grassy openings, swinging right at a Y-junction after 0.2 mile, where the unmaintained York Pond Trail breaks away. Cross several rivulets and Bunnell Brook at the bottom of shallow ravines. Half a mile into the trek, swing abruptly left, enter the tree line, and begin to climb out of the valley. Ascend a moderately steep grade at first, but the ter-

rain moderates quickly. The trail soon approaches Bunnell Brook and then follows the streambed westward for several miles, sometimes close to the bank, sometimes well above the tumbling water, but always within earshot of the stream.

The stream and the trail aim directly for a saddle between the three tree-covered humps of Mt. Terrace on the south and big-shouldered Mt. Cabot to the north, with its broad swaths of frost-fractured rock talus. The 2-mile push through the woods to the col is never difficult. The going is pleasant underfoot much of the way, but can be wet in spots during a wet summer. The once virtually abandoned route has been restored and is well trafficked now that the lower stretches of the Mt. Cabot Trail are no longer open to the public.

After an hour's ramble in the forest, the

Cabot cabin

day hiker, rather than trekkers' pushing farther uphill toward the summit. South facing, Bunnell Rock heats up comfortably warm in the summer sun and is blessed with a view filled up with the Franconia Range peaks 30 miles away. The vista is expansive and is most welcome after the long tramp through the forest below without a just reward.

Reluctantly, leave Bunnell Rock and ascend on a moderate and rather uniform pitch toward the summit cabin, passing an occasional patch of sunlight streaming into small pockets of treeless rock rubble. In this terrain, the intrepid souls among us bushwhack off the trail into the talus slope swaths on the more easterly side of the peak. It will take some effort to pick your way through the scree, but excellent views to the east, far into Maine, are exposed.

On the main trail, broad, elongated switchbacks make easy work of the elevation gain. The path eases its angle and swings by a recently built composting toilet and reaches a small, utilitarian cabin that has a certain backcountry charm all its own.

The cabin served as the living quarters for the watchman who spent his days in the cab of a steel fire tower that once stood just a few score feet uphill from the little building. The cabin still has a small porch. It is a pleasure to sit here on summer evenings, watching, if you are very quiet and still, the resident snowshoe hare grazing on the poor fixings growing about the place. The small main room holds a table with benches, a counter, and little more. It was the kitchen in its heyday. Photos of the former tower still grace the walls. Through the only interior doorway in the structure is a tiny bunkroom that sleeps eight, the bunks crowded side by side and two tiers high, outfitted with stiff, synthetic rubber mats.

Years ago, the cabin featured a woodstove and a rainwater catch, but they are

babble of the stream becomes a memory. The trail crosses a height of land, dips a minute, and sneaks up on the Kilkenny Ridge Trail, a little more than 2½ miles from the trailhead. The Kilkenny Ridge Trail was built in the 1980s over 20 miles of mountainous terrain from Jefferson to Stark. At the trail junction, move straight ahead, running now on the Kilkenny Ridge Trail. In a minute or two, pass the abandoned eastern miles of the Bunnell Notch Trail on the left. Fifteen minutes ahead, the Kilkenny Ridge Trail reaches the open upper portion of the Mt. Cabot Trail and merges with it. From here, they run as one to the summit.

The trek quickly becomes steeper and a bit rock strewn underfoot in places as the path bends in an arc toward the north. Break a little sweat in this section, but let the wind carry the moisture away at a granite perch that opens on the right, a favorite lunch break spot known as Bunnell Rock. When the Mt. Cabot Trail was still open to Lancaster, this stone haunt was the destination for many a

---

long gone. In reality, there is no water near the cabin and obtaining it takes some work. I'll explain how in a minute.

The Forest Service takes reservations and charges a fee to stay overnight at the cabin. Contact the Androscoggin Ranger District of the White Mountain National Forest at Gorham, New Hampshire, to book a date to stay on the mountain.

The cabin affords a view to the southwest and west, made possible by occasional clearing of young growth. Far below in the Connecticut River Valley reposes the built-up center of Lancaster, the shire town of Coos County. To the west, far in the distance, stand Green Mountain peaks west of St. Johnsbury, Vermont.

Drop your backpack, take a breather, then run off for the summit a little less than ¼ mile away. Just 50 feet north of the cabin, enter a little clearing where the fire tower once stood and take in the vista to the east of the Pliny Range humps, the northern Presidentials, and a portion of the Mahoosucs. To the west, more terrain in Vermont shows itself, more so than at the cabin.

Two-thirds of the way along to very top of the mountain, a small sign points the way to water. But getting to the elixir of life requires bushwhacking down, down, down a thousand feet of indistinct herd path in messy forest debris to a minor seep of water that doesn't shout its presence. You can miss it, unless the single red surveyor-tape flag is still in place to signal its existence.

Drift up an easy incline to the very broad and rather flat summit of Mt. Cabot, the tallest 4,000-footer north of the Whites. Through-hikers on the Kilkenny Ridge Trail often camp on the summit rather than at the cabin. Evidence of encampment is everywhere.

Many accounts indicate that there are no views from the summit. But storms blowing at hurricane force over it occasionally hammer down swaths of the stunted trees growing atop the mountain. Five years ago, an unobstructed view out to the Franconia Range and well south to Mt. Moosilauke opened, courtesy of tree fall. It takes years for new growth to fill in the forest at this altitude, so that view should remain open for some time, and others may materialize.

Everyone wants to reach the summit, of course. Most people turn about and retrace their steps back to their car, but I recommend staying at the watchman's cabin overnight, if nothing more to take in the mountain environment around you as the sun sets in the west over the Green Mountains. But there is another reason to stay put. Nearby, little more than 2 miles to the north, stands one of the great mountain summits of New England: The Horn. I'll leave The Horn for the next chapter. Best to return to the cabin for a pleasant evening and a welcome rest.

9.

Unknown Pond Trail to The Horn

Location: Stark, NH

Distance: 8.2 miles one way to the summit of The Horn

Difficulty: Moderate to moderately steep along the entire route

Trailhead: 44°33'14.19'N, 71°24'36.10'W

GETTING THERE

Travel north and locate NH 110. Travel 5 miles east from Groveton to the village of Stark. Or travel nearly 20 miles west from the little city of Berlin. Half a mile east of the tiny town center of Stark, Mill Mt. Road cuts south from the highway, where a universal hiking sign is displayed on a post. Drive along Mill Mt. Road high into the Pilot Range, until the lane dips into a shallow saddle and crosses a bridge over Mill Brook. Just beyond the bridge on the right is a pullout. Park there. The trailhead is back across the bridge on the opposite side of the lane.

THE "MUST-DO" SUMMIT

Most of the White Mountain National Forest is contained within a 600,000-acre contiguous mountain realm that most all trekkers in the East are familiar with. There is, however, a separate, smaller 150,000-acre package of mountainous real estate known as The Kilkenny that stretches north of NH 2 for 20 miles and terminates on the shoulder of NH 110. The Kilkenny harbors two mountain ranges, the Pliny and the Pilot, each of which boasts a 4,000-footer. But the unincorporated township also masks a real treasure, one of New England's exceptional summits, a peak that few people include in their playlist because it doesn't quite hit the 4,000-foot mark. That summit is The Horn. I include Thee Horn in my must-do list because it is the single best New Hampshire summit between the Presidential Range and the Canadian border. "There ain't no doubt about it!"

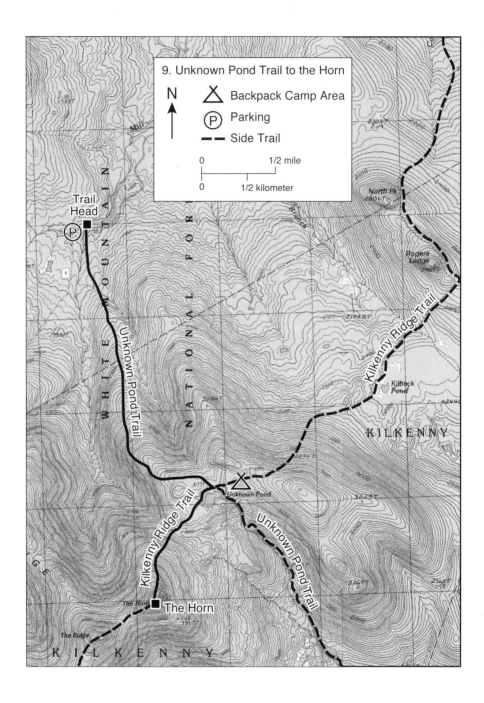

9. Unknown Pond Trail to the Horn

N

△ Backpack Camp Area

Ⓟ Parking

– – Side Trail

0   1/2 mile

0   1/2 kilometer

Trail
Head
Ⓟ

WHITE MOUNTAIN

NATIONAL FOR

Unknown Pond Trail

Kilkenny Ridge Trail

Kilback
Pond

North Pk

Rogers
Ledge

KILKENNY

Unknown Pond

Kilkenny Ridge Trail

Unknown Pond Trail

The Horn

The Bulge

KILKENNY

The Horn is a distinct pyramidal shape that rises out of a tall northern ridgeline that is anchored in the north flank of 4,170-foot Mt. Cabot. That high ground supports at its middle the viewless bowling-ball mound called The Bulge. The strikingly sharp form of The Horn terminates that ridge. Mt. Cabot and the Pliny Range peaks are very good at hiding The Horn from view from points south and east, so most people motoring into the North Country can't see it. Even those running NH 110 between Stark and Berlin can't readily get a glimpse of it. One has to cross the Upper Ammonoosuc River and travel along North Road in Stark before its lofty bell shape rolls into view.

The best and most interesting approach to The Horn, and by far the shortest, is along the western leg of the Unknown Pond Trail and a segment of the Kilkenny Ridge Trail. Midway along and at the junction of the two trails rests the exquisite cold glacial tarn that the Unknown Pond Trail takes its name from. From the shoreline of the Unknown Pond, visitors get an in-your-face look of The Horn as it towers over the placid but frigid waters of the lake.

Leave Mill Brook Road eastward and begin to climb in gently sloping terrain. Mill Brook runs below over the right shoulder. The forest is mixed hardwood to start, but soon the species mix dwindles down to white birch. Most of the trek uphill to Unknown Pond is a moderate push through a birch glade. The chalk white trunks vault up out of a carpet of dark green ferns. Such a limited palette of color is striking, a real pleasure to the senses. The squadron of birches stays with you much of the way. In fact, if you were to continue east on the Kilkenny Ridge Trail over the height of land and several miles out toward Rogers Ledge, the legions of white trees would march right along with you just about every foot of the

way; that is how extensive the birch grove is in the region.

Gradually the grade of the trail becomes steeper and remains at a uniform and moderate angle. As the elevation increases, Mill Brook falls farther and farther way in its tight ravine. At the height of land, the path crosses a little bony rim of rock and descends a few vertical feet to a sometimes moist passage.

On the level now, the trail reaches a junction on the right a little more than 2 miles from the parking spot. The Kilkenny Ridge Trail cuts away toward the south. The Unknown Pond Trail continues straight ahead, riding with the Kilkenny Ridge Trail for 300 feet or so in trees growing in the northern margins of the shoreline of Unknown Pond.

The route to The Horn is to the right at the junction. But for now, move east and spend some time at Unknown Pond. This is one of the larger high-elevation bodies of water in New England and its setting is splendid. Formed high in the mountains, when glaciers gouged out a shallow bowl and widened a bit by remnants of mammoth ice blocks left stranded in the mountains as the glaciers retreated, Unknown Pond is rarity. It is also shadowed by a major summit, the graceful steep-sided profile of The Horn.

Aquatic vegetation lines the shores in places. Tent camp sites dot some lengths of the north and east shores. Just beyond the pond to the east, the eastern leg of the Unknown Pond Trail slips right bound for York Pond Road more than a good 3 miles away. The Kilkenny Ridge Trail continues outbound bending northward. A few feet along stands a recently installed composting toilet. Make use of it if you must, for there is a bit of trekking left to do.

Once you've had your baptism at Unknown Pond, reverse direction and return to the first trail junction you encountered. Turn left now and swing around western edge of

Horn Trail sign   JOHN COMPTON

the lake, dropping out of sight of the water rather quickly and descending into a depression in the landscape and the lower flanks of The Horn. Cross a low moist area drained by a slowly moving rivulet and begin to climb off the ridge.

Once you're southbound on the Kilkenny Ridge Trail, the birch trees fast blend into a hardwood-softwood mix. The forest darkens as more spruce and fir come on as the elevation increases. There is a lot of vertical to climb, but the White Mountain National Forest trail planners who laid out the path and

the trailblazing crews who cut it ensured that the grade would never be steep or difficult.

The Kilkenny Ridge Trail gradually slabs the northwest flank of The Horn. Much of the way the treadway is forest duff underfoot. Occasionally, the path clambers on rock. The going is surprisingly easy, never tiresome, yet the elevation gain is impressive, nearly 1,000 feet.

An hour out of Unknown Pond, the trail crests the high north ridge that originates on Mt. Cabot's flank. The route flattens in a stand of stunted fir, the tops of the trees trimmed off 20 feet up each year by brutal winter winds howling over the exposed ridgeline. The second the trail levels a spur trail leaves left. This is the short link to the summit of The Horn. The Kilkenny Ridge Trail bends abruptly right bound for The Bulge.

Take the spur path on the left and run what's left of the ridge. Gradually ascend 500 feet on a well-defined trail into a nest of large boulders. The mountain's bony skull is at hand. Inch toward the east around the base of a huge hump of granite that thrusts up out of the timber and exposes a flat, naked cranium to the sun.

At first glance, there does not seem to be a way to climb up onto the stony fortress formation. Rounding the east wall of the rampart, a handy route up appears. A few long strides and a scramble and the summit is attained, and there is nothing but one or two small, scruffy spruce trees growing in the north edge of the ledge to block a 360-panoramic view of northern New Hampshire, Maine, Vermont, and Quebec.

I think of the view from The Horn as a primordial vista. Scan from horizon to horizon. What do you see made by man? Hardly a thing. What do you see carved by glacial ice sheet ice? Lots!

The Horn, if nothing else, is a learning tool. From its summit, you can get a good idea about the quirky habits of mile-high ice sheets and what the massive mantle of ice age ice did to the environment here more than 11,000 years ago. Look southward at the humpback of The Bulge and the dome of Mt. Cabot. Both exhibit plump-looking forms, well rounded and graceful. Look northward and things are very different. Below, a few miles away, is a raw wound in the landscape. It's the broad south-facing cliff of Rogers Ledge. Look up farther into the distance and there are more wounds in the mountains: the Devil's Slide at Stark Village, treeless ledges on the south flank of South Percy Peak and Bald Mountain, and great swaths of naked rock on North Percy Peak.

The Laurentide Ice Sheet that covered this region rounded off most of the summits in the region, leaving behind smooth, undulating mountain forms everywhere from horizon to horizon. But as the massive load of moving ice crested the tops of many a mountain, the crushing weight of the ice, unsupported on the southern flanks, caused the ice sheet to slump, and in so doing, the ice plucked rock off the south faces of the mountains. Repeated for millennia, this process sheered away whole sides of mountains. Indeed, some peaks visible from The Horn are, in reality, mountains cut in half.

To the southeast, over the high ridgeline of the Pliny Range, the saw-toothed peaks of the northern Presidential Range poke up into the sky. To the east and stretching far away to the northeast run the dozen summits of the Mahoosuc Range. In the north, almost all the acreage of the Great North Woods of northernmost New Hampshire (and there is a lot of it) is visible. To the west, the Pilots swing to the edge of the Connecticut River Valley, beyond which rear the Green Mountains of Vermont.

What makes this view so enchanting is that you have to really work to see any signs of human development, other than the occasional discolored patch in the forest that reveals where a recent logging cut had taken place. Think of it, there are very few places in New England where one can stand on a mountaintop and not see the thumbprint of humans. Such is the purview of The Horn.

10.

Rogers Ledge

Location: Kilkenny unincorporated township, NH

Distance: 8.2 miles round-trip

Difficulty: Easy to moderate

Trailhead: 44°35'48.26'N, 71°22'04.62'W

GETTING THERE

Take NH 110 that connects the community of Groveton on the west to the small city of Berlin in the east. From Groveton, travel eastbound through the village of Stark. Several miles beyond the little community, look for South Pond Road on the right. In the junction hangs a sign that denotes the federal recreational facility at South Pond.

From Berlin, motor eastbound. A dozen miles from the city pass the West Milan general store on the right. Continue another 3 miles and watch for South Pond Road on the left.

Drive uphill on South Pond Road until the lane levels out and then soon divides. At the junction, turn right and travel another mile to a park manager kiosk. Those who use the recreational facilities at the lakeside park must pay a parking fee. Those who utilize the Kilkenny Ridge Trail generally are not required to pay a fee, although that could be subject to change.

LAIR OF THE WORLD'S LARGEST CANINE

No one I know has ever met Capt. Robert Rogers's mammoth dog, who resides at his master's lair deep in the Kilkenny forest on the northern flank of the lofty Pilot Range. From his perch, Rogers's dog can survey for eternity one of New England's grand parcels of unpeopled real estate from a spacious and dramatic granite cliff ledge named for the reluctant hero of the French and Indian War.

At the parking area of South Pond federal recreation area, leave southbound along

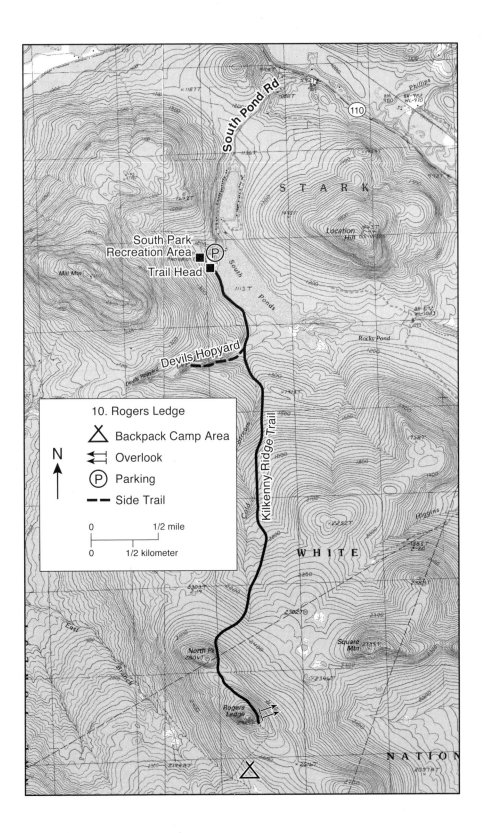

10. Rogers Ledge

△ Backpack Camp Area

⇄ Overlook

Ⓟ Parking

— — Side Trail

N

0   1/2 mile

0   1/2 kilometer

South Pond Rd.

110

S T A R K

Location
Hill

Phillips

South Park
Recreation Area

Ⓟ

Trail Head

Mill Mtn

South

Ponds

Rocky Pond

Devils Hopyard

Kilkenny Ridge Trail

Cold Stream

W H I T E

Higgins

Square
Mtn

North Pk

East

Branch

Rogers
Ledge

N A T I O N

the western shore of a beautiful body of water that, in summer, attracts local residents to its man-made sandy beach at the base of the parking lot. The path out of the little park—the 20-plus-mile Kilkenny Ridge Trail—is wheelchair accessible for a bit less than ¼ mile. It is perfectly flat and slips along a few feet above the water. Just beyond the last feet of the wheelchair path used to hang a swinging rope that I could never resist trying out, even with aging bones beneath my skin.

The trail becomes a pleasant woodlands footpath built upon the softened remains of old logging lanes that were, in turn, laid out on the backs of long-abandoned logging railroad corridors. Throughout its run southward to Rogers Ledge, it meanders though maturing hardwood forest.

Seven-tenths of a mile along, the trail branches. The Devil's Hopyard Trail turns away to the right (to learn more about this trail, see the next chapter) into a narrow gulch confined by vertical rock faces and clothed in rare plant communities. Cold Stream has been rolling largely unseen nearby, but it loops through the trail at two separate points. Cross the lower one on a bridge. The upper crossing requires a jog left. The bridge here is a phantom. It appears and disappears, depending on the whims of high water. At this writing, I have no idea if the bridge is in place or not. The last time I was through, there was no sign of a span anywhere.

Two and half miles into the trek, the trail swings off its southerly course, picks up a separate old and very indistinct logging route to the west, and then angles south once again and runs through forest glades and fern growing in perfectly level terrain. Half a mile farther along, a large pointed stake appears on the right, marking the a boundary between the town of Stark and the unincorporated place known as Kilkenny, or The Kilkenny, as the locals would say.

The wooden boundary pin heralds a coming change in the nature of the Kilkenny Ridge Trail. Much of the way, the march has been little more than a walk in the park. Level or undulating gently on an ever-so-gradual ascent toward higher county, the route begins to steepen as it mounts a ridgeline. For the first time, softwoods begin to muscle into the forest in greater numbers. Almost imperceptibly, the trail angles higher and higher over the course of a mile, until its pitch becomes moderately steep. No sooner does it begin to take some effort to climb, when the path turns sharply left and reaches its highest point, where the tree line narrows and sunlight streams into the forest. All about are stealth camping spots. This is a popular destination, by virtue of the multiple sites where people pitch their tents.

The Kilkenny Ridge Trail cuts east and follows the ridge a short distance, but the goal of this hike is right at hand. Leave the trail south through the last thread of trees and step out onto a granite shelf that straddles a much larger ledge a few feet below. Drop down onto the lower rock platform and stride out to the very edge of Rogers Ledge to take in the much-heralded panoramic view it affords from east to west.

It is not difficult to imagine, judging by the sweeping vista from the ledge, that the world before you could be untouched by human hands. One gets a sense that this country must have looked very much the same before settlers of European descent hacked their way into Coos County. Even the paper mill smokestack that stood out like a thin pencil line 15 miles to the east in the little city of Berlin is no longer visible. Dynamite charges leveled it once the mill closed and the infrastructure was sold for scrap.

The White Mountain National Forest boasts many a stirring view from the hundreds of peaks that populate its boundaries.

Rogers Ledge can takes its rightly place among the best of the best. But this ledge has one thing that virtually all the great vistas in the region does not, and that's the rock profile of Rogers's dog.

Don't laugh, for of the many stony profiles in the mountains that look like stern-faced forebears or Native Americans, elves, or imps, this rock visage is the best. Period! It is not terribly large, maybe only 10 feet long. And most hikers never see it, let alone know that it is right beneath their feet. But here is a faithful reproduction in natural stone of the immense head of a beagle or basset hound (whichever breed suits your fancy).

You must see it. Take a picture of it so you can share it on the web. For it is that good. To find it, you need only do a little work. Facing straight ahead into the view to the south, turn right (west) and walk to where the ledge narrows down to the woods line. Now you have to take a little risk. Bend out over the cliff edge (standing up, or better yet go down on all fours to be sure you maintain solid contact with the ledge) and look to your left right along the cliff face. Just under the ledge shelf, Rogers's dog's face hangs down at a steep angle firmly affixed to the granite out of which it was born.

When I discovered it, I couldn't recall ever hearing anything about it. I searched literature everywhere looking for a hint of the naturally carved canine, but I never uncovered a single word about it. As far as I know, I was the first person to ever photograph it and post it for mountain enthusiasts to see.

Enough of my egoistic rant; suffice it to say, Rogers Ledge and its stunning view are reason enough to trek 4 miles. The profile of Rogers's dog adds that little extra spice to the trip. And there is one more thing. Like so many south-facing cliffs and ledges in the mountains, Rogers Ledge's rocky skin heats up toasty warm in the summer sun. And like at some of the many other ledges I've visited in the afternoon, the warmth is inviting enough for you to stretch out and take a nap to refresh the soul for the return trip.

Because the way to and from Rogers Ledge ambles through such easy terrain, it takes no less time on the return trek to South Pond and the vehicle parked at the lot. If it has been hot during the day, top off your adventure with a dip at the beach at South Pond. I highly recommend it if the sweat has been running much of the day.

11.

Devil's Hopyard

Location: Stark, NH

Distance: 2.4 miles round-trip

Difficulty: Easy to reach, but tricky underfoot within the Hopyard

Trailhead: 44°35'48.26'N, 71°22'04.62'W

GETTING THERE

Locate NH 110 that links the small former paper mill community of Groveton on the west to the little city of Berlin in the east. From Groveton, travel eastbound through the village of Stark. Several miles beyond that little hamlet, with its picturesque covered bridge, look for South Pond Road on the right. In the junction hangs a large sign that denotes the federal recreational facility at South Pond.

From Berlin, motor eastbound. A dozen miles from the city, you'll pass the West Milan general store on the right. Continue for another 3 miles on NH 110 and watch for South Pond Road on the left.

Drive uphill on South Pond Road until the lane levels out and then soon divides. At the junction, turn right and travel another mile to a park manager kiosk. Those who use the recreational facilities at the lakeside park must pay a parking fee. Those who utilize the Kilkenny Ridge Trail generally are not required to pay a fee, although that could be subject to change.

AN OPEN WOUND IN THE MOUNTAINS

Sometimes in these old Appalachian chain peaks distinct, oddities hide within the folds of the mountains. Seeking them out is a pleasure because there are surprises in store. One such rare bit of real estate is the Devil's Hopyard, hidden away in the forests of Stark Township.

Sometimes mountains form imperfect unions. Most peaks transition smoothly from

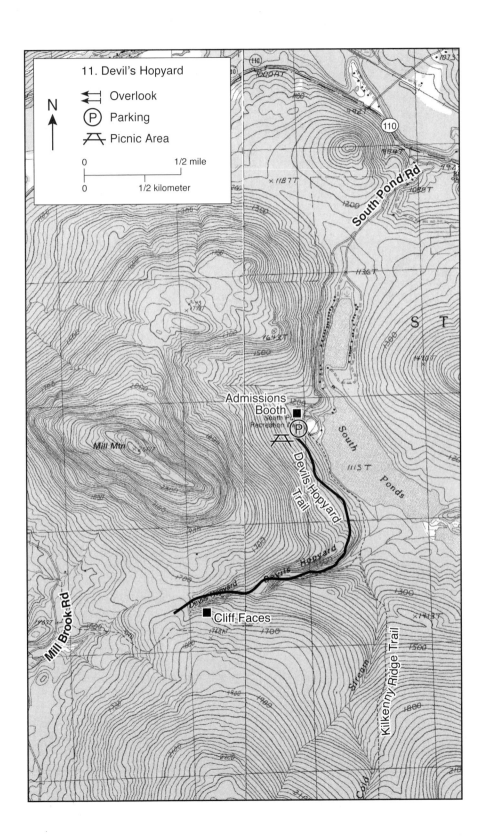

11. Devil's Hopyard

Devil's Hopyard   WILL LEAVITT

one elevation to another via a rounded saddle, but occasionally neighboring peaks don't get along and there is discord along the border. That seems to be the case at Devil's Hopyard, where Mill Mountain and an unnamed ridgeline don't match up well. Because of it, there is a deep and very narrow scar in the landscape that appears to be rent by seismic forces or grinding glacier ice, rather than by flowing water.

The Devil's Hopyard, therefore, is not a water-eroded canyon. Instead, it seems to be a ragged split in the earth, a geological anomaly, as if the creator saw fit to stab a knife down into the flesh of the mountains and leave a raw wound.

Regardless of its origins, the ragged gulch that is Devil's Hopyard is an easily attained destination, although you have to take care on the treadway because the path is lit-

tle more than a jumble of rocks that have fallen from the heights above over millennia.

Begin your trek at the parking lot at South Pond federal recreation area. You want to get going on the Kilkenny Ridge Trail that stretches from this point more than 20 miles to the 4006-foot summit of Mt. Waumbek, reluctant master of the Pliny Range. The Kilkenny Ridge Trail is off to the right, if you are facing the waters of South Pond. Turn your back on the structures in the park and pick up a wheelchair-accessible pathway that parallels the southwest shore of beautiful South Pond. Walk on a gravel-filled surface for about ¼ mile, until the trail becomes a woods-lined hiking path that was originally laid out down the middle of a long-abandoned logging track.

Trek ⁶⁄₁₀ mile to a trail junction. A sign indicates that the route to the Devil's Hopyard

The Kilkenny

is at hand. Turn right off the Kilkenny Ridge Trail and begin a short hike toward the Hopyard, always in the company of and crossing a small stream several times.

The trail rises ever so gently. Rounded hills begin to close in on both sides, and the terrain over each shoulder becomes increasingly steep.

Soon the world begins to exhibit a character something akin to haunting. Dimensions close off as the trail enters confined quarters between steep and even vertical surfaces. Direct sunlight is blocked by the tight terrain for all but an hour per day. Humidity rises. Moisture abounds and plants, mosses, and liverworts take full advantage of the wet. Beneath your feet, you may hear the sound of rushing water, but where is the stream? It's lost beneath a carpet of small boulders.

Here the air temperature drops considerably. Walk into the Devil's Hopyard on a hot day and find blessed relief from the heat within the walls of the gulch. Come in May and even June, and it is not at all unusual to find patches or even a carpet of crusty snow. In July, there may even be small clumps of hard ice wedged deeply beneath the rocks that pass for the trail.

The landscape in the Devil's Hopyard is often vertical, particularly on the left as you head westward deeper into the chasm. Cliffs, some 60 and 70 feet high, show their faces around bends in the route. The rocks below once resided high overhead. When the glaciers retreated from the region 11,000 years ago, fractured rock left behind fell off the heights and littered the floor of the Hopyard. Rocks have been falling ever since as winter gives way to spring each year in a three-month cycle of stone-breaking freeze-thaw, freeze-thaw.

The whole experience is not one of jagged rock and fractured stone. Organic material, too, has rained down off the cliffs and forests above and coated the rocks in forest duff. Although poor in nutrients, the light soils that have built up over millennia provide purchase for a host of very rare plants, some of which are only found sporadically in the northern Appalachians.

These plants build into elaborate caps of green in some places. Large boulders may exhibit living shingles of fungi and moss. Carpets of green stretch ahead and behind. The overall impression is that you have entered a northern temperate rainforest, something roughly like the Olympic rainforest of coastal Washington State. Only here, the atmosphere is decidedly colder.

Toward the rear of the formation, a bit less than ½ mile from the entrance to the Hopyard, round a bend under a sheer wall of rock. There is not a hint of transition zone between horizontal and vertical. The cliff rock bursts from the floor of the Hopyard at a 90-degree angle and soars above. I imagine this wall would be considerable challenge for free climbers who tackle such terrain without aid of safety rope and gear.

Unfortunately, the Devil's Hopyard ends too soon. Some who reach the back of the gulch clamber up the steep incline and bushwhack out rather than retrace their steps. Don't do that. Don't add to the erosion that is evident ahead and to the left. Turn around and head back from whence you came.

If, by chance, you have come into the Hopyard during a very wet summer or half a day after a heavy downpour, a small waterfall appears at the back of the formation. Water leaps over a ledge and crashes below, but you can't see the result. The terrain swallows all but a few feet of the falls. You can hear the loud tumult of water colliding with rock, but you can't witness it. The Devil's Hopyard keeps this waterfall all to itself, just as it does the stream that is always underfoot but unseen.

III. Androscoggin Flowage

Ice in Ice Gulch

The storied river of loggers and papermakers, the Androscoggin, receives copious runoff from ranges just north of the Presidentials, including the Crescent and the Mahoosuc. Both lengthy upland ridges with their taller peaks carry on their backs hiking trails aplenty.

Here we focus on three treks in the Crescent Range that reach some of the finer features. We have artificially limited hikes in the Mahoosucs to one trail fully in New Hampshire, rather than spilling over into Maine. But that one trek up Mt. Success is a dramatic one, with a finish that will raise the hair on your head.

These seemingly unrelated hikes do have one major factor in common. The terrain they wander in drains to a muscle-bound river that flows through the former paper towns of Berlin and Gorham.

12.

Mossy Glen

Location: Randolph, NH

Distance: 2 miles maximum, if traversing all routes in and around Mossy Glen

Difficulty: Easy

Trailhead: 44°22'34.81'N, 71°16'43.64'W

GETTING THERE

Mossy Glen is located on Durand Road, north of US 2 in Randolph. For this hike, Durand Road is accessed near the base of the long, steep grade on US 2 over the flank of Randolph Hill. If traveling west from Gorham and approaching the massive peaks of Mounts Madison and Adams, Durand Road is on the right, not far from the base of the western side of the hill. If traveling US 2 eastbound, look for Durand Road on the left in the flat as you approach that long uphill grade.

Once on Durand Road, you will come to a T-junction almost immediately. Turn left and drive about 1 mile, watching on the right for a white-painted Randolph Mountain Club sign that indicates Burnbrae Path.

A COOL DIVERSION

In the mountain community of Randolph, home to some of the most challenging trails in the White Mountains, residents and summer guests over two centuries created an intricate network of footpaths to all sorts of interesting points and features. Many of these trails were built to link the homes of residents and summer people alike so that folks could go on foot all over the town to visit one another. As a result, there are 100 miles of trails in the community and 30 miles of roads. What other community can boast such a pleasant fact?

A number of the trails in town find their way to the banks of Carlton Brook, a healthy stream that drains the western uplands of the Crescent Range. Before the brook empties into the Moose River at the bottom of the

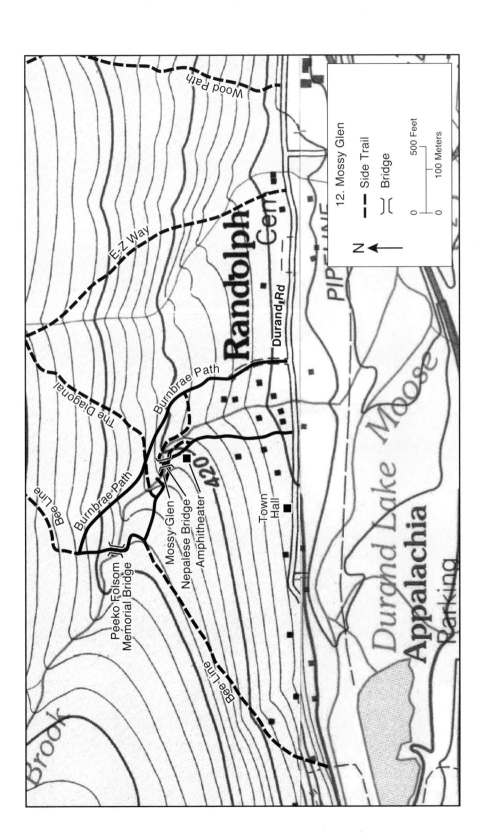

12. Mossy Glen

Side Trail

Bridge

N

500 Feet
100 Meters
0
0

Wood Path

E-Z Way

Randolph Cem

Durand Rd

The Diagonal

Burnbrae Path

Burnbrae Path

Bee Line

Burnbrae Path

Bee Line

420

Peeko Folsom
Memorial Bridge

Mossy Glen
Nepalese Bridge
Amphitheater

Town
Hall

Brook

PIPELINE

Durand Lake

Moose

Appalachia

Parking

Nepalese Bridge, Mossy Glen

valley, it passes through a ravine that seems like a grotto of sorts. The water pools, tumbles over small ledges to form falls, slides down tilted granite slabs, twists and turns, and provides high enough humidity at all times so that mosses and lichens grow in profusion. Hence the name Mossy Glen.

Once you see the Randolph Mountain Club sign on your right, stop before you reach it and park at the margin of Durand Road. Stride uphill on a gravel-filled driveway that reaches a small cluster of summer homes. Just as one of the homes comes into view, look for a trail that diverges uphill to the right. You are now on the Burnbrae Path proper, headed northwestward.

Immediately, the sound of the water greets your ears. Hike uphill on the high eastern slope above Carlton Brook to a junction with the Glenside Trail, a short footway that cuts left down toward the stream and into the base of Mossy Glen. For now, stay on the high side with the Burnbrae Path. In no time you'll reach a junction where the Diagonal Path cuts across Burnbrae. Again, stay with the Burnbrae Path and continue uphill, drawing nearer to the stream and then drifting away from it again.

One more junction appears. The Beeline, descending from Randolph Hill, makes for Carlton Brook. The Burnbrae Path ends at the junction. Turn left onto the Beeline and immediately descend toward the brook. A small, wooden stringer span, the Peeko Folsom Memorial Bridge, vaults Carlton Brook. The structure was named in memory of Phyllis Peek Folsom, a Randolph fixture, longtime Randolph Mountain Club member and descendent of one of the town's pioneer trail builders, W. H. Peek.

Below the bridge, the trail is never far from the stream. Things get interesting quickly. The pathway can be a bit moist and slick in the upper yardage. The Beeline now cuts away from the brook, and the path into the ravine goes by the name of Glenside; that is, I think it does. There are so many short link paths within Mossy Glen that I not positive I have the nomenclature correct.

Descend to a junction at a stream crossing, the Diagonal coming in from the left across the stream. Just below this point, the geology and the course of the stream create a pleasant ballet of rock and water. The water drops over a ledge and slips down a series of pitched slabs, rounding a crag in a graceful curve. Leave the trail in places and use some caution to get out on the slabs. Algae film on rocks can be a slippery as ice, so carefully pick only places that appear dry on which to plant your feet.

Carlton Brook steps, slips, and slides downhill through a modest gorge ringed with shady hemlocks and hardwoods. Even in hot weather, the confines are cool. Small pools intermingle with broad slabs of rock running with thin sheets of water that ensure high humidity.

Near the bottom of the ravine, a man-made feature appears. It's a bridge, but no ordinary trail bridge. This covered span has its origins a world away. The Nepalese Bridge, as it is called, is patterned after a structure in the mountainous Asian nation of Nepal. It is elegantly simple, made largely of natural, local materials, and has stood in this spot for 50 years without the aid of much maintenance.

Two Randolph summer residents in the 1960s came across a similar structure among Nepal's peaks, photographed it, and thought it might be a fine addition to the myriad pathways that crisscross the little White Mountains Township. A dozen people pooled their efforts and built a 40-foot version of the Nepalese span in what proved to be a most suitable setting.

The first thing you will observe when approaching from upstream is that the bridge stands well overhead, held aloft on its eastern side by a rock and concrete column. To reach the walkway on the bridge, climb a steep set of wooden stairs. Once you are up on the cross planks, the nature of the structure becomes apparent. It is built of just a handful of pine logs that hold up a steeply pitched roof of overlapping boards. The guardrail on each side is little more than long poles. The deck and superstructure above is held aloft by two steel I-beams.

Cross the bridge to ledges on the far side and immediately turn left and downhill to the stream. Turn right and enter a true, natural amphitheater with row upon row of seating carved into the slopes. To this day, the Randolph Mountain Club occasionally holds functions in this setting.

Leave the amphitheater and gorge through which Carlton Brook passes. Reach a grassy lane that drops downhill into the vicinity of several summer homes. Choose a driveway and descend to Durand Road. At the lane, turn left and walk a short distance to where you parked your vehicle.

Make the complete circuit of Mossy Glen in 45 minutes, or take your time enjoy in this little geological marvel. If you hike with young children or dogs, they'll find Mossy Glen very much to their liking. Short as it is, it is a nice little side hike that can be thrown in on a whim when hiking other trails in the area, particularly if the weather is a scorcher.

13.

The Ledge Trail Loop

Location: Randolph, NH

Distance: About a 3-mile loop hike

Difficulty: Moderate, steep in a few stretches

Trailhead: 44°22'27.78'N, 71°17'23.66'W

GETTING THERE

Motor along US 2 west of Gorham or east of Lancaster and Jefferson. From either direction, drive until the northern flanks of Mounts Madison and Adams tower high above the road. Continue until you see the only service station, Lowe's Garage and Cabins, at the foot of the mountains, but across US 2 north of the highway. Just to the west of the gas station, a road breaks north: Durand Road. Turn off the highway, where you'll immediately come to a T-junction. Turn right onto Durand Road and drive westbound for about 2 miles. Watch for two-tiered parking arrangement on the right, next to the road, that local residents use when visiting the town's recreational pond waterfront close by.

Across the road, look for a white-painted Randolph Mountain Club sign that announces Ledge Trail at the edge of a mowed clearing where a community sign marks the site of the former Ravine House, a famed summer guest hotel that once stood on the site.

SPYING ON GIANTS

The Crescent Range, as the late comedian Rodney Dangerfield often said, "can't get no respect." More than 2,000 vertical feet shorter than its dynamic neighbors, Mounts Adams and Madison, standing on the northern frontier of the Presidential Range, the peaks that make up a long, upland ridge that hems in the little community of Randolph will forever be in the shadow of giants. But a hiker can eavesdrop on what

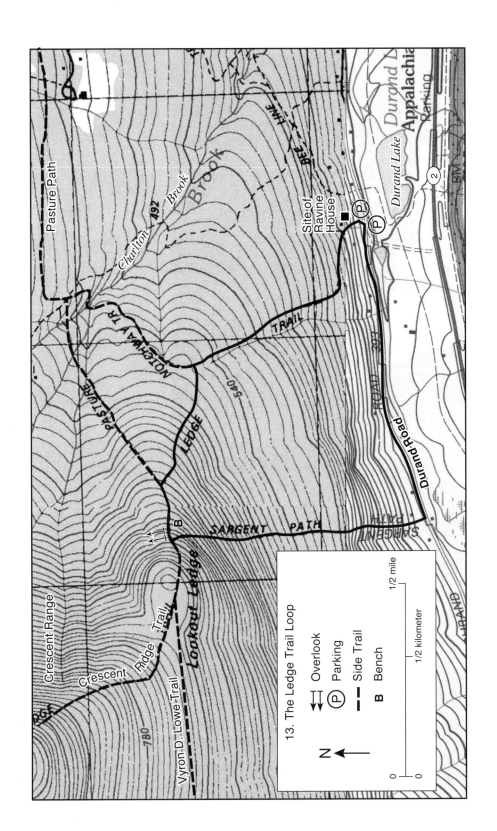

13. The Ledge Trail Loop

Overlook
Parking
Side Trail
B Bench

N

0   1/2 kilometer
0   1/2 mile

Randolph Valley

those leviathans are up to by trekking to Lookout Ledge midway up the south flank of Mt. Randolph.

Two driveways nearly merge across from the parking area on Durand Road. The Ledge Trail threads between the two, presents a single bog bridge span, and then climbs out of the valley quickly on a well-maintained pathway that sports a goodly share of exposed stones. Weather-worn orange blazes show in the trees. The route heads uphill at a moderately steep clip on a northwesterly course. The incline is steady but not taxing. The trail passes through maturing stands of hardwood trees and runs into a pinched gully and a trail junction ⁶⁄₁₀ mile from the road. Directly ahead, the Notchway leaves to the northeast to rendezvous with the Pasture

Path and the roads of Randolph Hill.

The Ledge Trail swings hard left and mounts a steep pitch on a wide but not terribly distinct track that was once a tote lane for logging. The path, now less stony underfoot, follows this remnant of the timber trade a short distance and then rises away from it. The degree of angle is more varied than below, but the elevation gain remains constant until the Pasture Path enters at an oblique angle from the right, a little more than a mile from the starting point.

West of the junction, the Ledge Trail becomes much steeper and rockier. Above the steepest section, the trail hugs the ridge as it slabs across its flank and the incline eases considerably. The track is framed by lots of spruce and fir, creating a dark passage until a ray of brilliant southern light strikes across the trail.

A log bench, a welcome bit of human engineering, appears at a spot known as the Eyrie. It rests above a steep drop that cleaves the forest apart a bit to admit the visage of 5,799-foot Mt. Adams in the distance. The view is restricted, but the reason for coming this way is a few hundred feet yet to the west.

Cross the height of land and begin a gradual descent just as the Crescent Ridge Trail diverges to the right. The Ledge Trail dips below the junction and immediately ends at a bald ledge of far greater dimension than that of the Eyrie. There's no bench here, but who needs it. The view is all that is necessary.

Outlook Ledge perches high above the Randolph Valley, with its twin strips, NH 2 and an old railroad line right of way. To the east, the vista expands to take in the southernmost peaks of the Mahoosuc Range and the northerly summits of the Carter-Moriah Range. The big Carter complex in that range is walled off from view by the whole of 5,366-foot Mt. Madison and its loftier neighbor.

Mt. Adams really commands attention, directly across the valley. It towers above Lookout Ledge as high as the valley is low. Front the cliff's vantage point, Mt. Adams flaunts its most striking feature: King Ravine. Hikers peer directly into the great gash in the mountain's north flank.

Time to throw off the daypack. Relax, eat and drink something, and enjoy the environment. No need to go anywhere all that fast.

Where the Ledge Trail ends, the Sargent Path begins. Climb back up to the head of the slab and turn left toward the west. Almost immediately, this new leg of the journey begins to lose altitude. The way also rounds a corner and heads almost due south.

The upper third of the nearly mile-long trail is quite steep and festooned with rocks that fell here in a slide millennia ago. The trail receives little formal maintenance. The blazing is worn and not easy to locate. Still, the course is not difficult to follow. The trail "suggests" itself on the higher slopes, follows an eroded wash for a while, picks up an ancient logging lane, and generally descends ever southward with few substantial swings right or left.

Because the Sargent Path is so direct, it deposits hikers out onto Durand Road in half the time it took to climb up the Ledge Trail to Lookout Ledge. Once at the road's margin, turn left and walk eastbound 3/4 mile, back to where your vehicle is parked. The trek along the road is uneventful, except Mt. Adams shows itself at openings in the trees and some beautiful summer homes are tucked into crannies here and there.

The loop hike is a good workout for the legs, for a morning or an afternoon. The trek leaves you time to pick up another hike for the day, if you'd like. Just don't hike it, as I did, when the air temperature at the edge of Durand Road was 90 degrees.

14.

Ice Gulch

Location: Randolph, NH

Distance: 6.5 miles

Difficulty: Moderate, steep in a few short stretches, and downright strenuous within the confines of the gulch

Trailhead: 44°23'19.50'N, 71°16'36.44'W

GETTING THERE

Pick up US 2 east or west to Randolph Hill, several miles west of the junction with NH 16 at Gorham. At the high height of land, with the northern Presidential Range peaks filling in the horizon to the southwest, look for Randolph Hill Road on the north side of the highway (right side if eastbound, left side if westbound). Turn uphill and travel 2 miles. The road through residential and summer homes bends left 90 degrees, then straightens out and runs a full mile arrow straight. Near the end of that mile, watch for a white-painted Randolph Mountain Club signs on the right. Ignore the first one, but when you see the second, turn off the road to the left and park in front of a rough-sawn board-sided single-story building with a metal roof. The sign states that you are at Boothman Spring Cutoff. Strap on your pack and cross the road where the sign is posted. A farm lane bordered by the occasional farm vehicle and outbuilding runs due north away from the road. You are on your way.

SUMMER HOURS ON ICE

The glaciers that once smothered every last acre of New England have not retreated entirely over the last 12,000 years. Not quite. Although you won't be able to stand on a mile-high, ice-age ice sheet these days, you can experience the depths of the cold that once gripped the northern latitudes in all seasons. Come to Ice Gulch for your dose of ancient frigidity.

This trek is a loop hike that ends with ½-mile road walk back to your vehicle. It

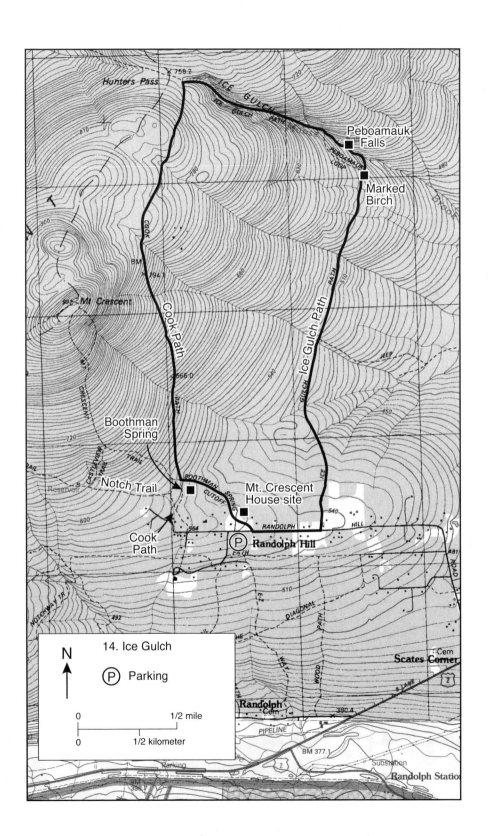

Peboamauk Falls

Marked Birch

Hunters Pass

Cook Path

Ice Gulch Path

Boothman Spring

Notch Trail

Cook Path

Mt. Crescent House site

Randolph Hill

Scates Corner

Randolph

Randolph Station

N

14. Ice Gulch

(P) Parking

0   1/2 mile

0   1/2 kilometer

encompasses three separate trails and a spur loop to a waterfall. But the main goal is a swing through one of the more challenging and geologically remarkable environments in all New Hampshire, if not New England.

Ice Gulch is a buried streambed that wrestles its way through a mile-long canyon framed by tall cliffs and crags. Since the retreat of the glaciers, those formations have been raining rocks into the very narrow gorge. Boulders large and small have been stacking up one upon the other for millennia, walling off the stream below and trapping winter cold in the depths, cold so strong and resistant to summer heat that ice remains tucked among the rock debris all year round.

When I last visited, late July temperatures were edging into the upper 80s on a cloudless day. Much of the rest of the nation was broiling; record heats were being set across the Midwest, South, and Southwest. The unaccustomed warmth of the North Country seemed ungodly hot in the forests of Randolph Township. All the more reason to trek into Ice Gulch.

That white-painted Randolph Mountain Club sign by the road points the track of the Boothman Spring Cutoff and to a junction with the Cook Path just beyond. Pace through the old farmstead to the occasional call of a rooster. The cutoff follows a farm lane a short distance, then scoots off it to the right, down a mowed path into the trees. Once under the canopy, the way becomes a woods trail and rises very gently to what was once an organized spring where good water could be had. Boothman Spring was once a picnic spot for guests who once frequented the Mt. Crescent House hotel that stood just a few feet to the east of the farmstead you passed through. The hotel is a distant memory now and no one cares for the spring, but

some stone refinements can still be seen.

Pass the large, flat slab of rock above the spring. You'll come to a junction with the lengthy Cook Path ½ mile from the road. Turn right, uphill. A vintage trail, the Cook Path rises on a due northerly course up the broad flank of the Crescent Range, the first elevations of consequence north of the Northern Presidential peaks of Madison and Adams. Boothman Spring Cutoff continues to the northwest a short stretch and ends at the Mt. Crescent Trail.

The Cook Path is all business. It serves one purpose, and that is to move hikers up the ridge to the head of Ice Gulch. Otherwise, there is little along the Cook Path to dwell on. It crosses three narrow brooks and three weed-filled logging tracks, climbing at a modest incline for nearly 2 miles when, upon crossing the last logging lane, it levels out just a bit below the height of land and runs through pleasant mixed forest that, in places, is plagued with wet ground. In a few sections, the trail has degraded to muck, and it takes a bit of ingenuity to sidestep the worst of it.

Nearing the vicinity of the head of Ice Gulch, the trail rises, dries out well, and then bends off its northerly course to an eastern heading. One last turn, and the bottom falls out of the trail and pitches at a very steep angle downhill. The Ice Gulch Path is at hand.

Unlike the stop at Boothman Spring, Ice Gulch is no picnic. The next mile is among the most difficult in the eastern United States, and that is not an exaggeration. Some hikers prefer to climb up through Ice Gulch to dampen down the effects of gravity. But most hikers choose to run the ravine downhill. Descending through the gulch, gravity is constantly needling you to miss a step or rely on a poor handhold. Make a mistake and it is easy enough to take a headlong tumble in this terrain. In fact, when I last

Ice Gulch pathway

the gulch or turn around. If hiking with children, choose a different venue.

The initial $\frac{1}{10}$ mile is the steepest portion of the entire trail. Clamor down at a sharp angle on boulders of manageable size, using your hands and even your rump to help in the descent. In the steepest section, approach the so-called Vestibule, a spring that never fails to bring forth water that is excellent to the taste.

The pitch continues and the way broadens a bit to accommodate larger and larger boulders, some of them the dimensions of a small room. Within the first few minutes, the view ahead and to the left reveals a towering, unbroken, and near-vertical escarpment. The wall to the right is largely masked by thick evergreen growth, so it is a bit more difficult to gauge its height and sheerness. But make no mistake, both sides of the gorge have contributed mightily to the rock maze you are now laboring to pick your way through.

Very gradually, the route becomes less and less steep but not less challenging. The bigger boulders make choosing a safe route more difficult. On a few rock faces, it is tough to find an adequate handhold. On two or three occasions, you may have to turn belly down to descend. Constantly, both hands and feet will need to be employed. On a warm day, it is very easy to work up a sweat sufficient to soak through a shirt.

But in more than a few places along the way, heat ceases to be a concern. Periodically, you'll enter refreshing pockets of cold air, as if the environment is air conditioned. It is, actually. Below your feet, small reservoirs of winter ice remain, sometimes hidden from view, sometimes readily witnessed. In several spots it's possible to crawl down into narrow rock confines for a full dose of winter chill.

Halfway through the gorge, the way levels out, but the boulder minefield soldiers on.

climbed the Cook Path toward Ice Gulch, I met a seasoned hiker whose leg was encrusted with blood from just below his kneecap to his sock. On the way uphill through the gorge he had lost his footing and had fallen. Nothing broken, he continued on.

His misfortune illuminates the need for extreme caution. Hikers must take their time in Ice Gulch and very carefully pick their route. Fading orange blazes help a little, but only a little. Once committed to the trek through the ravine, there are only two ways to go. The cliffs and very steep slopes on either side make it virtually impossible to climb out, so you have to either trek the entire mile through

Cross over a small rise in the terrain and the downward pitch resumes. Three-quarters of the way along, the country takes on a different look. It appears that sometime after the glaciers retreated from the area, the left palisade must have collapsed all at once. The path becomes a march along the lower edge of either a talus slope or the remains of a major rock slide that took down all the crags at once along a ¼-mile stretch. The boulders are smaller here and more uniform in size. Because of it, the going gets easier and it's possible now to make better time descending.

As the slide field dwindles down to the last rock stragglers, the lost stream appears and the terrain reverts to a forest glade. Pass a small spring, known as Fairy Spring, on the right and follow the stream bank downhill. Just under a mile from the head of the gulch, you'll reach a trail junction. The Ice Gulch Path cuts left steeply up an eroded hillside track, but don't take it. Choose the Peboamauk Fall Loop, instead running directly ahead and following Moose Brook downhill into the valley below. There is one more fine feature ahead down the wooded canyon: a waterfall.

The Peboamauk Fall Loop descends at a moderately steep pitch, crossing and recrossing the stream. Several of the crossings are necessary because of blowdown tangles on the banks. In high water, it might be wise not to attempt this spur trail at all.

Two thousand feet below Ice Gulch's last rock scramble, the trail approaches the top of Peboamauk Falls, a 30-foot cascade that takes its name from the Abenaki tongue. All accounts indicate the Native American word means "winter home." Cut left 20 feet and scramble out to the overhanging ledge, to watch Moose Brook succumb to the forces of gravity. The trail falls down a steep and somewhat slick incline to the outwash rocks below the falls. Pick your way around several large blowdowns and continue to the small but fairly deep terminal pool at the base of the falls. The brook cascades down within the confines of rock chute. When the water is high, this cataract rumbles because the sound of crashing water seems amplified by the shape of the terrain.

The way out from the falls is as steep as the pitch down. The last feet of the loop trail climbs the same steep slope you came down on, only the path is just a few feet farther downhill and to the west.

Scramble up the hill on less than stable footing. You'll return to the Ice Gulch Trail once again at a marked birch tree that boasts a now familiar white-painted Randolph Mountain Club sign.

The Ice Gulch Path swings southwest and maintains that heading for a full 2 miles, rising very gradually in elevation at first and then beginning a long, slow descent to Randolph Hill Road. The way is punctuated by three healthy streams. In times of high water, one or two of them could be problematical to cross. Several grassy logging routes interrupted the trail, too, but the entire outrun is a pleasant woods walk. The last footage drifts across mown lawn at the homestead of Sky Meadows. Pass to the right of the barn, to reach the road. Turn right and walk ever so gradually uphill nearly ½ mile back to your vehicle.

In all likelihood, the trip to and through Ice Gulch has taken longer than you had anticipated. There is no rushing through the boulder-strewn gorge. Time being cautious and resting is time well spent. When the sojourn is over, you've accomplished something substantial, for Ice Gulch puts everyone, veteran and rookie alike, through a rigorous test. Back at your car, you know you've bested one of the most difficult miles of trail in the whole of the Eastern United States.

Time to celebrate.

15.

Mt. Success Trail to the DC-3 Crash Site

Location: Success unincorporated township, NH

Distance: 3 miles to the summit, about another mile to the crash site, 8 miles round-trip.

Difficulty: Moderately steep and steep in some sections

Trailhead: 44°29'04.22'N, 71°04'10.88'W

GETTING THERE

Roll north to the small, former paper industry city of Berlin on NH 16. Pass auto dealerships and a Super Walmart on the left and the entrance to the Cascade paper mill complex to the right. Continue north until a set of traffic lights appears just below the city center. NH 16 continues straight ahead. Hastings Avenue cuts right, crosses a bridge over the Androscoggin River, and swings into the eastern boroughs of town. Drive nearly 2 miles, watching for the big green street signs on the right. As community buildings and homes recede and open paper mill–process landfill acreage comes into view, the road crosses a low height of land. Just beyond the sign for Success Pond Road shows itself on the right. Turn right, uphill onto Success Pond Road and travel a little more than 5 miles on a washboard surface. Spur roads will show themselves, but Success Pond Road is always the larger or wider of the lanes. The towering wall of the Mahoosuc Range soon stretches before your windshield. Always make for the peaks.

After traveling 5 miles, watch on the right for a good sign that points the way to the Mt. Success Trail trailhead. Turn right and stay right at a fork in the narrow lane. The way becomes grassy and weedy at its center but the going is good. This lane eventually ends in an old grass-filled log yard. It is a perfectly suitable place to park. The trail is at the head of the old yard and to the right.

Please note: Success Pond Road is a logging road. Big logging trucks have the right of way on the lane.

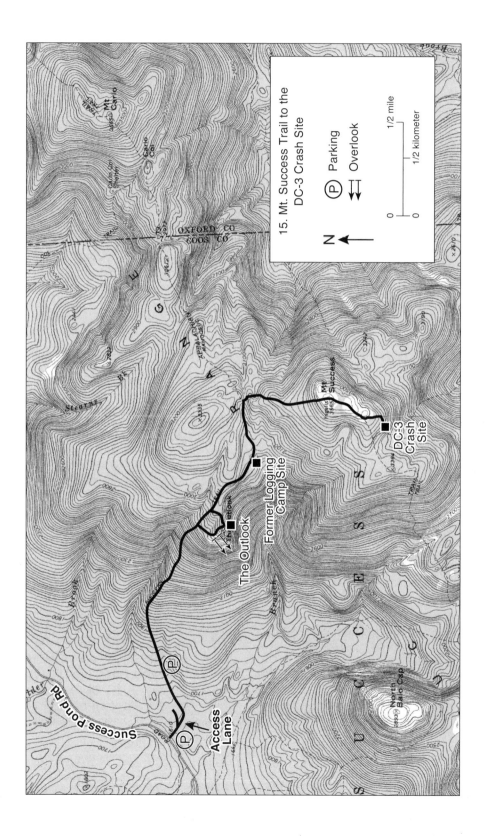

15. Mt. Success Trail to the DC-3 Crash Site

Parking Ⓟ
Overlook

0   1/2 kilometer
0   1/2 mile

N

DC-3 Crash Site

Former Logging Camp Site

The Outlook

Success Pond Rd

Access Lane

Mt Success
3565

North Bald Cap

OXFORD CO
COOS CO

THE TRAIL TO TRAGEDY

The Mt. Success Trail doesn't get top billing on the marquee of White Mountains footpaths, but it should. While many a trail has a single destination to some superlative feature, the Mt. Success Trail boasts access to three outstanding features. The Outlook cliff alone is reason to go, as are the blueberries on the ledges in late July. But farther up the line, Mt. Success's summit is an unheralded gem: broad, open, and commanding a 360-degree view of what is universally considered the most challenging terrain that the entire Appalachian Trail has to offer.

The summit, though, is not the final destination. The prize, if I should call it that, is the remains of a Northeast Airlines DC-3 passenger liner that crashed very close to the summit ridge in a snow squall in November 1954. The site is hallowed ground, for two of the seven people on board the plane died in the wreck. The twisted aluminum skin and framework and the separate broken sections of the craft's fuselage still remain where they came to rest. With only a little sleuthing and effort, you may find yourself standing in wild country and bearing witness to a tragedy that played out in an instant more than half a century ago.

Don your day pack and head up an easy grade in open hardwood forest, following blue blaze paint. In the early going, the trail occupies a very gradual grade, following a wash where recent heavy freshets have roughed up the water course considerably. The path threads along the edge of this seasonally dry defile, crossing it once, and then heads into an area where nearby woods were logged a decade ago. Sunlight stimulates growth in this section, and by midsummer growth has crowded in a bit about the trail. No bother. The going is still good, although the grade begins to sharpen as you reach the base of the peak.

Forest canopy closes in and the trail becomes a good woods walk. Much of the climb out of the valley is rather direct, tracing a fairly straight course with only the odd short jog to the left. As the hardwoods begin to mingle with birch and then spruce and fir, the way gets steeper. On several angled inclines, the trail has worn down to bedrock. Some sections may be wet and therefore a bit slippery. Use some caution, particularly if the forests are moist after a healthy rain.

Push ever upward toward a junction about two-thirds of the way up the mountain. The route to the right is a loop trail that swings west and returns to the main trail ½ mile on. Make the turn to the right. Don't pass this up. This loop path runs out to a series of ledges, the main one being a broad expanse of rock at the head of the Outlook, a big, near-vertical knob of granite that is a prominent feature on the side of the mountain, easily recognized through the windshield of your vehicle as you motored toward the peak.

The first ledge is tightly confined by trees and the view restricted. Keep going uphill and in a minute you'll crest the granite dome of the Outlook. Here, vegetation can get little purchase and the view is stunning to the south, west, and northwest, where the Northeast's loftiest elevations stand. Across the immediate valley below stands a poor twin cousin to the precipice where your feet a planted. An expansive valley, in which Success Pond Road snakes for miles, sweeps away to the northeast. In the midst of it sits a clearing with a conspicuous yet orderly array of large buildings. This oasis is a new federal penitentiary.

Mountain ranges, from the Carter-Moriahs and Presidential Ranges to the distant Whitcomb Range and Dixville Notch uplands far to the north, frame everything. Most all terrain to the east in Maine is walled off by

Mt. Success and the long Mahoosuc Range ridgeline.

Head east along narrower and narrower ledges, and if the season is right, pick blueberries along the way. In a few minutes, regain the main trail and turn uphill. Trek over a low height of land and enter a country of wet feet, where dozens of bog bridge spans string out over terrain that is marked by seeps, pour drainage, and filled-in bogs. At the head of this, on the right, someone has managed to set up salvage goods from a long-lost horse-logging camp. Leaning against a tree is a metal, horse-drawn, winter sled skid. It is accompanied by an iron side panel from a camp wood cookstove and several galvanized horse buckets that are losing their battle with the elements.

Spend five minutes slinking through the poor, moist acreage, when the trail pitches uphill again. Shortly the Mt. Success Trail meets the Mahoosuc Trail, a dramatic link in the Appalachian Trail, at a T-junction. To the left not far way is the Maine–New Hampshire boundary line at Mt. Carlo. For our purposes, turn right and head toward the nearby summit of Mt. Success. From the Outlook, the distance to the summit seemed a long pull, but the peak is really quiet close at hand.

Tread over a granite hump, level out, and begin a moderately steep push into the high country. Quickly, the spruce and fir lose height as the mountain levels off on a summit plateau of many acres. Suddenly the going is easy and a squat bony ledge thrusts up out of the flats at about the height of an average man. This elevation is marked by a stout signpost. You've reached one of two nearly identical topknot granite crests that crown Mt. Success.

Now the view doubles compared to the Outlook vista, swinging a full 360 degrees. The Great State of Maine heaves into view. To the north, Mt. Carlo and first-rate Goose Eye Mountain stand at attention. All the Carter-Moriahs stretch out, as does the spine of the Northern Presidentials down to Mt. Washington. The Dartmouth and Crescent Ranges tip their hats. The Pliny and Pilots, too. Know where to look and you can make out hazy low humps in the distance that command the very top of the Granite State.

Directly below, more bog bridges stride south across the plateau and disappear in a scrub forest summit shoulder. Drop down of the bony summit rib and cross the puncheon spans to the south. Cross through the wooded shoulder and ledges dominate once again, tipped very gently down toward the south and sporting a few low rock cairns.

About ¼ mile from the summit sign, watch on the left for a granite boulder about the side of a chest freezer sitting all by itself some 70 feet east of the trail. It is unmistakable. If you are watching for it, you'll recognize it. Once you've spotted it, pick your way over to it on what looks like a herd path. That's what it is. Now follow that unofficial pathway downhill into the trees. Drop only about 50 vertical feet below that boulder when suddenly a string of bright yellow blazes will appear. This blaze line is the boundary of the protected lands that surround the Appalachian Trail corridor in this region. At this writing, there is a red surveyor tape flag on a spruce bow as you enter this blaze line. Be sure to look around you, because you will have to return this way, and you'll want to pick up the herd path again to regain the summit.

Follow the yellow blazes to the south, the path staying fairly level as you pick your way along among the trees and blowdowns. After a few minutes, just about the time when most people would feel discouraged that they had made a wrong turn, the forest brightens with reflected light. Sunlight bouncing off aluminum shows the way.

Carlo and Goose Eye from Mt. Success

The yellow blazes run right up to Flight 792, an ill-fated Douglas DC-3 twin engine airliner. The flight originated in Boston with stops at Concord, Massachusetts, and Laconia, New Hampshire, and was making the last leg of the scheduled trip to the paper city of Berlin. This roughed patch of forest, less than 200 vertical feet below the summit, is where it came to rest.

The first impression is one of chaos. Trekkers stumble upon the very front end of the plane, approaching from the point where the copilot sat with an airline dispatcher directly behind, sitting in the jump seat. The section of the plane where these men were located when the craft hit the mountain was utterly destroyed. They were mortally wounded and knocked unconscious when the plane struck the ground, and died of their injuries during the night. The thought of it is sobering.

The wing on that side of the plane was torn away. The wing on pilot Peter Carey's side is still discernable as a wing. Where he was seated, the plane is nothing more than a tangle of wreckage, but somehow, despite terrible injuries, he managed to survive.

The airliner broke up into separate large fragments. Behind the cockpit and wing assembly area, the main bulk of the fuselage where the passengers were seated remains intact. While the front of the craft absorbed the bulk of the impact energy, a large chunk of the main cabin sustained little damage. It protected the three passengers and the flight attendant well enough that they escaped injury.

The aft end of the cabin broke away

where the galley wall ran. That big, round chunk of debris trails the rest of the debris by 20 feet or so. The tail assembly is nowhere in the immediate vicinity. It and the left wing sheered away when the plane first struck trees, and the debris is somewhere down the mountain a nasty bushwhack away.

Many who have come this way to see the wreck have left scribbling of their names inside the main cabin, some as early as 50 years ago, when finding the wreck was no easy chore. No way could I desecrate at place where tragedy struck so deadly.

When one is confronted with the wreckage, it is not difficult to imagine what played out in this remote place. Flying in a snow squall, the crew was relying on instruments to guide them into the tiny airfield in the town of Milan, just to the north of the little industrial city of Berlin. They were slightly off course and were reportedly low on fuel. At a critical moment, the plane dipped just below the ridgeline and the crew must have lost the glide-path beacon signal emanating from the airfield.

The pilot probably reacted hastily to the problem by pulling up the nose. But the airliner was too close to the mountain. The crew avoided a nose-in crash, but the tail likely struck the trees first and was torn away. The left wing followed. A second or two later, the plane nosed into its deathbed, skidded along for a moment and broke up.

It would take three days before rescue crews were able to reach the wreckage. The initial search effort focused on the Conway area. But the rescue switched to the Mahoosucs when the pilot managed to send a weak message over the radio the next morning, saying something to the effect of, "Down five miles . . . from Berlin Hill."

After staying huddled together against the cold overnight, the survivors took stock of their situation the next day. They discovered they were close to a broad, open summit. With great effort, they managed to haul aluminum shards and seat materials into the open, atop Mt. Success. When the weather cleared, they were discovered by planes crisscrossing over the Mahoosuc Range. On the third day, a helicopter landed on the mountain and removed the survivors to Berlin and the Androscoggin Valley Hospital there.

I can't say finding the wrecked airliner was exhilarating. My emotions were mixed. Most of us have been aboard aircraft that could just have easily suffered the same fate.

Once you pay your respects, it's time to retrace the steps back to the summit. If, for some reason, you miss the herd path route, simply bushwhack uphill and keep going until the trail or its cairns come into view. Head northbound and you'll be back on track.

On the way down, I doubled back to the Outlook one last time to find a party of five enjoying fat sandwiches and cold beverages. I told them about the wreck and how to find it. They changed their plans then and there. They simply had to try for the wreck. I ate more blueberries and took my time walking out and leaving a terrific day-hike behind.

IV. Nash Stream Forest

New stone stairway, Percy STEVEN D. SMITH

In the 1970s, when I first arrived in the country north of the White Mountain National Forest, there were but two hiking trails in the jumble of mountains that surrounded a devastated, heavily eroded valley through which Nash Stream drained. Back then Nash Stream Road followed the big brook northward into terrain savaged by a flood of water released explosively when the Nash Bog dam blew out in 1969. That road reached an old trailhead at Mile 3, which led to a path that ran straight up the hideously steep, naked granite flanks of North Percy Peak. Locals climbed the dangerous trail each August to harvest the carpet of blueberry plants on the mountain's expansive, domed summit.

Six miles farther up the line, the road passed a jeep track that ran up big Sugarloaf Mountain to a cabin near the summit. Above that cabin, on the summit ledges stood a fire watchman's lookout hut—not a fire tower—bolted to the rocks.

That was it. The nearly 40,000 acres of wild and beautiful country that has since become the Nash Stream Forest, New Hampshire's largest state forest, saw little hiking traffic. Today, there is a whole world of new hiking opportunities in that county, just a hop, skip, and a jump across NH 110 from where the northern boundary of the White Mountain National Forest plays out for good.

16.

Devil's Slide

Location: Stark, NH

Distance: Less than 0.5 mile to the cliffs

Difficulty: Moderate to moderately steep in the upper section

Trailhead: 44°36'15.03'N, 71°25'05.52'W

GETTING THERE

Locate NH 110 between Berlin and Groveton. From Berlin, travel west nearly 20 miles to the picturesque village of Stark with its long covered bridge, white-painted town hall, and schoolhouse crowded about the Upper Ammonoosuc River. From Groveton, travel 5 miles eastbound to the village. Pull off the highway, cross the covered bridge, and go to a T-junction directly below a massive and sheer granite cliff face called Devil's Slide. Turn left (west) at the junction. Motor about 1 mile, crossing a set of railroad tracks, a new residence on the right, and a tiny sandpit on the right. Just beyond the sandpit is a sandy pullout on the right. Park there.

FALLING FOR THE DEVIL

In none of the other pages in this guidebook will you find so much dramatic turf for so little effort. You can perch on the edge of infinity more than 300 feet in the air after, just 20 minutes earlier, your boots were planted on the edge of a road next to a cow pasture in the Upper Ammonoosuc River Valley. If you only have an hour to spend on trail in upper Coos County, you'll want to rendezvous with the devil at Devil's Slide.

The village of Stark is like few others in the eastern United States. Stark is blessed with a tiny cluster of classic New England structures, a much-photographed covered bridge, a decidedly charming bed & breakfast known as the Stark Village Inn, and a wild river with plenty of muscle running down the middle of it all. And there's a bonus, a big one. The town is tucked beneath a tall,

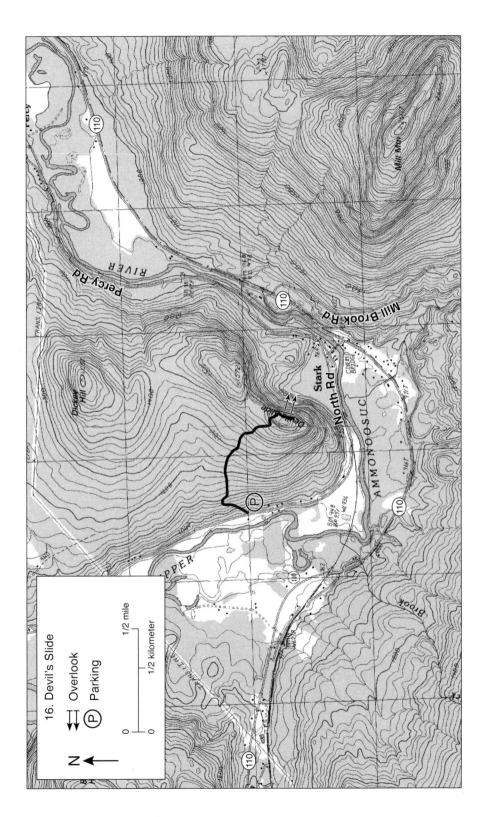

16. Devil's Slide

⇅ Overlook
Ⓟ Parking

0   1/2 mile
0   1/2 kilometer

N ←

Stark Bridge, Devil's Slide   JOHN COMPTON

wooded hill. But it's no ordinary forested knob. No, something violent happened here to create a most unusual backdrop. For all intents and purposes, Devil's Slide appears to be a small peak that has been cleaved in half—and one of those halves has utterly disappeared.

That's exactly what we have here. The great mile-high Laurentide Ice Sheet that covered New England until 11,000 years ago bulldozed through the region, and in so doing, literally ripped away the rounded south face of the hill. It was a clean kill. A thorough job. The short hike up the little mount presents plenty of evidence of that violent act.

Before the hike, simply pull off NH 110 and park the car in the schoolyard. Have a look at one of New England's most quaint hamlets, named for Revolutionary War general and hero John Stark, whose famous "Live Free or Die" utterance is the Granite

State's official motto. The original township was granted under the name of Percy. That moniker still graces another small hamlet in town, a road, and twin peaks to the north. But John Stark's bigger-than-life persona won the day, and the name Percy was dropped in favor of Stark.

Stark will not disappoint. From the arched burial vault and little cemetery on the hill across the road, to the 150-year-old covered bridge over the river, to the B&B across on the far bank, little Stark exudes an abundance of charm. All of it is framed by looming cliffs just feet away to the north.

Once you have parked at the unmarked trailhead off North Road, the trail will be directly ahead and you can angle easily uphill to the right. Step on the trail under a steep high bank, at the top of which is perched an outbuilding or box trailer presided over by a yappy small dog. Follow pink surveyor-tape flags into the woods. Begin to climb immediately out of the valley on a shallow grade.

This trail is easily followed but was never really formally cut. It follows a track down which moisture collects and occasionally runs in wet weather. Pick your way along the route, following the obvious right of way and the flagging. Step over or around a few blow-downs and come upon a very narrow gravel lane. Turn left uphill on the lane. The grade steepens. Follow the gravel just 100 feet or so west to a point where the trail swings toward the northeast.

Walk on an indistinct woods path now, keeping the pink surveyor tape in sight. The way underfoot is pressed into the soils, but in spring or in leaf fall, the route can seem obscure. Bend northward as the trail steepens and loops in an arc around to the rounded north flank of the little peak.

As you climb rapidly now, the forest turns over quickly from hardwoods to spruce and fir as the upper portions of the mountain are attained. After a brief steep push, the angle softens considerably and the trail loops over the northwest shoulder of the mountain below its true summit.

Ahead the dark confines of spruce and fir lighten to the south. Abruptly, forest converts to thin air. The trail ends at the edge of the Devil's Slide's great south face. Herd paths run uphill and down. Turn downhill along the cliff and descend 30 yards or so to a perfectly flat landing at the very edge of the finest outlook on the peak. There are no trees along the edge here to block the view. In fact, there is nothing to block a body's falling straight down several hundred feet to scree slopes below.

The first impression is disconcerting. It seems very odd that, with so little effort, you could gain such elevation that the town directly below looks like a cardboard village on an HO-gauge model train layout. From this height it is easy to see just how small Stark

really is. The tiny town is an afterthought in the landscape. To the south is the lofty Pilot Range in the Kilkenny division of the White Mountain National Forest. The pyramidal mountain named The Horn stands out readily against its round-topped neighbors, The Bulge, and 4,170-foot Mt. Cabot. Lower down, the pugilistic nose–like formation of Rogers Ledge cuts a fine figure. Close by, just above the village, stands Mill Mountain, which hides a fire tower watchman's cabin near the summit. The tower that once stood there has long been removed.

The view west is blocked by trees, but you will be able to see quite a distance to the east up the Upper Ammonoosuc River Valley, and identify summits in the Mahoosuc Range.

On occasion, peregrine falcons nest on the cliff face below. Bushwhackers have been known to try the extremely steep gullies in the lower and more eastern segments of the cliffs, and ice climbers give routes on Devil's Slide a go once in a while.

The best policy for getting down is to return the way you came. There is an old trail down a much steeper section of the north face, but it is very difficult to locate now. If you can't get enough of vertical terrain, it is possible to trek close to the cliffs for 700 feet, until the ledges give way to soils and forest to the east. You can pick up an old logging skidway on the east flank and drop down to Percy Road. A 10-minute road walk would bring you back to your vehicle.

But if you would rather hike trail instead of pick your way through the bush, simply return from whence you came. The whole effort takes under an hour. Because the climb is so short, may I suggest bringing a lunch up to the cliff and enjoy a picnic on high. That way, there will be no rush to leave, and you can revel in the view and in the good fortune of having chosen such a fine little hike with such a big reward.

17.

Bald Mountain Notch Loop

Location: Stark, NH

Distance: 8 miles to complete the loop

Difficulty: Easy much of the way, moderate in one lengthy section

Trailhead: 44°37'30.36'N, 71°21'48.38'W

GETTING THERE

Travel 7 miles from Groveton Village or nearly 15 miles from Berlin on NH 110. Two miles eastbound past the classic New England hamlet of Stark, look for Bell Hill Road on the left. Coming from Berlin, look for Bell Hill Road on the right, 0.25 mile beyond the entrance to South Pond federal recreation area.

Turn northbound, across the bridge over the Upper Ammonoosuc River. Cross a set of railroad tracks to a junction. Turn left at the junction onto Percy Road. Travel 0.25 mile. The old Stark landfill will appear on the left. Just beyond and down a slight decline in the road, a grassy lane cuts right. A bar gate stands near the road, and a tall post painted with a yellow blaze marks the route. Pull off the road on the right. Do not block the trail. You have reached the Bald Mountain Trail, the eastern portion of a loop hike in quiet Coos County forests.

SOLITUDE PERSONIFIED

I hadn't seen a black bear in 25 years. The last one I came in contact with was on a slab table in the fish hatchery cooler at Twin Mountain, New Hampshire, the unfortunate victim of a run-in with an automobile.

I wasn't thinking in terms of black bears when I sent a couple in their late fifties out to hike to Bald Mountain Notch, located in the southeast corner of the Nash Stream Forest. I had just met the couple. They'd asked me if I knew a readily accessible and fairly easy hike in the region, and so I sent them on their way toward the little-known notch in quiet forested country.

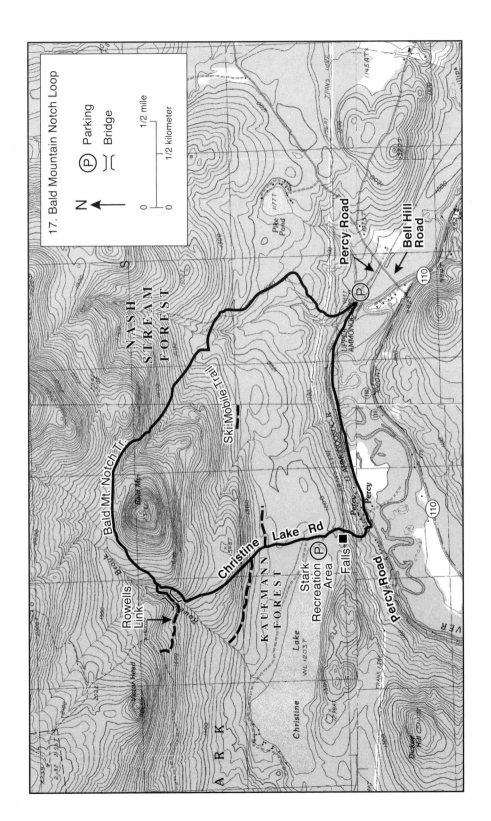

17. Bald Mountain Notch Loop

N

Parking

Bridge

0   1/2 mile

0   1/2 kilometer

NASH STREAM FOREST

Bald Mt. Notch Tr.

Ski Mobile Trail

Pike Pond

Percy Road

Bell Hill Road

110

UPPER AMMONOOSUC

Bald Mtn

Rowells Link

Brook

Christine Lake Rd

KAUFMANN FOREST

Stark Recreation Area

Falls

Percy

Percy Road

Christine Lake

Dicker Hill

PARK

A few days later I got a call from the fellow. He and his wife hadn't walked five minutes, when they came across two young bear cubs climbing a tree and a mother bear huffing nervously nearby. I thought the man was going to castigate me, but he was effervescent in his recollection of the encounter, excited really. He and his wife agreed that they had been very fortunate to have seen the big sow bear and her cubs on their home turf. I had to agree. I was disappointed it hadn't been me who had made the trek to Bald Mountain Notch that day.

I don't fear black bears in this region, and neither should you. This little tale should not discourage you from taking a long leisurely loop trek in wild country. Black bears are common but encounters are very rare. Meetings between humans and bears in the North Country almost always end with the bears sprinting away at astonishing speed.

So, slip your day pack on and head northwest into the little-hiked southeastern sector of the 39,601-acre Nash Stream. Pass the bar gate and pace through a clearing, a wide trunk-power line corridor. Enter mixed forest with a full canopy overhead. Ascend very gradually to a tight turn to the left. Pass blue state blazes on the trees and follow yellow blazes west in gentle terrain. Pass over a snowmobile bridge and disregard an indistinct lane to the right.

Keep the yellow blazes in sight and follow them uphill to the right at a T-junction in the trail. Climb to a left turn and begin a moderate ascent for a mile in mixed hardwood forest punctuated with white birch trees. The trail here is a very old and mellow logging lane that is a real pleasure to tramp. As the path increases in elevation, it rides on the edge of a deep ravine. In spring and fall, the route offers glimpses south to the high terrain in Kilkenny division of the White Mountain National Forest. For years, the view was substantial. A major ice storm in 1998 stripped many of the trees in this area of all but the strongest branches. But the forest rebounded and the view has diminished, particularly in high summer.

The trail grows increasingly steep but never difficult as it approaches a small peak ahead and on the left, known as Bald Mountain. After the steepest stretch, the trail moderates. It almost levels out when it approaches a tree on the left with a yellow-lettered sign tacked to its trunk. The sign reads STEVE'S TREE 1999. Somewhere in my memory, I recall having a conversation with a fellow who said he placed the odd plaque on the tree. But I can't remember the details.

But never mind the sign, because the path enters a delightful little pass between Bald Mountain and a bulky arm of Long Mountain to the northeast. Cross the height of land and immediately confront the refreshing west wind squeezing through the gap between the peaks.

Bald Mountain Notch is certainly not a feature to write home about. It has none of the drama or the size of the many famous notches in the White Mountains. Yet the little pass is delightful because it affords a substantial sense of isolation, and it is oh so quiet between the uplands. Descend gradually to a moist spot and bypass it on the right. At this point, the occasional intrepid peakbagger will leave the trail southward here and climb the steep terrain of low Bald Mountain. The peak is named for naked ledges all over its upper south flank and a ledge or two to the west. The views south are expansive eastward to the long saurian back of the Mahoosucs riding the Maine–New Hampshire line. Just as impressive is the vista to the northwest of North and South Percy Peaks and little Victor Head with its south-facing cliffs. It's a bit of a tough pull to reach the heights, as there is no trail up the

Rowell's Bridge rebuild   TRACY REXFORD

mountain. The effort to do so is well worth the trouble.

Continue on the track west on level and very gently declining terrain, still following yellow blazes in the trees. Swing a lazy turn or two until the path straightens for ¼ mile. Pass a wet slump over the right shoulder and move over trail that has had some recent ditching to drain moisture. Enter a small grassy opening. At the base of the clearing, stop. There is a trail junction here. The Rowell's Link drops down a little pitch to the right and takes the yellow blazes with it. The loop hike disregards that right turn and instead edges left away from the blazing.

But for now, it's time for a snack or lunch. So, do turn right and down a dozen vertical feet to another pathway that parallels Rowell's Brook. Swing downhill and walk just a minute to a log and plank span over the stream. Rowell's Brook bridge is just right for taking a little rest before continuing on. Nibble on something and rehydrate to the sound of the lively stream.

Refreshed now, stride back uphill and return to the loop hike route. Turn right. Walk on the level for a minute and then descend ⁴⁄₁₀ mile on a former snowmobile trail that has not been maintained in some years. The going is good but there are some blowdowns to step over. At the bottom of a moderately steep pitch, reach an opening that provides a parking spot for the vehicle of a camp owner who occasional comes this way. The tired old Emerson camp stands just across the stream on the right.

Follow a two-tire track downhill from the camp and slowly descend away from the

Rowell's Brook valley. The pathway soon levels and passes a wide woods lane on the right. Stride easily in flat country, pass another lane on the left, and go to a green-painted bar gate. Pass around the gate and drop down to a narrow gravel road. Move to the left along the road, and after 600 feet, look for a lane on the right. Make a hard right and walk into a parking area maintained by the town of Stark. This lot sits at the eastern end of mile-long Christine Lake.

Walk out onto the town beach at the edge of the lake. This body of water is a natural formation gouged out of the landscape by long-lost glacial ice. It is hemmed in by flat-topped ridges to the east and south. To the northwest, though, stand three peaks: little Victor Head, South Percy Peak, and, tucked behind the small mountain, North Percy Peak. The mountains form a graceful backdrop above the clean black waters of Christine Lake.

In late July and August, the water warms up sufficiently to attract families with youngsters who want nothing more than to swim all afternoon. After doing trail work in this region for two decades, I've found myself immersed in Christine Lake more than once.

Leave the lake and regain the gravel Christine Lake Road. Follow it downhill. Pass a small waterfall on the right, and soon you'll reach Percy Road, running east–west through the little hamlet of Percy. Turn left onto the narrow paved road and walk a long mile back to the place where you parked your car. Percy Road is little used, so the jog along the pavement is not the least bit objectionable.

You've made, essentially, a wobbly circle around Bald Mountain. If you are quiet, you have a good chance of seeing wildlife in the area. Open forests and some minor clearings permit browse to grow up, good forage for deer and moose. As few souls venture out in this country, you should have the woodlands to yourself all day.

18.

Victor Head Cliff

Location: Nash Stream Forest, Stark, NH

Distance: About 2.5 miles to the cliff face

Difficulty: Easy to briefly moderate

Trailhead: 44°37'40.90', 71°23'21.02'W

GETTING THERE

Leave NH 110 at Stark Village, cross the classic covered bridge, and turn right onto Percy Road. Travel 2 miles to the little hamlet of Percy and look for the Christine Lake sign on the left. Motor up a steep incline, level out, and continue a short distance until the lane bends to the right. Just before the turn, a drive leaves the road straight ahead. This is an access to a small parking area at the eastern end of the Christine Lake, a beautiful body of water tucked into an odd assortment of upland elevations.

Leave the parking area and return to the lane. Turn left. Hike 400 feet to where the road bends to the left. A wide woods path runs straight ahead. Leave the road and walk up a little rise to a green bar gate. Cross around the gate and trek in level terrain for ½ mile, ignoring a wide opening on the right halfway along. Soon you'll come to a junction with another woods lane, this one on the left. Turn left and trek a long mile under overhanging tree canopy. Pass a junk truck on the left. Cross over a snowmobile bridge at Rowell Brook, and eventually you'll arrive at a T-junction at the old, grassy logging tote lane known as Jimmy Cole Brook Road. Cross directly over the old way and enter the Old Summer Club Trail. Walk another ½ mile on very pleasant woods trail to yet another, less distinct junction. You have reached the Victor Head Cliff Trail.

THE RAVEN'S ROOST

After 2 miles of ambling on old, softened logging lanes running through a green sea of

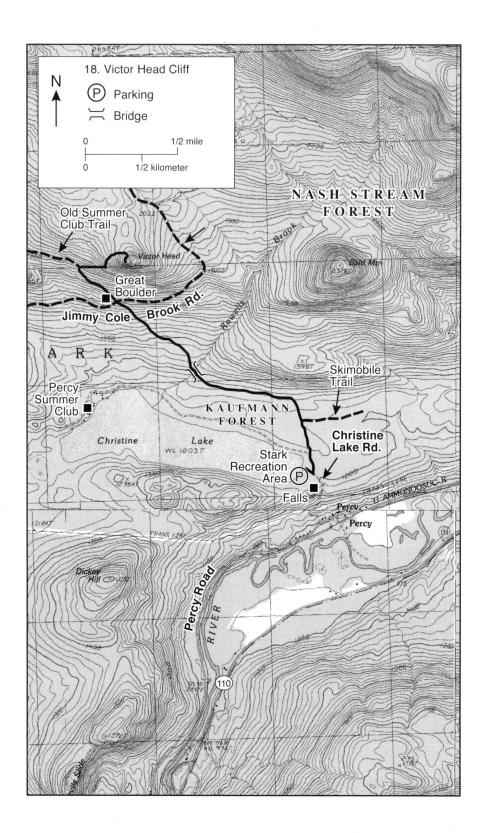

18. Victor Head Cliff

N

P Parking

⋈ Bridge

0   1/2 mile

0   1/2 kilometer

NASH STREAM
FOREST

Old Summer
Club Trail

Victor Head

Great
Boulder

Jimmy Cole   Brook Rd.

Bald Mtn

A R K

Skimobile
Trail

Percy
Summer
Club

KAUFMANN
FOREST

Christine   Lake
WL 12037

Christine
Lake Rd.

Stark
Recreation
Area   P

Falls

U. AMMONOOSUC R.

Percy

Percy Road

RIVER

Dickey
Hill

110

110

Victor Head view, north   STEVEN D. SMITH

hardwoods, reach a true hiking path. A Cohos Trail sign in a tree and yellow blazes point the way north to South Percy Peak, but you have other plans. Although you can't see the little pointy 2,200-foot peak known as Victor Head, it is close by. Almost invisible standing amid mountains 1,200 and more feet higher, Victor Head makes up for its diminutive size by presenting to the world a scruffy south face whose forehead is a granite cliff ledge.

Turn to the right off the Old Summer Club Trail you've been walking on and immediately enter a footpath that begins a moderate ascent in an easterly direction. Forty years ago, this path was cut by a logging skidder's dragging logs through the forest. Now forest debris and new growth have narrowed the route down to a trail.

In the steepest terrain since leaving the Christine Lake parking lot, the trail suddenly veers left and angles steeper still for a minute then moderates. Meandering through mixed forest, the path approaches the little summit pyramid. The original route ran directly at the elevation and it required a bit of fancy footwork and a handhold or two to reach the summit. But the old pathway was abandoned nearly a decade ago for a more circuitous route that can now be easily managed by adults and children.

The way cuts to the east and rises easily onto the summit plateau, just an acre or so large. The trail jogs through an S-curve cut around a blowdown jumble from 10 years ago. At the top of the last bend, turn right just a second to the north summit ledge. The spruce and fir part here, and there is an excellent view to the north of the twin, scarred summits of the Percy Peaks, two of the more conspicuous conjoined elevations in the White Mountain region.

Reverse direction and head south a few dozen steps. The path approaches a narrow granite slab pitched slightly downhill. The slab ends are a square edge. Beyond is the domain of flies and birds.

Victor Head cliff and a score of similar precipices in northern New Hampshire is a product of the Laurentide Ice Sheet that ground down the White Mountains for millennia before retreating 11,000 years ago. As glacier ice overtopped Victor Head, the great ice sheet lost its footing on the south side of the little peak. With nothing to support its fantastic weight, the ice slumped repeatedly, and in so doing, plucked rock of the south faces. Eventually, the ice created vertical cliff faces. Within 10 miles of Victor Head are half a dozen similar features, all facing in a southerly direction, including Devil's Slide and Rogers Ledge.

Victor Head cliff ledge is not spacious, yet plenty wide enough to support half a dozen trekkers for lunch and for lazing about like turtles in the sun. The vertical drop is about 50 feet, but the slope below is hideously steep and pitches again and again over sheer faces. A tall spruce managed to anchor itself on the terrain far below, and its top rocks in the breeze just off the edge of the ledge.

It will have taken you an hour at most to reach this destination. For little effort, you receive a major prize. The vista from Victor Head cliff is inspiring. In the foreground stretches mile-long Christine Lake, a narrow glacial gouge in the landscape, filled with waters sparkling in the sunlight. It seems close enough to dive into, but don't take me up on it. Your leap would fall far short, as the lake is farther off than it appears.

The full width of the Pilot Range is visible west to east, including the nose bulb of Rogers Ledge, the tall triangle that is The Horn, The Bulge as round as a bowling ball, and the broad dome of 4,180-foot Mt. Cabot. To the east rise the undulating uplands of the Pliny Range, but they are overshadowed by the serrated edges of the upper elevations of the Presidential Range. Due east are the northern folds of the Carter-Moriah Range and the southern high ground of the Mahoosuc Range.

Little human habitation is discernable from the perch. You will likely have the place to yourself because the feature is little known and is overshadowed by more imposing geology in the region. But little Victor Head is a hidden gem, one so easy to attain. It is the perfect half-day hike. Families can manage it easily enough, as can many a senior citizen.

On my way up the Old Summer Club Trail to the Percy Peaks, I never fail to take the detour to Victor Head. In May, birds of prey nest below and you can witness their coming and going. In summer, ravens call their own the ledges below. And in July and August, when the sun is high, the granite ledge becomes toasty warm, delightful enough to ease you to nap on the cliff edge.

In all my treks to the Victor Head, I have never encountered another soul. I think of the little peak as my own bit of personal real estate. That's folly, of course, but it does bode well for if you want a short promenade to a terrific outlook and have a good measure of peace and solitude, to boot.

19.

Old Summer Club Trail

Location: Nash Stream Forest, Stark, NH

Distance: About 8 miles round-trip

Difficulty: Lengthy; moderate to arduous in some sections

Trailhead: 44°32'40.90'N, 71°23'21.02'W

GETTING THERE

Travel to the village of Stark on NH 110. Turn off the highway where the covered bridge crosses the Upper Ammonoosuc River. Motor over the bridge and turn right immediately onto Percy Road. Drive 2 miles to the tiny hamlet of Percy. As you enter the little collection of homes, look for a standard green street sign that states Christine Lake Road is on the left. Turn left and begin a steep climb up a narrow paved road. Pass under a power line and motor by a small falls on the left. The road flattens and turns to a dirt surface. Shortly, the way bends to the right, but stay straight ahead and enter a parking lot for the recreational area of the town of Stark. Park there.

A HISTORIC ROUTE TO SOUTH PERCY PEAK

On the shore of the small public beach of beautiful Christine Lake, cradled by peaks and flat topped ridges, hikers who wish to tackle South Percy Peak can get a good look at their quarry to the northwest over the waters. Nearly a mile away, on the western corner of the lake, one can see a cluster of buildings that were once a part of an exclusive summer club. A century ago, summer residents and guests visiting the camps managed to cut and blaze more than 3 miles of trail up the southeast flank of South Percy Peak to the col between the mountain and its taller and more robust neighboring twin, North Percy Peak.

Today, that long lost trail has been approximated and cut to the very col where the

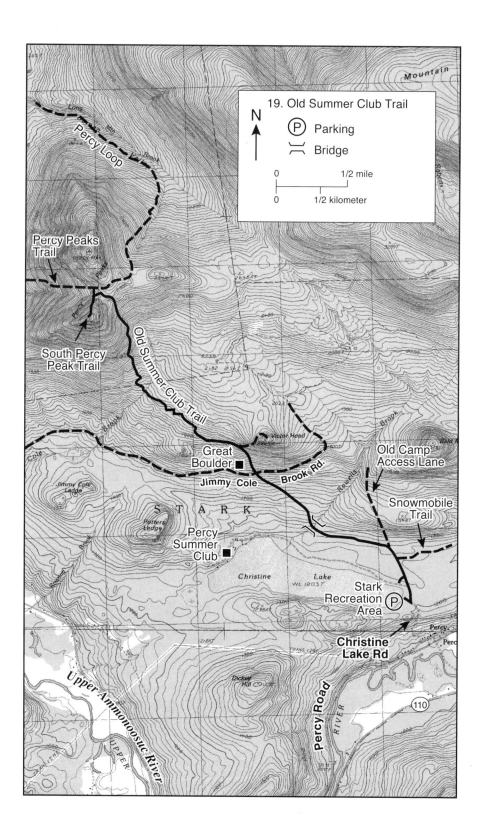

19. Old Summer Club Trail

N

Ⓟ Parking

⨆ Bridge

0 _____ 1/2 mile

0 _____ 1/2 kilometer

Mountain

Percy Loop

Percy Peaks Trail

South Percy Peak Trail

Old Summer Club Trail

Great Boulder ■

Jimmy Cole   Brook Rd.

Old Camp Access Lane

Snowmobile Trail

S T A R K

Jimmy Cole Ledge

Potters Ledge

Percy Summer Club ■

Christine   Lake

Stark Recreation Area Ⓟ

Christine Lake Rd

Dickey Hill

Percy Road

RIVER

110

Upper Ammonoosuc River

old trail reached at the foot of South Percy Peak's upper slopes. The Cohos Trail Association, bowing to those camp owners and guests who first cleared a pathway four generations ago, named its new trail the Old Summer Club Trail. Half a mile longer than the original because the pathway does not descend to the camps on the eastern end of the lake but leads to the public parking area at Christine Lake on the western edge, the Old Summer Club Trail is probably every bit as challenging as and perhaps even more interesting than the original. Certainly the restored trail comprises a host of rugged features that make the trek a worthy one.

The Old Summer Club Trail is a pathway that can be said to be divided into two separate sections. The lower half of the trek is unmarked but very easy to follow, as it runs on old grassy and wooded logging tote roads until it reaches an abandoned east–west lane known in these parts as Jimmy Cole Brook Road. Across that road, a trail sign marks the entrance to the new woods trail and yellow blazing appears immediate and marks the trail the rest of the way.

At the public parking area at Christine Lake, exit the entrance lane and make a hard left onto Christine Lake Road. Walk 400 feet to a point where the road begins to bend to the left. Ahead, just at the turn, a wide woods path ascends gradually into the woods of a 5,000-acre protected area known as the Kauffman Forest. Take it, and in a minute you'll be at a green metal gate. Walk around the gate and continue northward on a lane with a grassy surface. Pace along in pleasant surroundings, soon passing another grassy route that shuttles off to the right. Stay straight ahead. About 15 minutes into the walk on the old tote lane, the trail splits. Instead of continuing straight ahead this time, turn abruptly left on the level and walk under forest canopy for a bit less than a mile, passing a long-abandoned wrecked vehicle on the left, crossing over a snowmobile bridge over Rowell's Brook, and on an uphill grade, reaching a crossroads at grass-filled Jimmy Cole Brook Road.

Trek directly over the road and into the woods. A trail sign marks the way. Take a few steps and you will notice a massive glacial erratic boulder on the left, shouldering a yellow painted blaze. You are now on the formal woods trail brushed out and maintained by the Cohos Trail Association. In its lower section, the new stretch still follows an old but narrower tote lane that has softened to a trail. It climbs at a modest grade for 10 minutes' hike to a trail junction. The Victor Head Cliff Trail cuts right uphill and disappears around a bend. Stay straight ahead on the Old Summer Club Trail, ease over a height of land, and walk on gently undulating path until the old lane ends abruptly and new wood trail turns uphill to the right. In a minute, the true woods trail enters a glacial erratic boulder maze where big blocks of granite stand isolated or in jumbled clusters, the mixed hardwood forest growing all about the stone. The trail threads its way through this delightful feature for 10 minutes, sometimes running in the clear, sometimes wedged in between rocks, occasionally scrambling over them. In this section, the path makes one distinct Z-shaped set of turns on and off an old log skidder path. Watch the blazing and it will be a simple matter to navigate the jogs.

At the far end of the glacial erratic field, the path reaches the first of two branches of Jimmy Cole Brook, where you can obtain good water. Once over the second brook, the trail turns uphill for good on a moderate to moderately steep grade and rides the southeast flank of South Percy Peak. Soon the forest begins to transition to spruce and fir, exhibits one short switchback, and then

North Percy Peak NORTHWOODS STEWARDSHIP CENTER

runs on a fairly straight course ever upward until a ridge begins to show itself ahead. The trail makes a lazy bend to the left and rises more steeply to intersect with the ridge higher up the mountain. Now the path runs hard up against this steep terrain and the only way to gain the ridge is to scramble up a short, very steep, stony pitch, using both hands and feet.

The top of the ridge is actually a granite ledge that snakes toward the col between South and North Percy Peaks, stretching nearly the length of a football field. The trail runs right on the very edge of the ledge, in some places 30 feet above the forest floor. From it, you can obtain restricted views of mountainous terrain to the southeast. Thread your way long this low, serpentine cliff until the route passes over a little granitic knob that is always home to brown-capped chick-

adees. Drop quickly in elevation by 50 vertical feet, proceeding to a junction with the informal South Percy Peaks Trail, blazed in a deep, saturated red.

The Old Summer Club Trail ends here, but the hike does not. Turn left, pass through a fern-filled depression, and go up the northeast flank of South Percy Peak. The trail to the summit is really a herd path; it has never been formally cut or maintained. But the route is easy if somewhat steep to follow, as it rises directly up the mountain without so much as a switchback. As the trail approaches the summit, the way becomes a bit of a scramble over ledgelike granite blocks. But the ascent of South Percy takes little time, and just when you break a sweat you will reach open ledges just a few feet below the true summit.

The prize for your effort to attain the summit of South Percy is a front-row seat with a stunning view of neighboring North Percy Peak, that mountain projecting another 200 feet above. North Percy looks for all the world like a gigantic scoop of ice cream, but instead of a treat, it is a scarred monster with expansive, frightfully steep ledges where trees and scrubs can't get a foothold. If the forest does manage to cling to the rock, winter avalanches and spring mudslides inevitably carry the growth away. Because of its steepness, much of the upper reaches of the North Percy is denuded. South Percy, on the other hand, is able to maintain most of its coating of growth because its scores of ledge projections jut out just enough to allow soils to build up and roots to gain a hold.

A visit to the summit is not complete without a very short, easy bushwhack push over the summit to the highest ledges on the south side of the mountain, where the views off the Upper Ammonoosuc River Valley, the ranges of The Kilkenny, the upper thousand feet of the Presidential Range summits, and the undulating wall of the Mahoosuc Range can be savored. From this vantage point, you may actually be able to see your car parked at the west end of Christine Lake, a long sliver of water now far below.

On the return, you can add dramatic new terrain by detouring to the Percy Peaks Trail and swinging up to the summit of North Percy Peak. Whatever you do, be sure to retreat down the trail you came up on, and not descend on either the Percy Peaks Trail or the Percy Loop. Those trails will deposit you many miles and 1,000 vertical feet away from where your car is parked. Be sure to descend the Old Summer Club Trail. You'll be more than glad you did.

20.

Percy Peaks Trail

Location: Nash Stream Forest, Stark, NH

Distance: 4.4 miles round-trip

Difficulty: Somewhat strenuous climb up the eastern flank of the mountain

Trailhead: 44°40'01.73'N, 71°27'06.80'W

GETTING THERE

To reach the Percy Peaks Trail within the Nash Stream Forest in Stark Township, you'll need to locate NH 110 between Groveton and Berlin. Travel NH 3 or US 2 to Lancaster, New Hampshire. On the west end of town, NH 3 and US 2 diverge, NH 3 turning northbound toward Groveton and Colebrook. Drive about 8 miles north to the point where a large factory, the closed and shuttered Wausau Papers mill, comes into view behind a covered bridge and small steam switching locomotive and tender set up as a historic display. The junction of NH 110 is on the right. If traveling from the east, from the city of Berlin and NH 16, watch for NH 110 signs in the heart of the downtown and travel westward, taking care to follow the signs through residential city streets.

If traveling east from Groveton on NH 110, watch for Emerson Road on the left, a bit more than 2 miles out of town. If running westward from Berlin city, motor some 16 miles through the tiny town of Stark and watch for Emerson Road on the right, 3-plus miles beyond.

Once on Emerson Road, travel 3 miles on pavement until the road takes a dogleg turn to the right at the point where there is a cemetery on the right. Just as Emerson Road jogs right, Nash Stream Road cuts to the left. A good road sign marks the way.

Nash Stream Road immediately turns to a good dirt and gravel lane. Drive 3 miles, staying on the valley floor, and ignore spur roads to the left. As you approach a new but small bridge over Slide Brook, the lane widens out

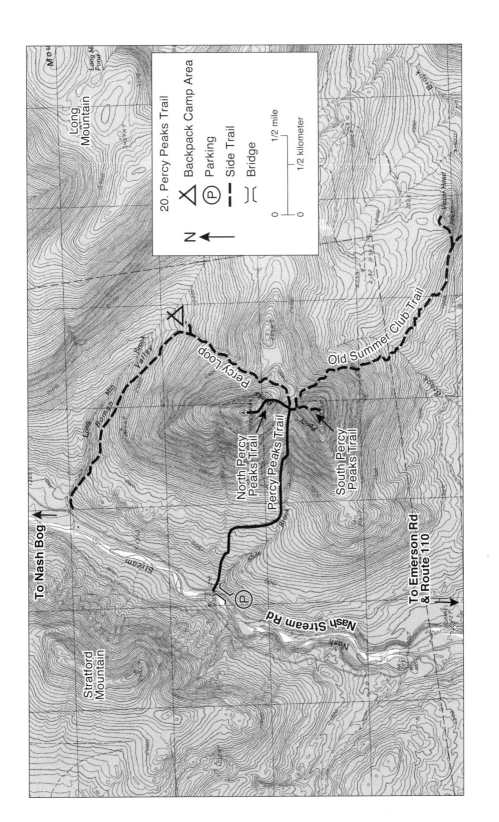

20. Percy Peaks Trail

△ Backpack Camp Area
Ⓟ Parking
▬ ▬ Side Trail
≍ Bridge

N

0   1/2 mile
0   1/2 kilometer

Long Mountain

Stratford Mountain

To Nash Bog

Nash Stream Rd

To Emerson Rd & Route 110

Percy Loop

Old Summer Club Trail

North Percy Peaks Trail

Percy Peaks Trail

South Percy Peaks Trail

into a parking area big enough to support three or four cars. Park there.

THE SWEET SIDE OF A KILLER

One of New England's more dramatic summits doesn't reside within the White Mountain National Forest, in Baxter State Park in Maine, or on the long spine of the Green Mountains. In New Hampshire's largest state forest, the 39,601-acre Nash Stream Forest just to the north of the Whites, stands a serial killer all of 3,418 feet in elevation that goes by the name of North Percy Peak. Viewed from the north, the mountain looks like a monstrous steep-sided gumdrop; from the west, it's a badly scarred hulk that can't hold its soils and sloughs off snow in avalanches that routinely denude the mountain's flanks. Motorists moving north on NH 3 at Groveton Village can't miss the mountain. The summit and its smaller twin neighbor, South Percy Peak, loom over the remains of the abandoned Wausau Papers mill on the banks of the Upper Ammonoosuc River.

People have been climbing North Percy for a century. Once early trampers discovered that the broad, rather flat summit was carpeted with acres of blueberries that ripen in August, hardy local residents made a yearly pilgrimage up the mountain with pack baskets and containers and picked their fill of berries in the warmth of late summer sun.

But North Percy gave up its sweet blue treasure grudgingly. The original trail directly up the mountain, formerly known as the West Side Trail and closed now for 30 years, ran a beeline up a terribly steep stretch of exposed granite ledges. At some point late in the 19th century came a report that someone slipped and fell to his death. Try as I may, I have not discovered a record of the death. But in the 1960s, a young man lost his footing on moist moss and lichen growing on the lower slabs, rocketed down the face of the mountain, and slammed into the trees below. He sustained mortal injuries.

Just before the turn of this century, the mountain claimed yet another victim, this one not *Homo sapiens,* but *Alcus alcus*–a moose. The smell of the rotting carcass filled the woods for more than a month.

When I first came to summit North Percy more than 40 years ago, I climbed the old route up the western slabs, a trek among the steepest I have experienced anywhere in New England or in the Adirondacks. Although it was bone dry when I was there, it was abundantly apparent to me just how dangerous the trek would have been in wet weather. Moreover, it would have been impossible to tackle the mountain without crampons, had there been any ice at all on the rock faces.

Today, North Percy Peak is safer than ever, but is still a challenge in the upper stretches. The Percy Peaks Trail, which follows the lower section of the old trail and the former Notch Trail to the col between North and South Percy, has recently been overhauled top to bottom. Crews from the Northwoods Stewardship Center at East Charleston, Vermont, staunched erosion, cut bypasses in the worst places, built grand stone staircases and retaining walls, replaced a log bridge, and stabilized terrain just below the summit ledges.

Park at a small parking lot at Mile 3 on the right side of Nash Stream Road, at the foot of a new bridge built over Slide Brook. Don your day pack and turn north over the bridge. Look for the entrance to the trail to the right just beyond the bridge. Ascend in easy terrain directly away from the road, cross a log span, and slip near to the high bank that cradles Slide Brook.

After a ⅓-mile jaunt on an easy incline and a stretch of long-lost log skidder lane, the trail begins to rise in earnest. The old path

Percy Summit sign   STEVEN D. SMITH

was heavily eroded in several places, but new bypasses and restoration work has improved the route substantially.

Approach almost to the very edge of Slide Brook at one point, then turn left away from the stream for good. Here, long ago, I came down to the brook to get water and almost ran headlong into a moose that had just climbed down the far bank and was hustling across the water. The creature swept by about a dozen feet from me. We were both quite surprised.

In the vicinity of the turn, the forest begins to transition from eastern hardwood to coniferous evergreens. White and silver birches dominate the landscape here at first but soon have to compete with spruce and fir. Working now in steeper terrain, approach and pass on the left a massive glacial erratic

boulder. The trail relaxes a few minutes but then approaches the lowest moss-slickened reaches of the massive slabs that rise a thousand feet above. Until recently, the trail clawed its way steeply uphill in eroded soils and root tangles to the right of the exposed rock. A relocation cut moved the path a bit more to the southwest and diagonally along the mountain's flank. The new stretch greatly improved the footing and eased an ascent into an open granite scar, steep enough to prevent soils from building up on the rock. Pick your way along a fracture seam in the slab, taking some care as you go.

Regain the forest and approach the col between the twin peaks. The incline eases in a stretch of open mature evergreens and leads to a junction where yellow blazes show themselves. To the right, a path descends to the south toward South Percy Peak and the Old Summer Club Trail junction nearby. Stay straight ahead for about 200 feet. Reach a second trail junction at a tight turn to the left. The route ahead is the Percy Loop coming up from the cold northern flank of North Percy Peak. Ignore Percy Loop and turn hard left uphill for a five-minute rigorous climb to the base of North Percy's summit cone.

The forest growth ends abruptly about 2 miles into the trek. Looming above is nothing but naked granite, slabs so steep that you have no choice but to lean into the mountain as you ascend, following indistinct orange plant blazes that have just about eroded into invisibility.

The trek up the slabs is a cardio workout. Just when the acetic acid in the calves begins to burn, the steepness abates, scrub growth finds places to anchor to, and grand vistas open. Think of North Percy as climbing a giant gumdrop, and you are now gaining the rounded summit. Herd paths swing through low mountain blueberry and scrub spruce and converge on the very summit at a rock cairn that holds up a big sign the states you are at North Percy Peak, elevation 3,418.

Although lowbush blueberries grow on many summits in the Northeast, few mountains boast a carpet of the fruiting plants acres in expanse. Come this way in early August, and in most years, you may eat your fill of the berries before descending. More than a few families in the region have known about North Percy's fruit cache for generations, so sometimes you may witness people picking fruit and filling containers on the summit.

The blueberries are only a part of the riches on top. Mineral collectors periodically scour exposed ledges for quartz and other semiprecious crystals and stone. And there is a wealth of unrestricted views in all directions, including an overlook down onto badly scarred twin neighbor South Percy Peak some 200 vertical feet below, and to long, lean Christine Lake to the southeast of the smaller mountain. Everywhere, mountainous country is cleaved by a band of farm fields that straddle the Connecticut River Valley to the west and southwest. Except for the village of Groveton far below, where the abandoned Wausau Papers mill sits cold and useless, there is little human habitation to be seen.

Once you've made your acquaintance with this fine summit, do one more thing before you leave. Move over to the west edge of the mountain, scurry down a few dozen feet, and have a look down the hideously steep former West Side Trail, about as steep a bit of real estate in northern New Hampshire that can be tramped without a rope.

Don't descend the old trail, please. Go down the way you came up. If you have a little extra ambition, try dodging down the Percy Loop trail that shows up on the left in the little dogleg turn 15 minutes off the summit. The Percy Loop (see the following chapter) has its own rewards and provides a route down to an organized campsite and eventually out to Nash Stream Road, about a mile north of where you parked your car for earlier in the day. By walking southbound on the road, you can reach your vehicle in 15 minutes. That way you don't have to retrace the entire route you ascended hours before.

In the country north of the White Mountain National Forest, North Percy Peak is one of the more beloved summits in the heavily forested realm known as The Great North Woods. If you love tramping about in the Whites, you ought to add North Percy Peak to your list of must-climbs. You will not be disappointed.

21.

Percy Loop

Location: Stark, NH

Distance: 2.2 miles to the summit of North Percy Peak, 5.4-mile loop

Difficulty: Moderate to very strenuous on the incline below the summit

Trailhead: 44°40'43.02'N, 71°26'44.75'W

GETTING THERE

To reach the Percy Loop trail within the Nash Stream Forest in Stark Township, you need to locate NH 110 between Groveton and Berlin. Travel NH 3 or US 2 to Lancaster, New Hampshire. On the west end of town, NH 3 and US 2 diverge, NH 3 turning northbound toward Groveton and Colebrook. Drive about 8 miles north to the point where a large factory, the closed and shuttered Wausau Papers mill, comes into view behind a covered bridge and small steam switching locomotive and tender set up as a historic display. The junction of NH 110 is on the right. If traveling from the east, from the city of Berlin and NH 16, watch for NH 110 signs in the heart of the downtown and travel westward, taking care to follow the signs through city residential streets.

If traveling east from Groveton on NH 110, watch for Emerson Road on the left, a bit more than 2 miles out of town. If running westward from Berlin city, motor some 16 miles through the tiny town of Stark and watch for Emerson Road on the right, 3-plus miles beyond.

Once on Emerson Road, travel 3 miles on pavement until the road takes a dogleg turn to the right at the point where there is a cemetery on the right. Just as Emerson Road jogs right, Nash Stream Road cuts to the left. A good road sign marks the way.

Nash Stream Road immediately turns to a good dirt and gravel lane. Travel 3 miles and reach a small bridge over Slide Brook. Just before the bridge is the parking pullout for Percy Peaks Trail. Don't stop here. Continue

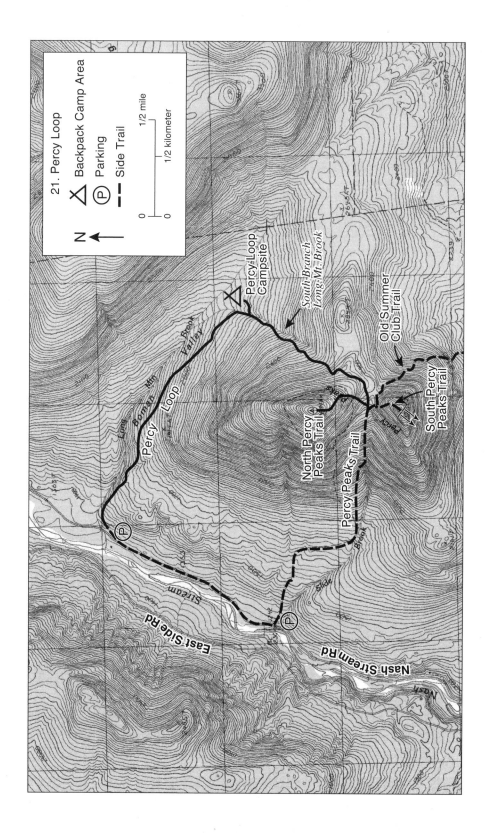

21. Percy Loop

Backpack Camp Area △
Parking Ⓟ
Side Trail - - -

N ←

0   1/2 mile
0   1/2 kilometer

Percy Loop Campsite △

South Branch
Long Mt. Brook

Old Summer
Club Trail

South Percy
Peaks Trail

North Percy
Peaks Trail

Percy Peaks Trail

Percy Loop

Long Mtn Brook Valley

Percy
Brook

Slide Brook

Stream

East Side Rd

Nash Stream Rd

Nash

on for another full mile. On an uphill grade, watch for a small, sandy pullout on the right and a birch tree sporting a Percy Loop sign and yellow blaze. At the foot of the tree is another Percy Loop sign. If you go too far, you will pass over Long Mountain Brook. Park at the pullout. Behind the tree, on the right, the trail cuts into the spruce and immediately begins to climb out of the valley.

A LOOP HIKE OF THE DRAMATIC PERCY PEAKS

North of NH 110, the domain of the White Mountain National Forest ceases and the wild terrain of the Nash Stream Forest, New Hampshire's largest state woodland tract at 39,601 acres, and the equally large Bunnell Reserve stretch away to the north. To reach deep into this country, Nash Stream Road stretches north 11 miles, running in a beautiful stream valley that had been utterly destroyed in 1969, when the large log and stone crib impoundment, the Nash Bog dam built at Mile 9 along the road, collapsed during a drenching two-day rainstorm. Trees and undergrowth have healed the wounds, but clues of the scouring of the landscape is evident everywhere along the road, if you scout the understory as you motor north.

The Percy Loop trail trailhead is located at Mile 4 along the road, about a mile north of a small, new bridge built over Slide Brook, just a few feet north of the parking pullout for the Percy Peaks Trail. Make note of where the Percy Peaks Trail's position in the woods on the right. The hike spelled out below will drop you down the Percy Peaks Trail to Nash Stream Road, so you may walk back to your car a mile along the road at the end of your loop hike.

Continue on one more mile to a point where the road pitches gradually uphill and crosses atop a large culvert built into Long Mountain Brook. A few feet south of the stream, where the Percy Loop enters the woods, is a recently built, sandy pullout on the right, large enough for two automobiles. Look for the Percy Loop trail sign in the birch tree at the head of the pullout and a low signpost at the foot of the trail.

The Percy Loop provides the easiest access to the bold, conical twin summits called the Percy Peaks. On this hike, the destination is North Percy, the larger of the two mountains, although peakbaggers can readily summit both peaks in no time. North Percy is heavily scarred with great, exposed granite ledges, many of them very steep. The peak boasts a broad, rather flat summit crown several acres large. The land on top is, in reality, a blueberry barren, and the picking is almost always good the first week of August.

Don your day pack and begin your hike with the prattle of Long Mountain Brook on your left. Immediately, the trail pitches up at a moderate angle and remains so for ½ mile. The pathway provides fine footing. It was once a logging tote road, but has mellowed well over a generation to a support a young foot trail that is as pleasant to the eye as it is to the feet. Ascend eastbound, leaving the brook far below, slipping through mature mixed hardwoods interspersed with spindly cherry that has a maddening habit of keeling over during the winter and blocking the trail.

Twenty minutes into the climb, cross a knoll and enter a more gradual grade, flanked on the left by the moderately steep pitch into Bowman Valley, which separates North Percy from Long Mountain. Cross a sometimes moist depression and occasional seasonal rivulets to a point where the trail seems to level out and come to an abrupt end at the foot of a badly eroded ravine. The former logging tote road has been severed here by the winter runoff turbulence of the little south branch of Long Mountain Brook. A few feet before the trail disappears at a granite slab

Percy Peaks   JOHN COMPTON

wet with good fresh water, a new woods footpath cuts uphill abruptly to the right, swinging southward.

Ascend rapidly for just a minute; you'll come to a junction. On the left, a spur trail leaves at a campsite sign and crosses the branch stream. Detour off the main trail for 300 feet, descending gradually to Percy Loop Camp, an organized tenting site complete with a tent platform, a composting latrine, a sign kiosk, and access to water in all seasons. The camp, built by the Cohos Trail Association and located in a white birch grove, is at roughly the halfway point to the summit and is a good place to stop, take a break, rehydrate, and enjoy a snack.

Back to the main trail, continue uphill. Lose the little stream quickly and begin to climb steadily and directly south through the transition zone where eastern hardwoods begin to give way to cold boreal forest species. As spruce, fir, and birch come on strong, the trail underfoot changes abruptly. Enter a boulder and scree field, a rock debris

minefield built by granite scaling off the very steep, naked north ledges of North Percy Peak and accumulating for thousands of years.

Use caution in the boulder warren, particularly if the terrain is wet or icy. Pick your way, using your hands as necessary to steady yourself. On occasion, look up and catch glimpses of the hideously steep north flank of the mountain towering above, and from which all this granite debris underfoot fell over the course of 12,000 years.

At the head of boulder field, the Percy Loop moderates in steepness, soon almost levels out for a stretch, and slips over a ridgeline. The forest brightens as restricted views to the southeast open and the sun reaches directly into the more southerly slopes. The path drops in elevation for a few seconds and then rebounds, slabs the eastern flank of the mountain, and meets a junction with the Percy Peaks Trail.

At the junction, turn right and uphill on the Percy Peaks Trail and make for the summit of perhaps the most dramatic peak north of the White Mountain National Forest. The century-old trail climbs at a moderate pitch in stubby spruce and fir forest, until the trees end rather abruptly at the base of a very steep granite slab hundreds of feet wide and high. Look closely for old and eroded orange plant blazes on the rock and begin an arduous 400-foot climb up the slabs, leaning into the steepness of the hill.

In wet or particularly in icy conditions, the slabs on North Percy can be perilous. North Percy is a killer. The slabs under the now closed-up section of the original trail on the western flank of the mountain claimed at least one life half a century ago, when a young man slipped on wet moss growing on the granite and rocketed down the steep incline. Unable to stop his descent, he slammed into the trees 100 feet below the point where he lost his footing. A second account of a death on the mountain from the late 1800s, I never have been able to verify.

Approaching the top of the mountain the grade eases a bit where some scrub trees and lowbush blueberries gain a hold. At the very summit, a low rock cairn supports a handcrafted sign signifying you have reached 3,418 feet of elevation.

The summit of North Percy is rather flat, several acres in expanse, and carpeted with blueberries. The first week of August, the summit is a riot of blue fruit if it has been a normal rainfall year. The view from many points on top is unobstructed, and it is a grand view. To the south, over the Pilot and Pliny Ranges in the Kilkenny district of the White Mountain National Forest, the tall summits of the northern Presidential Range are clearly visible. To the east runs much of the chain of the 30-mile Mahoosuc Range, but some mileage is hidden behind the nearby hulking whaleback massif called Long Mountain, which stands another 200 vertical feet

higher than North Percy. To the north, you can see all the high terrain of the Dixville country and the peaks of the Connecticut River headwaters realm at the top of the Granite State. A westerly view reveals the Goback and Northwest Peaks Ranges in Stratford and Columbia Townships, respectively, the Connecticut River Valley with its open farm fields, and the horizon-to-horizon spine of the Green Mountains.

Many people come this way when the blueberries are ripe, and mineral collectors comb the ledges for quartz and semi-precious stones. Pockmarks in the rock reveal where collectors have chiseled out some rare find.

In fair weather, it a pleasure to languish for an hour or more on the fine summit. But there are miles to go. Take care working your way back down the slabs on the same route you ascended. Retrace your steps to the junction with the Percy Loop Trail, but instead of backtracking down it, turn hard to the right and stay with the Percy Peaks Trail.

In a few hundred feet, pass by a junction on the left with the Old Summer Club Trail that accesses South Percy Peak, and begin a descent into the valley (the terrain is spelled out in detail in the previous chapter). The descent is rapid, challenging in one or two places, but the trail is in excellent condition now that it had been refurbished in 2010 and some heavily eroded sections bypassed.

In less than two hours of your leaving the summit, the trail bottoms out at Nash Stream Road. Turn right and begin a long mile walk back to your vehicle, completing the loop hike. The entire trek is a bit more than 5 miles in length, but picks up one of the most endearing summits in New Hampshire's Great North Woods. Throw in an extra hour and the summit of South Percy Peaks, and you have, for a little extra work, netted two terrific summits with exceptional views for your efforts.

22.

Pond Brook Falls

Location: Stark, NH

Distance: Less than 0.25 mile round-trip, but add more than 0.5 mile if you add a walk down to Trailblazer Bridge over Nash Stream. If you tackle the bushwhack to Waterhole Brook beaver bog, add another long mile.

Difficulty: Easy

Trailhead: 44°40'43.02'N, 71°26'11.66'W

GETTING THERE

To locate Pond Brook Falls within the Nash Stream Forest, you need to find NH 110 between Groveton and Berlin. Travel NH 3 or US 2 to Lancaster, New Hampshire. On the west end of town, NH 3 and US 2 diverge, NH 3 turning northbound toward Groveton and Colebrook. Drive about 8 miles north to the point where a large factory, the closed and shuttered Wausau Papers mill, comes into view behind a covered bridge and small steam switching locomotive and tender set up as an historic display. The junction of NH 110 is on the right. If traveling from the east, from the city of Berlin and NH 16, watch for NH 110 signs in the heart of the downtown and travel westward taking care to follow the signs through city residential streets.

If traveling east from Groveton on NH 110, watch for Emerson Road on the left, a bit more than 2 miles out of town. If running westward from Berlin city, motor some 16 miles through the tiny town of Stark and watch for Emerson Road on the right, 3-plus miles beyond.

Once on Emerson Road, travel 3 miles on pavement, until the road takes a dogleg turn to the right at the point where there is a cemetery on the right. Just as Emerson Road jogs right, Nash Stream Road cuts to the left. A good road sign marks the way.

Nash Stream Road immediately turns to a good dirt and gravel lane. Motor 6 miles to the point where the road crosses a culvert that carries Pond Brook. Immediately beyond the humped-up lane over the culvert a parking pullout appears on the right. The short

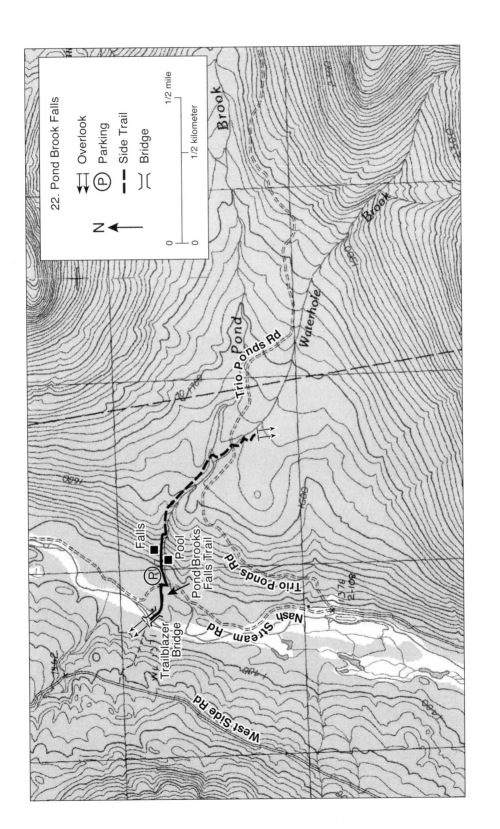

22. Pond Brook Falls

Overlook
Parking
Side Trail
Bridge

N

0
0

1/2 mile
1/2 kilometer

Brook

Brook

Waterhole

Trio Ponds Pd

Trio Ponds Rd

Falls

Pool

Pond Brooks
Falls Trail

Trailblazer
Bridge

Nash Stream Rd

West Side Rd

path to the falls slips around an earthen berm to the northeast.

SLIP-SLIDING AWAY

With the summer sun low on the western horizon late one afternoon in the Nash Stream Forest, I came across a through-hiker sitting naked on smooth granite slabs tilled toward the sun. All the worldly possessions he had taken with him on his trek, from his socks to his sleeping bag, were scattered about on the stone, drying in the sunlight. He had chosen a fine place to dry out after several days' hiking in steady rain.

The lone trekker reclined on a huge baby bottom–smooth granite slab that supported a large slip falls called Pond Brook Falls, the only substantial waterfall within the New Hampshire's largest state forest. Like most people who come this way to the falls, the bare-ass hiker was in no hurry to leave.

The walk into Pond Brook Falls is the shortest trek highlighted in this guide. The base of the falls is only 300 feet from the edge of Nash Stream Road. You get a lot to like for little effort. But the real prize here actually resides near the top of the falls, and getting there is not the least bit difficult but can be tricky. If high water is thundering over the rocks, the slabs become slippery and even dangerous.

Follow Nash Stream Road to about Mile 6, to the parking pullout on the right. In the spruce is a Pond Brook Falls sign. Once out of your car, follow the narrow trail to the east around a large stone and wander into cool, forested surroundings. Immediately, the rumble of the falls will greet your ears.

Pace along on the level for 200 feet on path that was substantially eroded by tropical storm flashflooding, when the trail begins to pitch uphill, rounds a little bend, and divides. To the right, a herd path runs a few dozen feet to a black pool agitated by a fat jet of water squeezing between large two boulders stacked at the bottom of the falls. The pool is deep enough for a good plunge, but the waters can be frightfully cold in all seasons except, perhaps, the first week of August.

Leave the pool behind, pace back to the main trail, and work uphill to a low berm of tree roots and soil that forms a divide between forest and granite. Ahead, sunlight pours into a realm of rock and fluid that makes up a complex bit of geology that's one-third waterfall, one-third grand water slide, and one-third flooded stairway.

Scramble onto the smooth skin of the water and ice-polished granite, pitched up at a 20-degree angle, climb 40 feet, and have a seat where that naked hiker baked his rear end and belongings in the sun. Before you, water sprays over broken ledges and skims in thick sheets over the slabs that funnel the liquid into the narrow flume between the boulders below. Any youngster looking at this big slide falls would instinctively want to race uphill and then jump into the drink and body surf into oblivion at the bottom. I don't recommend it, for obvious reasons, but the thought of doing so is enticing.

Twenty-five feet above, the slabs are divided by a small knoll that anchors a dozen trees. To the right of the knob, the slabs are interrupted by a little shelf 18 inches high. In low flow, the sun beating on the gray granite can heat the little bath to a comfortably warm temperature. Immerse yourself here and relax as the falls slips along beside. And you have a view of the valley below and out to the flank of 3,000-foot Stratford Mountain.

Swing to the left around the knoll and take some care hop-scotching up the rock outcroppings to the point where the Pond Brook reunites at a kettle hole, a natural round granite tub formed by small rocks swirling round and round in a natural depres-

Pond Brook lower falls   JOHN COMPTON

sion. Eroded over millennia by the stone tum-
blers, the kettle hole is nearly as circular as
natural forces could make it. Try your luck in
it in early August. You can sit in it up to your
chest while water splashes over a series of
steplike granite ledges and boulder rubble
just upstream from the tub.

In summer, when water levels in the brook
are usually low, the slabs of Pond Brook Falls
offer firm footing the full length of the falls.
But in periods of high water, the smooth
slabs can be slick enough to cause a loss of
footing. Climbing uphill poses less of a problem than does descending. In tough conditions, move a few feet to the north, into the
woods. An old trail built more than a decade
ago by Stratford High School students can
still be followed down off the falls.

The short jaunt to and from the falls need

not be the end of outing. Rather than take
off in the car, swing out to the road, turn right
(north) and walk just 40 feet to the junction
of a side lane on the left. Walk down the two-
tire track until two metal gates hove into view.
Swing around the gate on the left and stride
down to the beautiful mountain stream that
drains the valley. Spanning Nash Stream is
Trailblazer Bridge, a 90-foot snowmobile
bridge supported beneath by arched steel
beams that are substantial enough to hold
up a skyscraper.

Mosey out onto the span to its far end.
Upriver, the southern major peak of the Whitcomb Range rises over the valley and the
fast-moving water. Downriver, to the southeast, the impossible profile of North Percy
Peak shows itself. From this angle, the heavily scarred mountain is a narrow, steep-sided

Pond Brook Falls

Pond Brook upper slides JOHN COMPTON

mixed hardwoods and softwoods. Move up-hill on gentle terrain for ¼ mile, watching for the confluence of Pond Brook and Water-hole Brook. Waterhole Brook enters the main stream at the far bank. Just above the con-fluence, several large boulders stand in Pond Brook, each close to the other to allow pas-sage to the other bank.

On the far bank of the stream, follow Wa-terhole Brook, now a short distance to the edge of Pond Brook Road. Cross the road, turn downhill a few feet, and then stride into a grass-filled skidway. Stride a few dozen feet and look to the right. Find a red surveyor-tape flag and follow the flags through a small stand of trees to a raspberry cane clearing. Stay to the left at the clearing and pick up an indistinct right of way just below the re-mains of a long-abandoned beaver dam. Climb up on the dam wherever the trees part and you can sense a view northeastward. On the dam, you can see across a large, drained bog that once held a beaver pond. In the dis-tance, the fine south summit of Mt. Whit-comb rises high above the bog.

Mt. Whitcomb is rarely climbed, as there is no formal trail to the summit. Rarer still are those who bushwhack to the mountain's multiple cliff ledges for a dramatic view down the Nash Stream valley.

The beaver bog and environs of Water-hole Brook are a moose haunt. Moose drop-pings, hoof prints, and browsed vegetation signal that the largest member of the deer family is common in the area.

Whichever course you take at Pond Brook Falls, a five-minute sojourn or an hour-long bushwhack, there is little chance you will be disappointed. If exploring the many features of the Nash Stream Forest, put Pond Brook Falls among those items at the top of your list.

gumdrop shape, its western flank looking for all the world like an Olympic ski jump outrun hill from hell.

The bridge is a good point to begin a tub-ing run southward, provided the water level isn't anemic because of a dry summer. Not into tubing? Enjoy a fine afternoon in the sun on the bridge while Nash Stream talks you into continuing northward to explore more terrain that few people ever explore.

If you could use a bit more of a challenge or like to explore new terrain, continue uphill from the top of the falls. Bushwhack above the north bank of Pond Brook, following it in

Nash Stream Forest

23.

East Side Trail Loop

Location: Nash Stream Forest, Odell unincorporated township, NH

Distance: About 5 miles to complete the loop

Difficulty: Easy but somewhat lengthy

Trailhead: 44°44'11.73'N, 71°26'22.33'W

GETTING THERE

To reach the East Side Trail within the Nash Stream Forest in the town of Stratford and Odell unincorporated township, you'll need to locate NH 110 between Groveton and Berlin. Travel NH 3 or US 2 to Lancaster, New Hampshire. On the west end of town, NH 3 and US 2 diverge, NH 3 turning northbound toward Groveton and Colebrook. Drive about 8 miles north to the point where a large factory, the closed and shuttered Wausau Papers mill, comes into view behind a covered bridge and small steam switching locomotive and tender set up as a historic display. The junction of NH 110 is on the right. If traveling from the east, from the city of Berlin and NH 16, watch for NH 110 signs in the heart of the downtown and travel westward taking care to follow the signs through city residential streets.

If traveling east from Groveton on NH 110, watch for Emerson Road on the left, a bit more than 2 miles out of town. If running westward from Berlin city, motor some 16 miles through the tiny town of Stark and watch for Emerson Road on the right, 3-plus miles beyond.

Once on Emerson Road, travel 3 miles on pavement until the road takes a dogleg turn to the right at the point where there is a cemetery on the right. Just as Emerson Road jogs right, Nash Stream Road cuts to the left. A good road sign marks the way.

Nash Stream Road immediately turns to a good dirt and gravel lane. Travel 9 miles, staying on the valley floor and ignoring spur roads right or left. At Mile 9, Nash Stream

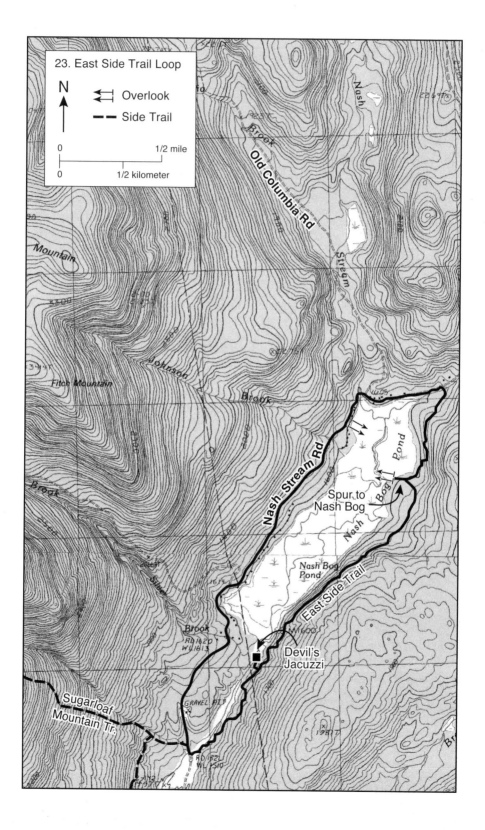

23. East Side Trail Loop

N

⇇ Overlook
– – Side Trail

0 — 1/2 mile
0 — 1/2 kilometer

Old Columbia Rd

Nash

Stream

Mountain

Fitch Mountain

Johnson

Brook

Brook

Nash Stream Rd

Spur to
Nash Bog

Bog

Pond

Nash

Nash Bog
Pond

East Side Trail

Brook
RD 1620
WL 1613

Devil's
Jacuzzi

Sugarloaf
Mountain Tr.

GRAVEL PIT

RD 1521
WL 1510

Road crosses a good-size bridge over the water. Park on the right just before the bridge. The trailhead is just to the right of the south end of the bridge at the base of a stone stairway.

THE SCENE OF AN ECOLOGICAL DISASTER

A hike on the East Side Trail and the loop back to your car along the narrow, camp-lined Nash Stream Road begins at the scene of an ecological crime. The second you step from your car and make your first footfalls on the path, you will notice evidence of a disaster at your feet. Rounded stones jumbled together, spindly and sickly birch, and reindeer moss are prima facie evidence of a great tribulation that befell the Nash Stream Valley four decades in the past. About ½ mile upstream from the trailhead once stood a massive log and stone crib dam, built a century ago to create a head of water so that cut logs could be more easily driven down the stream to paper and sawmills far down river. But after three days of heavy rains during the summer of 1969, and despite the efforts of dam controller Ralph Rowden to open all the sluice gates and kick out every head board at the top of the dam, the dam failed all at once. More than 70 acres of lake waters languished behind the dam, but once the structure collapsed, it only took a few hours for the entire lake to drain away. In so doing, the fantastic forces unleashed scoured the valley floor raw, undermined hillsides, and caused landslide after landslide. To this day, the land is still healing.

So when you start your hike, look about and take note of the aftermath of disaster about you. But fear not, the dam was never rebuilt, and you will have a pleasant overland hike ahead of you, accompanied by rugged channel of Nash Stream and the wildlife haven that is Nash Stream Bog, a wetland that was once the floor of the long-lost lake.

Strike out northbound away from the bridge along the east bank of the Nash Stream, a fine trout brook festooned with boulders and cold pools. Pace along on the stream bank and detour through flood boulder rubble to the point where the trail curves right and climbs a shallow grade. Over the height of land, the trail levels out, now well above the stream, and drifts along for 300 feet before falling rapidly down two separate drops that deposit you close to the stream again, but about 20 vertical feet above the waters. Cross a wet spot on bog bridges and turn upriver in tight spruce growth.

Now pay attention. Watch for a junction ahead, flagged by a double yellow blaze and a sign that reads, DEVIL'S JACUZZI. Leave the main trail here for a few minutes and cut left downhill. As you turn, you will notice a huge boulder, 15 feet tall, which sports a stone cap, as if some giant fashioned a head covering for the great stone. Drop into a boulder maze and thread a narrow trail for 200 feet. Swing around another giant stone and step out onto a somewhat level stone shelf right on the edge of Nash Stream.

You have arrived at Devil's Jacuzzi, a natural formation in the stream current that mimics a big, commercial hot tub. Three granite slabs form a box and a fourth slab below the current forms a seat. Because of the way the rocks align, fast-moving water slips into this formation and rolls, trapping air that boils to the surface as if there were Jacuzzi jets beneath the waves. The effect is arresting, and the first impulse is to strip off your pack and clothes and to step into the "tub." Go ahead, but if it isn't the first week of August, the water can be bone-rattlingly cold. And while you are enjoying your plunge in the Devil's Jacuzzi, take a look upstream. Just above are two very large round boulders with scars on their flanks. These boulders once stood

Nash Bog

within the Nash Bog dam. When the dam failed, they rolled downstream and lodged here.

Back on the main trail, move northward through an S-curve, pass one more immense glacial erratic, and begin to climb into higher terrain. Leave the tight spruce behind and stride in very pleasant open hardwoods that are lit on the left by sunlight flooding into a broad, treeless environment beyond the tree line. The trail now runs parallel to Nash Bog, a wildlife-friendly habitat, the floor of which was once the lake bottom. The East Side trail undulates easily up and down on its way north for 15 minutes' hike, then bends into a wide Z-turn. At the base of the turn, a spur trail cuts directly out to the bog, where moist ground stops you. Nearly 70 acres of open terrain greets you, and across the bog,

3,600-foot peaks hold sway west and north.

Five minutes north of the Z-turn, the trail leaves the woods and enters are narrow grassy meadow, once a logging landing. Ignore the opening to the right and move directly ahead across the meadow until it narrows into a former logging lane, widens once more, and narrows again. Walk on the level through grass, wildflowers, weeds, and occasional alder stands until the path is severed by fast-moving Pike Brook. Step across the stream on sizable rocks and continue to the narrow upper last mile of Nash Stream Road. The route of the Cohos Trail turns right here; for this hike, turn left, southbound, and stroll nearly 3 miles back to your vehicle. Although it's a road walk, it is less than dull, because the route passes scores of old summer camps that were once built as lakeside bungalows. When the dam breached, the camps were left high and dry. But the treeless bog permits good views to the north and west to Mt. Muise and the Whitcomb Range peaks.

The walk is a fanciful lesson in American rural culture. The camp owners are proud of their little abodes and often give them tongue-in-cheek names. At one point you'll pass a sign that reads, MAYOR OF ODELL. Odell is the unincorporated township you are walking through. Permanent population: zero.

More than 2 miles along the road, a gray-painted bungalow comes into view on the left that boasts a sign: BROKEN DAM CAMP. Turn left off Nash Stream Road, walk the drive by the camp and a second one, and follow the indistinct lane into the woods. Once in the trees, you'll notice you are moving along on top of an increasingly tall, earthen structure—the former Nash Bog Dam. Stride atop the dam as the earth below falls farther and farther away, until the structure surface crumbles and a steep tail dives downhill to the bank of Nash Stream. At the water, the freezing cold Silver Brook enters on the left.

Directly ahead across Nash Stream, four or five massive dam timbers still poke out of the steep embankment on the far side. They are all that remain of the very large crib dam once stood here, creating a lake that was 25 feet deep at the face of the dam.

The last road-walk leg of this long but easy loop hike is a trek down a long hill. At the crest of the hill, North Percy Peak shows itself 5 miles to the south, the mountain's extremely steep west face looking for all the world like a Nordic ski jump outrun hill. At the base of the hill, pass the Sugarloaf Mountain Trail on the right, cross Nash Stream on the stringer bridge over the flow and reacquaint yourself with your car.

Some who come this way do so to fish Nash Stream. Others come to tramp in quiet surroundings in terrain that is frequented by moose. Nash Bog and its environs are excellent moose habitat and the great creatures are often seen moving through this region. In fact, the East Side Trail is a popular thoroughfare with the animals, as evidenced by the discrete piles of moose pellets (droppings). And the bog is home to scores of songbird species.

24.

Sugarloaf Mountain Trail

Location: Nash Stream Forest, Stark, NH

Distance: 4.4 miles round-trip

Difficulty: Somewhat strenuous climb up the eastern flank of the mountain

Trailhead: 44°44'12.10'N, 71°26'21.47'W

GETTING THERE

To reach the Sugarloaf Mountain Trail within the Nash Stream Forest in Stratford Township, you'll need to locate NH 110 between Groveton and Berlin. Travel NH 3 or US 2 to Lancaster, New Hampshire. On the west end of town, NH 3 and US 2 diverge, NH 3 turning northbound toward Groveton and Colebrook. Drive about 8 miles north to the point where a large factory, the closed and shuttered Wausau Papers mill, comes into view behind a covered bridge and small steam switching locomotive and tender set up as a historic display. The junction of NH 110 is on the right. If traveling from the east, from the city of Berlin and NH 16, watch for NH 110 signs in the heart of the downtown and travel westward taking care to follow the signs through city residential streets.

If traveling east from Groveton on NH 110, watch for Emerson Road on the left, a bit more than 2 miles out of town. If running westward from Berlin city, motor some 16 miles through the tiny town of Stark and watch for Emerson Road on the right, 3-plus miles beyond.

Once on Emerson Road, travel 3 miles on pavement until the road takes a dogleg turn to the right at the point where there is a cemetery on the right. Just as Emerson Road jogs right, Nash Stream Road cuts to the left. A good road sign marks the way.

Nash Stream Road immediately turns to a good dirt and gravel lane. Travel 9 miles, staying on the valley floor and ignoring spur roads right or left. At Mile 9, Nash Stream Road crosses a good-size bridge over the

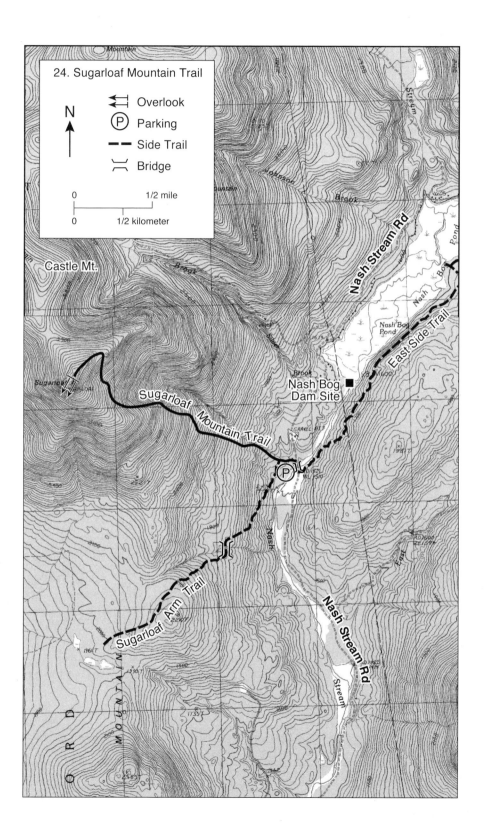

24. Sugarloaf Mountain Trail

N

Overlook
Parking
Side Trail
Bridge

0   1/2 mile
0   1/2 kilometer

Castle Mt.

Sugarloaf

Sugarloaf Mountain Trail

Nash Stream Rd

East Side Trail

Nash Bog Pond

Nash Bog Dam Site

GRAVEL PIT

Sugarloaf Arm Trail

MOUNTAIN

Nash Stream Rd

Johnson Brook

Brook

water. Fifty feet beyond the bridge, the trail-head parking spot sits off to the left. Park there.

THE COMMANDER OF THE GREAT NORTH WOODS

The first thing I'll do if I win a $200 million lottery (fat chance) is restore to the summit of Sugarloaf Mountain in the 36,601-acre Nash Stream Forest, the watchman's observation cab on the exposed naked summit ledges, right on the very spot where the structure once stood. I still miss the little building, even though it has been gone for a generation. But the view from the summit of Sugarloaf is as marvelous as ever, a showstopper, for trampers who don't mind the rather dull and laborious slog up and down the mountain's moderately but continuously steep eastern flank.

For those who like their views panoramic and their peaks pointed, like Goose Eye, The Horn, or Chocorua, Sugarloaf should fill the bill. To reach the trailhead, simply motor nearly 9 miles north on Nash Stream Road to the point where the lane crosses the only large bridge over Nash Stream. Just 50 feet ahead on the left is a little pullout adjacent to an untraveled lane to and beyond a camp, a route that was once the jeep service road that accessed the fire tower watchman's living quarters and summit observation cab. Park, but don't block the drive. Follow the yellow blazes west, pass a little private camp on the right, cross a rivulet, round a gate, and walk through a small field. Reach the woods line and immediately the trail splits. To the left cuts the Sugarloaf Arm Trail, a snowmobile trail and through-route of the Cohos Trail. The Sugarloaf Mountain Trail stretches straight ahead and begins to pitch uphill right away at a moderately steep angle.

There are few features along the 1.5-mile-long once-service road, other than the trail was recently refurbished with a multitude of water bars and water division channels, and the growth impinging on the trail clipped back. Ascend at a maddeningly constant angle that never relents until the forest brightens at a small clearing where, a generation ago, the fire watchman's quarters stood to the right side of the trail. All that is left now is the rotting flooring of two small buildings that once stood here. Thirty feet to the left is a good spring where you may obtain water in any season, even in dry summers.

Once beyond the remains of the little buildings, things get more interesting. The trail pitches uphill once again in spruce and fir and approaches a ½-mile-long ridge that links Sugarloaf to an indistinct summit called Castle. Upon reaching the ridgeline, the trail turns to the left and now rises very gradually in pleasant boreal terrain to flat slabs of rock. As the slabs broaden out, the forest is pushed aside and grand visas open.

Stride out to the highest point among the narrow band of slabs to the very spot where the former fire tower cab was once anchored. Steel pins still reveal the anchor points. Unlike virtually all other fire towers in the East, Sugarloaf tower wasn't a tower at all. The summit was so exposed and the view so unobstructed that a steel superstructure was dispensed with and the watchman's cab was perched on a low deck affixed directly to the summit slabs.

When I first hiked up to the summit of Sugarloaf in 1971, I spent a memorable hour with the ranger who manned the station. Handing me a pair of binoculars, he pointed out a tiny dot in a bog pond far below to the southwest. In the middle of the bog were ripples and a moving object. The binoculars revealed that what I was seeing was a moose, the first I had ever witnessed.

He also mentioned that he had a resident porcupine, living beneath the building; if I was

Sugarloaf sign   CHAD PEPAU

lucky, I might see the creature. Sure enough, I did meet the permanent tenant of the tower, the minute I left the summit to descend. The quill pig was ascending the last feet of the trail as I started off and we had a bit of a standoff before he shrugged and waddled to and beneath his man-made home.

Today, the summit is structure free. The slabs drop away quickly at the head of the south flank, giving one the impression of standing on the bow of a ship. Below, the fine glacier-carved Nash Stream Valley sweeps away to the south, flanked on the east by the long, undulating ridge of the Whitcomb Range; the taller and hulking mass of Long Mountain, and the always interesting twin cones of the Percy Peaks. To the west is a gash in the landscape between West Peak and the imposing Goback Range,

a jumble of both rounded and pyramid summits that cut off the Connecticut River Valley from your view. The wound in the landscape is Stratford Notch. To the north, over the encroaching spruce, stands the 3,600-footer Gore Mountain, and farther off, the tallest peak north of the White Mountain National Forest, Bunnell Mountain. Fine summits each, they shoulder no foot trails whatsoever but can be approached by bushwhacking along log skidder tracks.

Sugarloaf is no tramp. At 3,701 feet in elevation, it is bested only by Bunnell in this northern country. Sugarloaf has such a graceful profile when seen from almost every direction, and a commanding presence at the southern leading edge of the tall Northwest Peaks Range, too, that it positively dominates the region it stands in. Because

Sugarloaf, ecophotography   JERRY MONKMAN

the mountain nearly matches the height of the summits in the Pilot Range farther to the south, you have an unobstructed view of the upper above-tree-line slopes of Presidential peaks Madison, Adams, and Jefferson.

Once on top, charmed by the panoramic view, it is easy to forget the uninspiring trek up the mountain. You must remember that reaching such a fine spot takes no more than two hours—a short effort, really, to attain so fine a vista. Because of that fact, Sugarloaf is becoming popular once again. When the summit cab was in place and one could hike up and visit with the ranger, the peak was frequently climbed. Once the structure was removed, people stopped coming. But that's

changing, as more and more trekkers are seeking out a wilderness or solitary experience, rather than hiking with the masses that frequent the high peaks of the Presidential Range and the Franconia Range, an hour's drive or more to the south.

The view to the east has change considerably recently. Beyond the Whitcomb Range are the unsung summits of Kelsey Mountain and Owl's Head. These uplands and Dixville Peak farther to the north have become foundations for more than 30 huge wind turbine towers, standing nearly 400 feet tall. Renewable energy technology has come to the Great North Woods because anemometer (wind velocity) tests in the region place the ridges of Coos County in the 99 percentile bracket for wind speed and wind availability for inland sites. This fact made wind technology feasible in this region.

That corporations wanted to build wind towers on nearby high ridges in the area should tell any trekker in no uncertain terms that windy conditions are the norm on peaks like Sugarloaf. Pack a rain shell with you when you come into region to hike, and you should be fine. And speaking of wind, what would be better than standing in a good, stiff breeze on a hot day in August on the summit of Sugarloaf?

25.

Gadwah Notch Trail

*Location: Nash Stream Forest, Odell
unincorporated township, NH*

*Distance: Various day-hike trip lengths, but
5.5 miles overall one-way. It's 1 mile to
Cathedral Meadow, 1.5 miles to Moran
Meadow, 2.2 miles to Muise Bowl, and
about 2.7 miles to Bulldozer Flat.*

*Difficulty: Moderate, but lengthy with
1,500-feet elevation gain to Gadwah
Notch and about 800-feet gain up
Baldhead Mountain all the way to the
Baldhead lean-to. There are several short
but steep pitches along the route, as well.*

Trailhead: 44°45'57.07'N, 71°24'41.02'W

GETTING THERE

Travel north on NH 3 to Lancaster, NH. Continue north 10 miles to the outskirts of Groveton Village and the junction of NH 110. Turn right (east) on NH 110 and travel 2 miles to the junction with Emerson Road, a secondary paved road on the left. Turn left onto Emerson Road and travel 3 miles to a junction at a hard right turn in the lane adjacent to a cemetery (on the right). In the turn, stay straight ahead and leave Emerson Road. A sign in the junction island states Nash Stream Road. Immediately turn left onto this good woods road.

Nash Stream Road has a dirt and gravel surface. Travel on this lane for 11 miles, ignoring a few lanes on the left or right. After Mile 9, the lane passes a series of small camps near the road. Pass these camps and continue on a narrowing but good surface until the road appears to end at a Y-junction where two gates seal off vehicle progress.

Park here, but do not block the gates or the access to the last small camp at the junction. The Gadwah Notch Trail begins beyond the gate on the left. There is a trail sign at the foot of the gate and bright yellow blazing in the trees and on rocks on the road.

LEAVING CIVILIZATION
TO FEND FOR ITSELF

The Baldhead Notch Trail is a 5-plus-mile trek well suited for unfettered day hikes of varying lengths with plenty of fine features or a trek with an overnight stop at the Baldhead Mountain lean-to at 3,047-foot elevation. The very remote structure boasts a

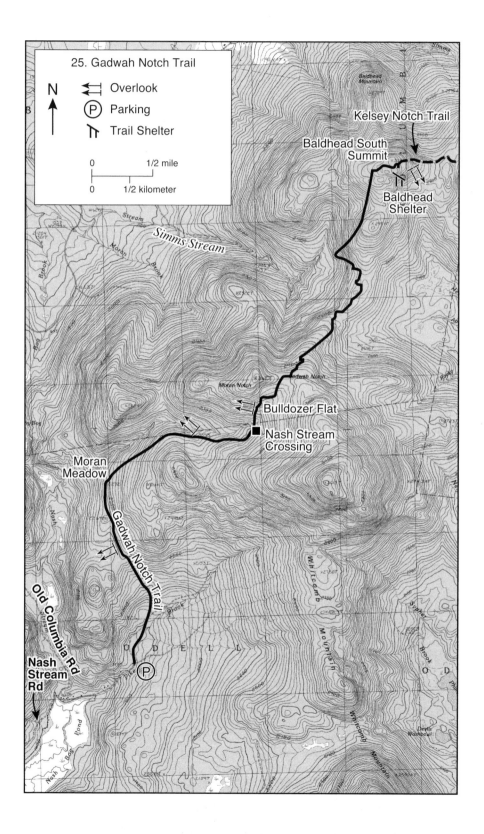

25. Gadwah Notch Trail

N

⇆ Overlook
Ⓟ Parking
⋔ Trail Shelter

0 ————— 1/2 mile
0 ————— 1/2 kilometer

Kelsey Notch Trail

Baldhead South
Summit

Baldhead
Shelter

Simms Stream

Moran Notch

Bulldozer Flat

Nash Stream
Crossing

Moran
Meadow

Gadwah Notch Trail

Old Columbia Rd

Nash
Stream
Rd

40-mile view south down a U-shaped glacier-carved depression called the Phillips Brook Valley to the Presidential and Carter-Moriah Ranges on the horizon.

Step around the so-called Headwaters gate, where the Gadwah Notch Trail sign stands, and begin a level trek on a narrow, untraveled woods lane that is accompanied by Pike Brook on the right. Hike in easy terrain and fine mixed forest for ¼ mile, when the lane begins to pitch up in elevation. Climb out of the valley on a moderate and steady incline for 2,000 feet. Ahead, the lane brightens and then levels out at the head of a broad field of a dozen acres called Cathedral Meadow. To the west, a long 3,600-foot ridge punctuates the atmosphere, headed by the graceful profile of 3,701-foot Sugarloaf Mountain and topping out at 3,724 feet on the wooded summit of Bunnell Mountain. To the south, the Whitcomb Range rises through gaps in the tree line.

Cathedral Meadow is the first in a series of every higher mountain meadows on the Gadwah Notch Trail that are superb habitat for many creatures, including moose, eastern coyotes, white-tailed deer, and black bears. Some day-hikers simply end their trek at Cathedral Meadow and have a picnic before returning to their cars. But a good deal more terrain and greater vistas lie ahead.

Continue straight ahead on the lane, now filled in with low grasses. Stay on the level, walking at ease ½ mile through woods on both sides, until the track turns abruptly to the right and uphill. While the trail turns right, there is a second meadow clearing ahead, called Moran Meadow. Smaller than Cathedral Meadow and lacking a view, it makes up for its lesser status particularly in June and July, because it is festooned with the blooms of thousands of wildflowers.

Turn uphill on the old grassy woods lane that is the Gadwah Notch Trail and leave Moran Meadow behind. Climb easily but steadily another ½-mile, until the lane again levels out. A large, bowl-like environment, framed by high ridges, opens up as the lane begins to become indistinct underfoot. You have entered Muise Bowl, named for Mt. Muise that stands 3,610 feet to the right (east) of the natural amphitheater. Walk straight through the natural depression, passing a place-name sign in a spruce on the left, and begin a very gradual rise. Keep to the high side in the open spaces, walking parallel to the woods line on the right.

Turn around. Behind you are the Moran uplands close by and the big rounded summit of Bunnell Mountain in the distance. You are standing in a place that few people have ever seen. This was once the domain of loggers and was rarely visited by anyone of foot. But the Gadwah Notch Trail, part of the 165-mile Cohos Trail through-hiking trail system in the region, opened this area to hiking boots. Under most circumstances, you will be here by yourself. Because it is so removed from any well-traveled road and blocked from civilization by a string of ridges and mountains, human noise rarely intrudes into this space. Here you can hear the continental silence that once prevailed all over America before the advent of modern civilization. Under the best circumstances, you can actually hear the sound of your own body at work.

Now the lane ceases to be anything but a wide grassy corridor through low spruce, ascending modestly. Depending on the human and moose traffic in recent weeks, you may have to watch your step in a few places as the way narrows the higher the elevation. Cross several seeps and cross another flat headed by a large rotting log pile on the right. Walk before the logs, slip through a raspberry patch, and descend to a stream crowded with logs that were once placed in the streambed to allow heavy equipment to move across. This rivulet is the upper stretch of Nash Stream. Water here is very good to the taste.

Cross the stream and begin an uphill pull on good footing to what is deemed Bulldozer Flat, an open, slightly pitched clearing covered with small stones, caribou moss, and an occasional rock cairn. This clearing, with a big place-name sign in a spruce tree at the head of the flat, is ideal as a lunch spot because the view from this 3,000-foot elevation is expansive, the best vista except for the one from the lean-to still more than 2 miles away. Bulldozer Flat is a fine destination for a day hike. It can be reached by most hikers in two hours, and the walk out to the car is all downhill.

Ten years ago, I had the good fortune of sitting at Bulldozer Flat in the early morning, when a large bull moose ambled southward into the clearing. He did not see me seated at the woods line and crossed directly in front of me and set up shop, browsing on young maple saplings 30 feet downhill. So for 10 minutes or so, I got to watch the great fellow nibble away on his breakfast, while over his shoulders the sun slowly illuminated the great wall of the Northwest Peaks range, the highest major range in New Hampshire north of the White Mountains. For me, that morning was one of the finest in all creation.

A set of rock cairns runs east through the meadow directly toward the summit of Mt. Muise standing due east of Bulldozer Flat. Head in the direction of the mountain and watch for the piles of rocks as you go. Some 200 feet out of the flat, the trail turns abruptly left and up a slight pitch and begins to march away northward. Now the pathway seems more and more like a woods trail, with blazing on the rocks and trees and direction arrows posted. Very gradually ascend on soils and rock outcroppings for ¼ mile, when suddenly the trail veers into the forest and becomes a distinct woods trail. The entrance is marked by several large yellow blazes and an arrow. There is no missing the turn.

Walk up to a rock knob, cross over it, and descend in dark spruce to a wet corridor that has been bridged with puncheon spans of hewn timber. Walk on a stretch of bog bridging until the trail reaches dry ground and follow a zigzag pattern through tight spruce and fir forest growing in the heart of Gadwah Notch. Gadwah is a shallow swale between two uplands, and the depression is crowded with young growth, maturing trees, and dead snags that resemble the masts of sailing ships. In high-elevation fog, this stretch can seem forbidding, but in good weather one can see how hard it must be for trees to make a suitable living in the cold, moist, and acidic environment within the notch.

After a series of S-curves, the trail seems to straighten a good deal and begins a steady descent in more open, mixed forest. Soon the yellow blazing in the trees is accompanied by royal blue paint, the color of New Hampshire state blazes. The trail follows a state boundary line downhill (north) for nearly ½ mile in pleasant forested terrain to a sudden and sharp right turn to the east, just beyond a blue-painted metal boundary pin. Follow the good blazing east a short ways to a flat where the trail makes a broad S-turn around a fallen snag, slip over a rise, and enter a fine stretch of ridge line in open hardwood forest. Amble along in comfortable surroundings and soon reach a straight stretch that runs a football field length before turning abruptly left up a little pitch. The trail now runs north again on the ridge for several long minutes before turning a hard left and descending 300 feet to an open area. Turn right in the opening and make a long U-shaped turn to the left. Follow the blazes to the lip of a drop. Descend on the steepest ground on the trek so far, cross a rivulet on

Crew peeling logs   NORTHWOODS STEWARDSHIP CENTER

a bog bridge, and continue downhill. Cross an indistinct logging skidway and keep falling into the Sims Stream Valley.

The trail bottoms out in a wooded flat, makes a series of easy turns, and reaches a blue-painted metal pin. The path turns a hard right (north), soon crosses several bog bridge spans, enters a narrow corridor wedged between tight spruce, and then begins to climb out of the valley. The going is easy to moderate uphill on good footing, following a very old and indistinct logging skidway.

Five minutes out of the valley and the trail passes an immense yellow birch tree, a boundary tree marking a property boundary corner. Because it stood at a corner and marked the location, the tree was never felled. It is one of the largest yellow birch trees in the Granite State.

Pass by the tree, ascending easily, and you'll soon begin to climb in earnest the south flank of Baldhead Mountain's south peak, the tallest of four upland rises that make up the mountain. The trail here is in very good condition and easy to follow. Yellow blazes mark the way, but they are shadowed by blue state blazes and old red Champion International Corporation blazes, as well.

The climb up Baldhead is moderate, punctuated by two short, steep pitches at different elevations. But the going is generally easy, as the trail rises about 800 vertical feet in about a mile. After a 15-minute uphill push, the trail flattens for a moment, crosses a draw, and reaches a critical right-hand turn that is well marked. In the turn is a steel plate and steel pins affixed to a tree. This is a boundary marker of the old Franconia Paper Company, a relic from logging times more

Bulldozer Flat. Mt. Bunnell

than 70 years ago. Throughout the climb, the trail has been confined to state property in the 36,000-acre Nash Stream Forest, but the 90-degree turn to the right here sets you on a course across private land owned by the estate of the late Fred Foss, an early and strong supporter of new foot trails in the region. The New Hampshire Fish and Game Department is now in negotiations to buy this land and set it aside as a habitat to protect rare species. That's a good thing, surely.

The Gadwah Notch Trail now turns abruptly east and begins to ascend a narrow arroyo where the last water on the trek may be found in all but dry years. Fill water bottles here if you must, but treat or filter the water before drinking. Cross the wet, climb a short pitch, level out, and begin the final push uphill toward the summit of Baldhead.

In open mixed forest, make easy turns and ever upward progress. Loop around a blow-down tangle. You'll soon crest a narrow false summit with restricted views through the trees. Descend off the narrow height of land, cross a little depression, then rise onto the southeast ridge and move off toward the true summit.

Suddenly a glint of metal will show through the trees; it is the roofline of the Baldhead lean-to. You approach it from above, passing a little rock knob, then turning off the trail to the right (south) to the lean-to. It resides in a clearing at 3,047-foot elevation

The Baldhead lean-to boasts a 120-degree view of some of New England's highest mountains. Forty miles away stand Mounts Madison, Adams, Jefferson, and Washington. To their left rises the Carter-Moriah Range with the deep chasm in its midst, that of Carter Notch. Various summits of the Pilot Range are visible, as are Long Mountain, peaks in the Whitcomb Range, Mt. Muise close in and to the right (south southwest), and Owl's Head and Kelsey Mountain to the east. Newly built wind turbines now stand on these two summits.

The lean-to is a sturdy post-and beam structure that was donated by the late Thomas Abbott of Sanbornton, New Hampshire, to the Cohos Trail Association. It sleeps five comfortably, six with some shoehorning. Nearby is a rather exotic latrine with decorative door built by one Karl Vornberger of Holderness, New Hampshire.

If you hike often and tramp many miles, Baldhead could be a day hike. But getting here and getting back to the trailhead would take the entire day. Most people who come this way spend the night in the lean-to. And why not? It is as quiet and wonderfully remote a spot as can be had in New Hampshire, in much of New England for that matter. There is no settlement anywhere close at hand. The only lights on the horizon at night are the string of yard lights at the New Hampshire State Prison at Berlin, 30 miles away.

It is best to time your visit to the lean-to to coincide with the full moon. It illuminates the Phillips Brook Valley far below and gives black form to the mountains huddled beneath the blue night sky. I have been here when two eastern coyote packs, each on either side of the valley, began calling to each other from bivouacs several miles apart on adjacent summits.

I have been asleep in the lean-to only to have a moose tramp past after midnight. And I have been here in snow in early October.

The only drawback to visiting the lean-to is that there is no water available on the summit. If it is a dry year, there may not be water readily available to you for several miles. So always bring in 2 quarts of water with you when overnighting at the lean-to.

If you are day-hiking, you must return from whence you came, but if you are through-hiking, you can continue northbound, passing just to the left of the mountain's 3,087-foot, blowdown-infested summit. The lean-to is the starting point north for the remote Kelsey Notch Trail. That pathway brings you 2-plus miles downhill to the old Kelsey Notch Road, which gives access to the old fire service lane that runs up and over the summit of nearby Dixville Peak and out to the Balsams Wilderness Ski Area, built on the northwest flank of Mt. Gloriette. To reach the Baldhead lean-to from Dixville Notch, you would have to trek more than 7 miles south and overcome some 2,000 feet of vertical elevation gain.

The Gadwah Notch Trail through to the Baldhead lean-to is recommended for those who really would like to get away from the crowds patrolling the trails in the White Mountains. Most days, you will have the notch trail to yourself; the lean-to, too. If you remain quiet during your trek, you have an excellent chance of seeing wildlife in the many meadows and in the boreal or hardwood forests. Pick a day of fine clear weather so that you may enjoy the many vistas that give the trail its fine character.

26.

Baldhead Mountain Trail

Location: Columbia, NH

Distance: About 5 miles round-trip

Difficulty: Moderate with an occasional short steep pitch

Trailhead: 44°49'01.94'N, 71°24'14.46'W

GETTING THERE

Bungy Road, in the town of Columbia, is 7 miles east of the village of Colebrook or about 5 miles to the west of Dixville Notch off the south shoulder of NH 26. Turn south across a bridge across the Mohawk River and run on asphalt a mile to a Y-junction.Stay to the left and continue over a ridge and down into the valley of Sims Stream. After a dogleg turn to the right, the road turns to a dirt surface. Run a mile past the dogleg into a broad clearing surrounding beautiful Far Cry Farm, at the foot of 3,600-foot mountains. The clearing soon comes to an end as the road rises into the forest, levels out, and then begins a lazy descent through parcels of private land supporting about a dozen hunting camps.

As the dirt lane levels out, it passes a last camp on the left accompanied by an odd-looking, small, barnlike building on the opposite side of the road. Ahead 200 feet, a rough logging lane cuts left. Take that turn and enter a narrow tote road that can be tough on a sedan but easily managed by a pickup or jeep. Half a mile from Bungy Road, the road leads to a grassy clearing with a rutted track ahead but to the left. Park here. That indistinct lane eastbound is where you want to go.

BUSHWHACK CHALLENGE

Of all the foot paths highlighted in this guide, this one is not a formal trail but a discernable route to a remote peak that ends at a lean-to near the very summit of 3,097-foot Baldhead Mountain, an unheralded and

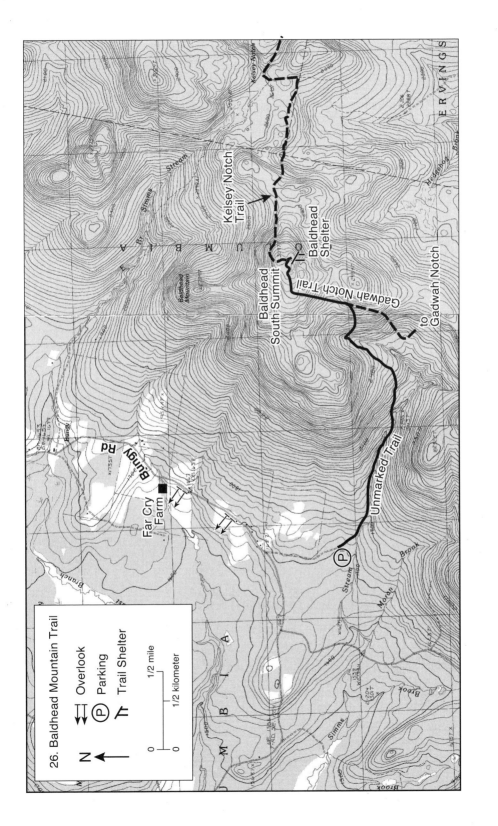

26. Baldhead Mountain Trail

N

Overlook
Parking
Trail Shelter

0   1/2 mile
0   1/2 kilometer

Kelsey Notch

Simms Stream

Kelsey Notch Trail

Baldhead South Summit

Baldhead Shelter

Gadwah Notch Trail

to Gadwah Notch

Unmarked Trail

Far Cry Farm

Bungy Rd

Baldhead Mountain

Brook

Moxn Brook

Stream

Simms Brook

Brook

ERVINGS

COLUMBIA

little-known topknot with a marvelous view southward.

The so-called Baldhead Mountain Trail follows a heavily eroded former logging lane and log skidder run on the mountain, running in pleasant woodlands, open abandoned farm fields, a wash filled with boulder rubble, until it threads the upper reaches of the Cohos Trail to a lean-to destination.

If you pay attention to the directions here, you will have no trouble getting to Baldhead, but you will need a single brightly colored object—a bit of surveyor tape, a handkerchief, or what-have-you—to place on the trail or hang from a tree at one point. More on this later.

Leave your car behind in the small, grassy clearing and move uphill easily into the trees on an old logging route that the forest is closing in around. In a few minutes, as the lane rises a little more steeply, you'll arrive at a deep gully running down the middle of the way. In some places, the road has been completely washed away. Stay to the right side and continue eastward until you leave the gully behind and the silver ribbon of Sims Stream shows itself close by on the right. Follow both the lane and water upriver in a rather pleasant setting for ½ mile. Slip around some downed growth toppled by heavy snowfall in a bend. Soon you'll reach the first of two crossings over Sims Stream.

Here the stream can be crossed easily in all but high water, in spring or after a heavy summer thunderstorm, by picking your way across stones in the channel. If water is thundering, choose your path very carefully. You don't want to be knocked off your feet here, because the stream narrows a bit directly below and picks up speed. Topple over here and you could be in for a difficult ride or worse.

On the far side, the lane continues uphill

but its surface deteriorates immediately into a moonscape of boulder rubble. Ten years ago, the lane was fully intact and easy to access. Now you must scramble over and around legions of smooth granite rounds laid bare during a mountain flood midway through the first decade of our century.

Soon you'll move above the mass of boulders and regain the old skidway for a minute, until the second crossing at Sims Stream shows itself in a depression. Descend a few feet to large rocks in the stream. Again, in high water, this can be a troublesome crossing, more so than the first one, because the stream is confined to a narrow sluice here and moves faster.

Scramble 8 feet up a step-eroded embankment and stride into an alder thicket. Take the path of least resistance through the tangle. Emerge in a minute and regain pleasant footing on the old tote way. Climb up a moderate grade into a grassy field, the remains of haying acreage that no longer see the sickle bar of a tractor.

Move uphill easily, always staying on the high side of the field near the tree line on your left. The field widens out to the right. Watch at your feet for an occasional rut or small, eroded depression. Pace through a little patch of forest, stepping around a deep gully that hides the iron remains of an old wood-fired cookstove. Enter an eastern extension of the farm fields, staying "high" and keeping the forest on the left shoulder. As you rise toward the woods ahead, the north flank of 3,610-foot Mt. Muise looms, filling the southern horizon and creating what looks like an immense bowl. In autumn, during peak foliage season, this spot is a delight to the eye.

With the fields behind you, enter the mixed forest and begin a moderate ascent on the eroded track. Level out to a degree and slip along on good footing through the

Baldhead lean-to under snow

woods, a branch of Sims Stream well below. The route is easy to follow but can be muddy and soft in places after rains.

Cross a narrow rivulet and approach the mountain proper. The route pitches uphill at a moderate level, passes a rotted iron cook-stove on the right, scrambles up a rock-strewn pitch, and reaches a tight dogleg turn to the right. Change direction abruptly, to begin a sharper angle of ascent on a track made by a log skidder long ago. The way becomes steep, bends around a gradual left turn, and runs for 30 seconds on indistinct track until the way suddenly meets a well-defined trail.

You have now reached the well-worn track of the route of the 165-mile Cohos Trail, in this section known as the Gadwah Notch Trail. Now that you have gained this pathway, turn uphill to the left. But before you do, you *must* do something that will ensure your safe return to your car later in the day or after an overnight stay at the Baldhead lean-to still a mile ahead.

Earlier, I told you to bring something that you can use as a visual signal, a bit of sur-veyor tape, a handkerchief, or something similar. You will want to set out your signal here to remind you to get off the Gadwah Notch Trail section of the long-distance Cohos Trail. If you descend to this point with-out something to flag your memory, it may be difficult to recognize that this is the point where you have to leave Gadwah Notch Trail. If you hang your signal securely and promi-nently, finding your way back downhill will not be the least bit problematical.

If by chance you still miss this junction on

your way out later, a very big clue that you have gone too far will show itself two minutes to the south. A truly huge yellow birch tree stands alongside the path. It is a boundary tree, left standing to mark a property boundary. It was never felled and has grown into one of the largest yellow birches alive in New England. If you see that tree, you've gone 500 feet too far. Reverse direction and find your route out.

Okay, you've placed your visual cue on the trail. Head north uphill on true woods trail. Drop into a rocky gully, rebound, and enter a steep pitch in tight spruce and fir, following multicolored blazing: red, blue, and yellow. Yellow is the blaze color of the Cohos Trail. From now on, follow the yellow blazing to the summit.

Crest the steep pitch, enter pleasant mixed forest, and wander on moderate grades uphill, swinging through an S-turn at one point. The way is delightful at this point; the going gets a little easier as the trail approaches a 90-degree turn to the right at a boundary tree that boasts a metal plate stamped with the name of the long-gone Franconia Paper Company. Turn right and follow a narrow gully uphill to a seasonal steam crossing. Scramble up a small rock ledge and begin a rather lazy meandering ascent high on the southwest flank of Baldhead Mountain. Swing around a blowdown tangle and reach a false summit with restricted views south. Immediately drop off the little knob, cross a dip, and rise onto a level ridge. Trek this blowdown-prone exposed elevation until the flash of metal greets your eye ahead and below the pathway. The Baldhead lean-to is at hand.

Leave the main trail and descend 5 vertical feet to the site of the lean-to. Swing around the south side of the structure and behold a dramatic viewpoint. A sweeping vista opens southward down the beautiful Phillips Brook Valley, lined with 3,500-foot summits. Beyond, 40 miles in the distance, the northern Presidential and the Carter-Moriah Ranges reach the sky. Seated on the lip of the floor of the lean-to, you'll understand why you took the effort to come this way. The view is showstopper, a fine present for the visitor from so modest a mountain. Baldhead is only 3,097 feet in elevation, and until the Cohos Trail was built, no hiker ever stumbled into this remote corner of Columbia Township, New Hampshire. That's all changed, and for the better.

Remember, the Baldhead Mountain Trail is not a formal trail. You won't discover it on any map anywhere. But it is not difficult to find nor unduly difficult to ascend. If you like to undertake a little challenge and tramp where few people ever do, this trek may very well be just right for you.

V. Dixville Notch

Mt. Gloriette ski area rocks

Like to get the blood racing a bit, do you? Few places in the Northeast will get the heart rate up like standing on the edge of a 700-foot drop: Table Rock cliff in ragged Dixville Notch.

Smallest of New Hampshire's "great" notches, Dixville Notch is its most dramatic—and for good reason. The big, nasty gash in the landscape was born of cataclysm, when glacial ice dams held in check by the ridges in the region more than 12,000 years ago ruptured repeatedly and allowed vast ice-locked glacial lakes to drain all at once through a low saddle in the ridgeline. In what could have been just a matter of days, torrents of glacial melt water tore away rocks, cutting through the strata as if a knife through flesh.

What was left behind is marvelous hiking country today, bristling with cliff ledges, harboring waterfalls, a chain of ponds, a flume gorge, and even a world-class grand resort hotel known fondly in these parts and around the globe as The Balsams.

27.

Kelsey Notch Trail

Location: Dixville and Columbia, NH

Distance: 2.4 miles to Baldhead Mountain summit and lean-to, one-way from where the trail meets old Kelsey Notch Road. Add another ½ mile or so one-way if you park at the Dixville Peak junction. The round-trip is more than about 6 miles to and from the junction.

Difficulty: Easy to moderate to moderately steep and strenuous in a few short spurts

Trailhead: 44°49'13.10'N, 71°20'37.37'W

GETTING THERE

Travel north on NH 16 to the tiny community of Errol. Turn west (left) and then about 5 miles to Log Haven Campground on the left. Look for a newly restored and widened forest lane on the left a hundred feet or less beyond the grounds of the little resort.

If starting from the west, from Colebrook, take NH 26 through Dixville Notch. About 3 miles east of the notch, look for Log Haven Campground on the right. Just before the campground, watch for the wide forest lane on the right.

Leave the highway southwestward onto a former logging road that serves as a snowmobile trail in winter and as an access way to wind turbine towers on Dixville Peak and summits to the south.

This road has experienced severe washouts in the past, but is being maintained now by Brookfield Renewable Power, Inc. Drive several miles to a junction. Pass the lane entering on the left. Continue straight ahead and climb out of the valley. At about Mile 4, you'll come to a second junction. The lane to the right runs up Dixville Peak. Ignore it.

Park your vehicle off the traveled way, just west of the junction. The GPS trailhead coordinates posted above show this area as the place to park. However, if you have a four-wheel drive vehicle, you can continue to the west, downhill to a solid plank bridge that is strong enough to carry loaded logging trucks.

If the way continues to look good in the valley, continue through a slight depression and begin to climb out on an easy grade. The

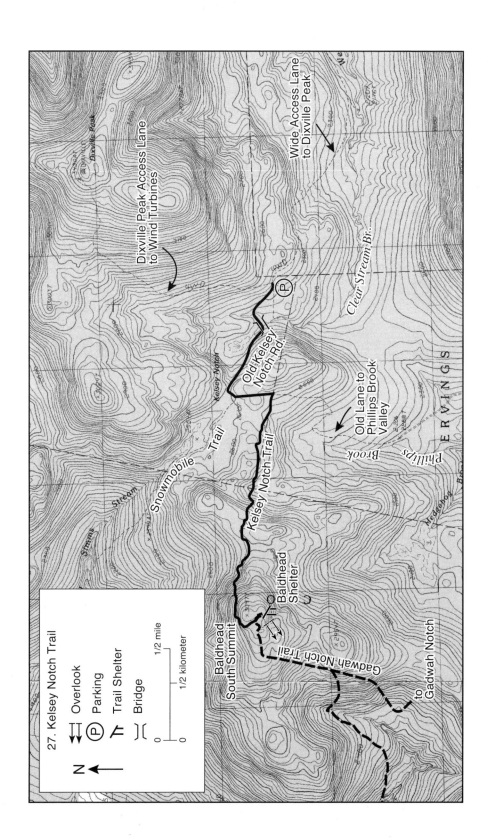

27. Kelsey Notch Trail

Overlook

P Parking

Trail Shelter

Bridge

N

0   1/2 mile
0   1/2 kilometer

Dixville Peak Access Lane
to Wind Turbines

Wide Access Lane
to Dixville Peak

Old Kelsey
Notch Rd.

Snowmobile
Trail

Kelsey Notch

Kelsey Notch Trail

Clear Stream Br...

Old Lane to
Phillips Brook
Valley

Phillips Brook

ERVINGS

Hedgehog

Simms Stream

Baldhead
South Summit

Baldhead
Shelter

Gadwah Notch Trail

to
Gadwah Notch

Dixville Peak

P

Mt. Muise

road is very narrow here but easy to maneuver over, provided your vehicle is not extremely low to the ground. When tight terrain begins to open out into a broad flat, pull off the lane and stop. Look for a great deal of yellow blazing on the left (south) that shows the way in to the Kelsey Notch Trail.

If you decide to walk in from the junction for Dixville Peak, the trailhead is only about $\frac{4}{10}$ mile away.

STAIRWAY TO LONESOME

Kelsey Notch isn't on the map. It is far removed from far removed. Once the site of the first east–west horse path between the Connecticut River to the west and the Magalloway and Androscoggin Rivers to the east, the path fell into disuse after the turnpike through Dixville Notch was opened in mid-19th century.

Poor land for farming, it was never settled. But the wild region grew its fair share of trees, and so the Kelsey Notch country became working forest. It still is, to this day. The logging roads that snake through the region are testimony enough to that fact.

The real beauty of Kelsey Notch is its isolation. The domain is cut off from NH 26 by the sprawling mass of Dixville Peak. The very sparsely settled hardscrabble neighborhood of Bungy, in Columbia Township, is 3 miles away by foot. Other than Log Haven Campground back from whence you came on NH 26, there is no habitation whatsoever to the north and northeast. To the south, the country is filled up with New Hampshire's largest state forest, which not a single permanent resident calls home.

Although the wind farm service road has been extensively rebuilt and is much wider than the original road, its margins will soften with age as grasses and weeds hide the work of bulldozer blades.

Kelsey Notch is often wind-whistle quiet. Before the wind turbine system was built, I had never met a soul in this country. That was and, surprisingly, still is its appeal. Take the time and effort to drive into the Kelsey Notch, and you will have the Kelsey Notch Trail to yourself. Guaranteed!

It's not that the Kelsey Notch Trail is never used. It is a part of the 162-mile Cohos Trail. Through-hikers ramble along it in the summer and fall. But the pathway is not your average day-hike destination. The trek to the top of little-known Baldhead Mountain and the six-person lean-to isn't a bushwhack, and offers a fine and just reward at the end.

Despite its isolation, the Kelsey Notch Trail is actually well maintained by the Cohos Trail Association. Leave your car and look for a mass of yellow blazes alongside the dirt lane pointing the way south. Rise up off the road to a granite slab. Cross it and discover the Kelsey Notch Trail sign in a spruce directly ahead. Walk on an old logging skidway in level terrain. The footing is good in most places, a bit moist in a few sections. Bypass the moisture on either side of the track and move southward in forest pocked with weedy openings.

Less than ¼ mile from where you left the Kelsey Notch Road, the trail makes a 90-degree turn to the right and leaves the skidway. Your route now roughly follows a boundary line that separates Dixville from the unincorporated township of Ervings Location. Indistinct red blazes can be seen on occasion peering from old healed ax blazes in the trees.

Meander on an easy decline in open forest with restricted views to the south. Continue to what seems like an overgrown field at its base. Drift uphill easily across this opening, a habitat that is favored by white-tailed deer. I have seen them often in this area. The opening also affords a good look at 3,610-foot Mt. Muise in the distance, which offers a classic New England mountain profile from this vantage point.

Pace into young forest, pick up another skidder path, and follow it to yet another such pathway, heralded by a little granite slab marked with an angled yellow blaze. Descend easily on the old skidway to a depression at the very base of Baldhead Mountain. Stay "high" to the right on the trail if the season has been wet, and gain the northeast flank of the peak.

Just as the trail is about to pitch uphill, look for a small pocket that collects seep water in most seasons. This is the last reliable water on the trek. If you need water, you'll have to obtain it here.

Immediately, the trail rears up at a moderately steep angle. The route is clear underfoot. The way is well marked and sees enough traffic to be easily discernable in the ground.

Think of Baldhead as a series of terraces one above the other. As you will see, the route is marked by short, fairly steep inclines interspersed with stretches of flat or easily rising benches. The first push uphill is more sustained that the ones above, but is less steep. However, it does level out and lulls you into a sense of well-being.

The trail also has a tendency to make unexpected changes in direction. These changes are always clearly marked by yellow blazes in the shape of 90-degree angles.

In short order you will get a sense that there is a rhythm to the ascent. Cross a flat area, turn 90 degrees, move off in another direction entirely, and then reach a steep incline that takes a minute or so to mount. Finish the exercise and repeat. Because the trail twists and turns and makes repeated leaps in elevation, restricted views repeatedly come and go. Although the route is confined to the forest, its layout is interesting and keeps you alert to changes. It avoids a cold mountain bog in one in spot, then skirts what appears to be a clearing in the forest 100 feet away. That's what it is. Leave the trail, if you like, and investigate. A logging clear cut created a wide vista to the north on the other side of a low rise. Crest that rise, and the high ridges and modest mountain summits of northern Coos County show their profiles.

Back on the trail, you'll soon cut an S-turn through an open and grassy moose bedding area. In 10 minutes, round a hillock and enter a tight and dark ravine. Climb the steepest pitch yet, grabbing a small tree as necessary to aid your ascent, and haul yourself up onto the last leg of the trail before the very summit. The way is moderately steep, running in spruce and fir now that the elevation approaches 3,000 feet. Still the going is good, the trail well delineated by brick red evergreen needles and bright yellow blazes.

The flank of the summit knob rubs your left shoulder for a minute and then the path turns left steeply uphill a dozen feet and flattens. You have reached the south and principal summit of a complex of four separate uplands. The top is quite broad and wooded. Trek on fairly level ground toward the southwest. Rather than run over the very summit, the trail skirts it a few dozen feet to the north to avoid a blowdown tangle at the mountain's highest point. Swing around a fallen tree and watch for the shine of metal in the forest ahead. The glint among the dark tree trunks is the first indication that you are closing in on the Baldhead lean-to and its stunning 100-degree view to the south.

At a minor rock outcropping, the path to the lean-to drops 6 vertical feet, but if it's a clear day, the view will bring anyone up short.

Chad Pepau in Kelsey Notch

The Baldhead lean-to is situated at the very head of a long U-shaped valley at the bottom of which flows Phillips Brook. The valley was carved by a glacial tongue. Numerous wooded peaks flank the valley and form a foreground against which progressively taller mountain ranges reach skyward. Dead south stands Long Mountain. The Pilot and Pliny Ranges in the Kilkenny division of the White Mountain National Forest overtop Long Mountain. Slightly to the southeast, the massive forms of the northern Presidential Range exceed everything else in elevation. And just to the east of Mounts Madison, Adams, and Jefferson stretches the Carter-Moriah Range, its serrated spine cracked by the deep wound that is Carter Notch.

The Presidential Range peaks are 40-plus miles distant, as are the Carter-Moriahs. To the west Owl's Head and Kelsey Mountain hide the Mahoosuc Range from view. Atop those two peaks, a service road has been laid out. Its purpose is to shoulder heavy trucks that will soon be moving into place huge steel tubes, equipment, electric generators, and turbine blades. Brookfield Renewable Energy, Inc. has permits to erect more than thirty 400-foot wind turbines in the Dummer Ponds region to the east-southeast, all the way to Dixville Peak. In short order, big electrical generators spun by the turbine blades will be generating clean energy and feeding that power into the New England power grid.

The reason the wind turbines will be built here is often evident when perched at the lean-to on Baldhead Mountain. The peak and the surrounding terrain are often buffeted by wind. The lean-to has a partial front built on its open side, because of the ferocity of the breeze at times.

Of all potential wind energy sites in New Hampshire, other than at the seacoast, the high ridges of Coos County withstand the highest wind velocities on more days of the year than does any other locale. Total wind potential tests pegged the ridges nearby in the 99-percentile category. It doesn't get much better than that if you are a wind-energy engineer. And so, now, when you reach Baldhead, great turbine blades are looping in the breeze on the peaks nearby. The big towers compete with the splendid view that can be had from the lip of the lean-to.

On the summit, there is one luxury. The lean-to has a companion structure, a one-holer latrine hidden down a very short path to the southeast. No dismal trap, the Baldhead latrine boasts a world-class privy door complete with moon and stars, and the interior is airy, thanks to large, screened openings.

Were it not for its extremely isolated perch, Baldhead summit and its lean-to would be visited more frequently because of the view and because the structure can sleep five comfortably, six in a pinch. But the remoteness of the site is a decided plus. It's never crowded here. If you spend the night under the full moon, you might hear the coyote troops that live in the valley calling among the peaks, or hear the heavy thud of moose footfalls as one of the big creatures plods by on the trail at night.

If your purpose is to day-hike in unexplored territory above the Whites, then the Kelsey Notch Trail up Baldhead Mountain should be on the list. Getting to the trailhead is an adventure in and of itself. And the trek up to the lean-to is challenging enough to make you feel a solid sense of accomplishment upon arrival.

28.

Mt. Gloriette to Dixville Peak

Location: Dixville, NH

Distance: About 7 miles round-trip

Difficulty: Moderate and steep terrain

Trailhead: 44°51'19.70'N, 71°19'18.08'W

GETTING THERE

Locate NH 26, an east–west highway that intersects with NH 3 in the heart of Colebrook Village or NH 16 in the hamlet of Errol. This road is the northernmost east–west route maintained by the state and runs between Colebrook on the west to Errol and beyond to the east.

Midway along from both directions stands the Balsams Grand Resort Hotel. If approaching from the west, from Colebrook, motor about 10 miles and climb a very long hill on the approach to Dixville Notch and the hotel. At the height of land, a large, well-appointed sign signaling the Balsams Wilderness Ski Area stands on the right. Turn right down the access road to the ski area and drive to the ski area base lodge parking lot and leave your car there. If approaching from the east, drive through Dixville Notch and swing alongside Lake Gloriette and the Balsams Hotel, across the waters on the far shore. Just before the highway will begin a long descent into the Mohawk River Valley, the large sign for the Balsams Wilderness Ski Area appears on the left. Turn down that access lane and drive to the base station lodge parking lot.

SPRAWLING SENTINEL OF DIXVILLE

Ski areas don't get rave reviews as hiking venues. No one writes guidebooks about ski trail hikes, and this author is no exception. But some alpine ski slopes offer great treks and outstanding views, and the start of the tramp to the summit of Dixville peak fits that billing.

Dixville Notch

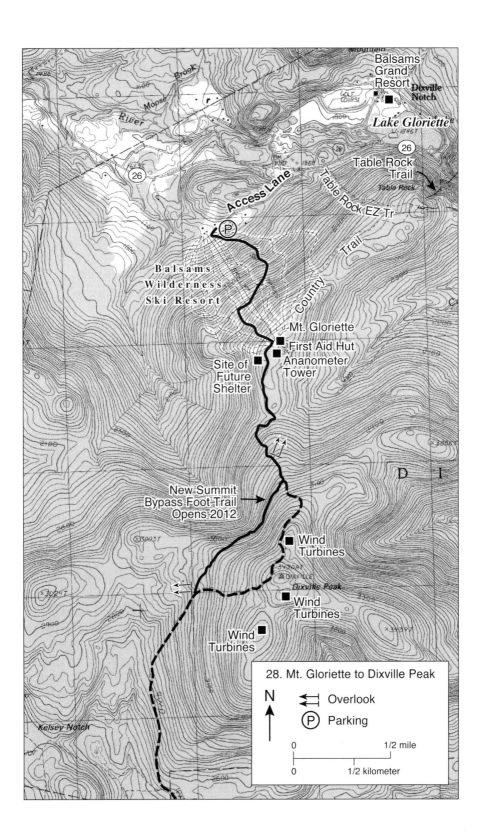

Balsams Grand Resort

Dixville Notch

Lake Gloriette

Mountain

GOLF COURSE

26

Table Rock Trail

Table Rock

26

Table Rock EZ Tr

Access Lane

River

Mosse

Brook

26

P

Country

Trail

Balsams Wilderness Ski Resort

Mt. Gloriette

First Aid Hut

Site of Future Shelter

Ananometer Tower

New Summit Bypass Foot Trail Opens 2012

DIXVILLE

Dixville Peak

Wind Turbines

Wind Turbines

Wind Turbines

Kelsey Notch

D   I

28. Mt. Gloriette to Dixville Peak

N

⇄ Overlook

Ⓟ Parking

0   1/2 mile

0   1/2 kilometer

Now that you've parked at the base of Balsams Wilderness Ski Area, you are standing facing southeast before Mt. Gloriette, a long-arm extension of taller and broader Dixville Peak to the south, not fully visible from this vantage point in the parking lot. Balsams Wilderness is 1,000 vertical feet from head to foot and is perched in high country that routinely gets heavy doses of snow as many as five months a year. The ski area does not quite reach the true summit of Mt. Gloriette, which stands off toward the east and is obscured by the form of the ski area ridge and boreal forest growth.

Pick a route up the mountain on any one of the dozen trails. The two chairlift lines offer the most direct going. Set off and climb a slope that is moderately steep without letup for the full 1,000 vertical feet, until you crest the mountain's rather flat and mile-long ridgeline. At the very top rises a little first-aid building beyond the last ski towers. Keep it in mind. It is often unlocked and you can dodge into it if the weather gets truly nasty on your way back down from Dixville Peak. Weather in far northern New Hampshire is notoriously finicky. So, too, this region gets 5 or 6 more inches of rain and snow, on average, than do the counties to the south.

The trek up to Mt. Gloriette's high ridgeline is uninspiring, except that as you ascend, the view to the northwest and north grows in volume. At the top, enjoy a sweeping vista of northern New Hampshire, Vermont, and southern Quebec. Canada is little more than 15 miles away from your perch.

Behind you, away from the view, stands Dixville Peak, now bristling with seven massive wind turbine towers, rising as high as 400 feet to the tips of their uppermost turbine blades. These huge power-generating windmills are just a few of some 36 turbines that have been erected on high, windblown ridgelines to the south.

Once you crest the mountain turn right (south) on open ski terrain and turn down the first left-hand opening you see. Look for yellow Cohos Trail blazes in the spruce trees and a large Balsams sign that states, TO DIXVILLE PEAK. Pace down what was once a service lane built when the ski area was initially constructed. The way has narrowed considerably over the years into a broad woods path that forms a link route between the ski area and the old fire road up and over Dixville Peak. Today, this path and the fire road are snowmobile trails in winter.

The little link is less than ½ mile in length and descends very gradually over most of its length. The going is good much of the way, with the exception of several spots where water tends to pool in depressions in all but high summer. Some recent ditching and trailside clipping have improved the going a bit, but be aware that you may encounter water. To avoid it, you may have to bushwhack a few dozen feet around the wet.

The link path comes to an end down a little pitch at the edge of the former Dixville Peak fire road, now a major snowmobile avenue that is groomed by big machines in winter. Enter right in the elbow of a dogleg turn. Stay straight ahead and uphill. Cross over a hump, descend a second, and then rebound and begin a long-mile pull up toward the summit of Dixville Peak. The summit can no longer be the objective here. It is off-limits because the power company wishes to limit direct access to the turbine towers. But the summit was never a great joy, anyway. The south flank of the peak always was the reason to venture this far, and today a new summit bypass foot trail swings around the summit and reaches the wide open terrain on the south-facing slope of the mountain.

The fire lane running up the north face of the peak was initially built as a means to get to an early fire tower that once graced the

Top of Wilderness Ski Resort

summit. It was removed long ago, but the leg anchors are still in place. They recently served as anchors for cables that held a tall anemometer (wind speed instrument) tower in place, but hellish winter winds nearly a decade ago now promptly felled the steel edifice, when one of the cables snapped free from its mooring. The lane was extended over the mountain and down into the Kelsey Notch valley to the south to serve as a fire break and as a logging tote road lower down the slopes.

The lane is wide with good footing all the way, but because the forest doesn't shade the route, it is exposed to the sun along its entire length. On hot summer days, this trek can be tedious and taxing because of the heat. But now you can leave the old service road and dodge down the new woods path, cut specifically by the power company to ac-commodate the long-distance Cohos Trail because that pathway can no longer loop over the summit.

This new mile-long trail runs in cool spruce and fir along the west flank of the mountain, always staying on the level at about the 2,700-foot elevation of the slopes. From the newly cut trail within the forest, there are no views of substance. Once the new path runs its course, though, and breaks out of the trees at the head of a wide switch-back in the newly rebuilt service road, the grandeur that is Dixville Peak is revealed.

A blue horizon beckons south to north-northeast. This vista from the south flank of Dixville Peak is all the reason necessary to make the trek up here over a ski area lift line and snowmobile right of way. On the clearest days you will be able to make out the north-ern Presidential Range on the edge of sight, the Kilkenny ranges, most of the major peaks in the Nash Stream Forest, the entire Northwest Peaks Range, Cleveland Notch, Vermont's Mt. Monadnock looming over the Connecticut River valley, and a few Canadian summits. And always, in the far background, runs the spine of the Green Mountains of Vermont.

The view comes courtesy of logging company harvesting and now power company cuts that have opened the flank to sunlight. At this elevation, growth grows back slowly, so there should be no worry about losing the view over the next few decades.

The view is now more complex than in recent years. The peaks immediately ahead—Kelsey Mountain and Owl's Head—are festooned with wind turbines, too, their great windmill blades rotating in the constant breeze.

Remember the anemometer tower that was toppled by fierce winter winds? It was set up to record the wind velocity over the course of several years, summer and winter. The recording device on the tower discovered that of all places in New England except the very seacoast, these high ridgelines in

Coos County were the windiest of locations. Consequently, plans were drawn up by industry to place a fleet of wind turbines here. Free energy, riding those wind currents, is being tapped here—clean energy to fuel the power-hungry Northeast.

I make a point of coming in winter, wearing snowshoes, although it is often easy to trek on the packed snowmobile trail without them. I'm not alone. Snowshoe rabbits haunt the peak. If you get down on your belly and quietly snoop about, you can occasionally catch a glimpse of one hiding under the snow-laden spruce bows. Oftentimes, the ice and snow crystal rime is so thick the trees look like desserts instead of denizens of the forest.

The return is fast and far easier than the ascent. As you descend you can view the country to the north from the wide lane. And at the top of the Balsams Wilderness Ski Area you have the fine view reprised. Drop down to your car, and if you are smart, drive over to the Balsams Grand Resort Hotel and order yourself a stiff drink in celebration of your trek into country few people ever see on foot.

29.

Table Rock Trail

Location: Dixville, NH

Distance: 1.3 miles on trail and 0.8 mile on NH 26 back to the parking pullout

Difficulty: Moderate climb on the trail's mile-long western leg, but an extremely steep descent into the notch on the eastern end

Trailhead: 44°51'41.41'N, 71°18'15.30'W

GETTING THERE

Motor eastbound from Colebrook Village on NH 26 near the top of the Granite State. Motor 10 miles to a long grade uphill. Climb until you see a large, well-appointed sign that states Balsams Wilderness Ski Area on the right. Pass by the sign and access road, but slow down. Just beyond the lane is a grass-lined pullout. At the forest edge, a trail sign heralds the west entrance to the Table Rock Trail.

If traveling westbound from Errol, pass through Dixville Notch, swing by Lake Gloriette and the Balsams Grand Resort Hotel on the right, pass the hotel's service lane on the right, as well, and then look left for the trailhead pullout a short distance before reaching the Balsams Wilderness Ski Area sign.

A STORIED TRAIL WITH TWO DISTINCTLY DIFFERENT PERSONALITIES

Dixville Notch is more reminiscent of the butte country of Arizona than the dense, eroded granite cores of New England's 200-million-year-old mountains. Much of the rugged pass through the mountains is composed of brittle metamorphic rock that is distinctly brick red in color. Throughout New Hampshire's North Country there are few such outcroppings, but in Dixville Notch, the fragile layers of mudstone are striking.

The Table Rock Trail has been in place on the truncated shoulder of Mt. Gloriette for more than a century. Like many an early trail in the White Mountains, the original route ran straight up the mountain, rising out of the

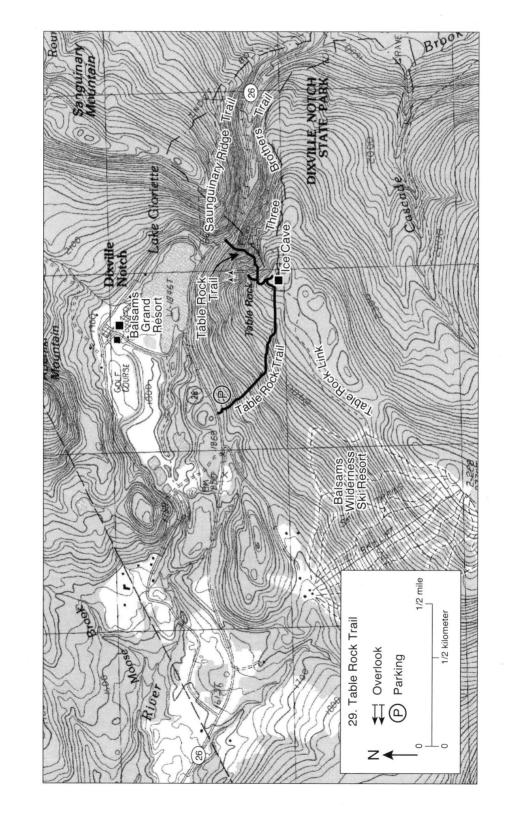

Sanguinary Mountain

Round

Lake Gloriette

Dixville Notch

Balsams Grand Resort

GOLF COURSE

Mountain

Brook

River

Moose

Saunguinary Ridge Trail

Three Brothers Trail

Ice Cave

Table Rock Trail

Table Rock

Table Rock Trail

Table Rock Link

DIXVILLE NOTCH STATE PARK

Cascade

Brook

GRAVE

Balsams Wilderness Ski Resort

P Parking

Overlook

N

0   1/2 mile

0   1/2 kilometer

Table Rock

in the early years of the 21st century. Recently, water drainage was improved and erosion control upgraded.

Climb in mixed hardwood in the lower sections. Spruce and fir increase in number the higher the elevation. Throughout the climb, there is no hint that you are moving close to terribly steep terrain over the left shoulder. The way is simply a pleasant woods walk, broken only in one spot by stepping stones around a seep.

No more than half an hour into the climb, the trail begins to ease and approaches a T-junction. To the right, a fine cross-country ski trail leaves for the upper reaches of the Balsams Wilderness Ski Area a mile away. But turn left here. The Table Rock Trail drops gradually downhill to the north and in two minutes reaches yet another T-Junction. The Three Brothers Trail approaches from the right. The Table Rock Trail cuts left and immediate drops steeply down a moist, well-used pitch for 60 feet.

At the bottom of the pitch you'll be confronted with two options: To the right, the eastern arm of the Table Rock Trail drops out of sight. A look down the chute should give you an early idea as to the steepness of the descent to come. But disregard the path down, for now. Directly ahead is a set of stone steps. Mount the steps and come to a level shelf. Walk a few feet, and the forest suddenly disappears. You have reached the backstage of dramatic Table Rock.

Table Rock is actually the upper flat but very narrow summit rocks of a spire whose foundation is grounded at the very edge of NH 26 nearly 700 feet below. Where it is anchored to Mt. Gloriette, Table Rock is comfortably wide at first, but it does not stay so for long.

Venture northward. Immediately the landscape disappears on both sides, lost to vertical cliff faces. As you advance, notice the

western head of the notch to a shallow saddle on the doorstep of the famed cliff named Table Rock, for which the trail is named. The pathway is so steep and so full of loose material that I don't recommend climbing it. Instead, your journey will start a short mile to the west on a route that is almost as old as the original.

Leave the parking pullout southward and begin immediately to climb out of the valley. The Table Rock Trail bends east right away and pitches up at a moderate angle that changes little throughout most of the course of the climb.

Throughout the ascent, hike on a well defined path that has benefited from the work of professional trail crews twice over a decade. Some of the pathway was rerouted snaking cracks in the reddish rock, cleaved apart ever so slightly each year by the action of ice. Things seem firm enough, but halfway along, the route begins to narrow down quickly.

Our peripheral vision always gives us clues about the nature of our immediate surroundings. Those clues help us orient with every step, and we walk confidently along, not giving the art of walking a thought. But midway out on Table Rock, there are no visual clues on either side, only empty space and yawning drops. The result is disorientation. Many people who come this far stop and can go no farther because they feel they have lost some substantial fraction of their sense of balance.

But there is a way to tough it out, if you really want to. The trick to moving to the very end of Table Rock is to focus ahead a dozen feet and keep your eyes riveted forward as you proceed slowly. As you go, the path chisels down from 6 feet, to 5, to 4, to 3. Finally, the last bit of terra firma is a rock that is point shaped like an arrowhead. Beyond it is only atmosphere.

Hundreds of feet below and to the right, NH 26 bends to the east, squeezed tight within the confines of the brutally steep slopes of Mt. Gloriette and Mt. Sanguinary. To the left, 700 feet below, are the placid waters of man-made Lake Gloriette, and hugging the shoreline, the classic form of a 19th-century New England luxury hostelry known as the Balsams Grand Resort Hotel.

Directly ahead and across the notch stand a collection of 3,000-foot peaks topped with gently rounded summits, real estate that has been the domain of loggers for more than one hundred years. Straight down, or nearly so, is NH 26. A fall from this vantage point would yield a terrifying few seconds of freefall and a resting place in a jumble of shattered rock scree.

Have a seat, sit tight to the last morsel of rock, and enjoy the rarified air. The setting is dramatic, about as thrilling as New England has to offer. A snack or lunch is in order, a celebration of your good fortune in having reached the last foot of Table Rock without turning back or falling to an untimely death.

Once you've mastered your surroundings, it's time for the last hurdle that the Table Rock Trail may throw across your path. Descend the stone steps at the entrance to the cliff and turn immediately left and steeply downhill. You have a bit less than 700 vertical feet to descend now, but every foot of it is very steep and the soils and rocks can be unstable. Take your time. Be careful not to dislodge rocks that appear to be badly eroded out of their anchoring soils. In wet weather, the route can be very slick and footing tough to keep. In fact, in wet weather, stay off this steep incline altogether.

There is no letup in the steepness of the descent until you reach the road and a small, sand-choked parking pullout. The original trail sign here has been removed for some time, and wisely so. The New Hampshire Division of Parks and Recreation would rather visitors utilize the much easier and more pleasant western route to Table Tock.

All that is needed now is to turn left and walk along the shoulder of NH 26 back to your vehicle not quite a mile away. Although the trek is along the road, the view across the waters of Lake Gloriette to the Balsams Grand Resort Hotel and the jagged face of Mt. Abenaki, just behind the hotel, is a sensation in its own right. Road walking doesn't seem so anticlimactic in Dixville Notch.

30.

Three Brothers Trail

Location: Dixville, NH

Distance: 5 miles round-trip

Difficulty: Moderate to steep in sections, particularly in the vicinity of Huntington Falls

Trailhead: 44°51'20.47'N, 71°17'07.24'W

GETTING THERE

Swing eastbound from Colebrook Village on NH 26 and pace off 12 miles to Dixville Notch. Climb the divide and descend through the notch and down its eastern narrow passage to the Dixville Wayside on the right (south) side of the highway. Or travel westbound on NH 26 from the hamlet of Errol. Approaching Dixville Notch in level terrain just before the road pitches uphill, look for the Dixville Wayside on the left, fronted by a state sign.

Pull into the wayside and park across from the old salt shed near the tiny Whittemore graveyard. Accompanying the little family grave plot is a large routed sign that spins a tale of woe about the original settlers in this remote and cold region of Coos County.

A FINE OLD TRAIL RESTORED

Dixville Notch was born of geologic cataclysm. The 5 miles of trails that ring this tiniest but most dramatic of New Hampshire's great mountain passes ride on rocks that were spared destruction on numerous occasions 11,000 years ago, when the Laurentide Ice Sheet that covered all of New England retreated from this region, melting away as temperatures across the Northern Hemisphere increased suddenly and substantially at that time.

Ice dams atop the mountains collapsed repeatedly in this area, allowing vast glacial lakes impounded by rotting ice to drain away suddenly in fantastic floods. Deluge after deluge carved the canyon we see today, perhaps in as little as a few days.

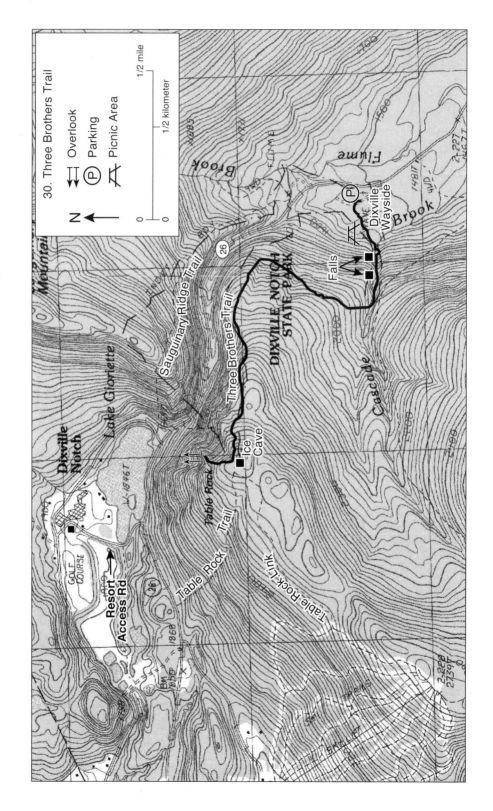

30. Three Brothers Trail

Overlook
P Parking
Picnic Area

N

0   1/2 mile
0   1/2 kilometer

Dixville Notch

Lake Gloriette

Resort Access Rd

GOLF COURSE

Sauguinary Ridge Trail

Three Brothers Trail

Table Rock Trail

Table Rock Link

Ice Cave

DIXVILLE NOTCH STATE PARK

Cascade

Falls

Dixville Wayside
P

Flume

Brook

Brook

Pull into the Dixville Wayside. An old salt shed appears on the left. Swing right and park at a little fenced compound that marks the tiny graveyard plot of the Whittemore family, the first settlers in this region who built a little log cabin nearby. The pioneers endured three brutal winters snowed in, cut off from all other habitation. When the matriarch died in midwinter, the surviving family members abandoned their holding and removed to the tiny hamlet of Colebrook, 12 miles away.

Hopefully, better weather will greet you upon your arrival. Don your backpack and walk across the parking area to the west and turn left up the first narrow gravel lane you come to. Enter a little picnic area and look for a creosote-laced post sporting a sign that indicates Huntington Falls and the pathway beyond. Trek a short distance, crest a little rise, and continue to a pool in a branch of Clear Stream that collects water at the base of the first of two waterfalls. This lower cascade is a braided affair, dropping 20 feet to the pool. Here the water is bone-chillingly cold almost every day of the year.

The trail leaps the brook. Pick your way across on exposed rock slabs and mount the far bank. Immediately, the Three Brothers Trail pitches steeply uphill and hugs the deepening ravine where the falls tumbles. Catch a fine glimpse of the lower falls as you ascend in dark evergreen forest.

Stay close to the clifflike ledge of the ravine. Several other vantage points open up with drops of 20, 30, and 40 feet, respectively. At the highest point, a second falls appears, this one falling much farther than the lower cascade, but it is so tightly confined that it appears like a sliver ribbon in a cave. Ten years ago, during a photo shoot for *National Geographic Adventure* magazine, the photographer and photo editor asked me to climb up into the upper falls, clamber around at the base of the cliffs, and

immerse myself in the shower of the falls. The shoot lasted an hour. I was blue when I emerged, trembling with cold. Unfortunately, not one shot made it into print.

Continue a steep ascent until the trail swings left with the stream and moderates. The chasm where the falls originate recedes behind. Crest a low rise, descend a few log stairs for a second, cut sharply left, and soon you'll regain the stream. Cross on exposed stones, but be careful if water is very high. This crossing can be dangerous when the stream is raging after a heavy summer cloudburst. Once in a great while, it is best to bushwhack upstream a ways to find a more suitable crossing.

Leave the brook for good now and begin a moderate push uphill in mixed forest on fine pathway that, a dozen years ago, had fallen into disuse because of lack of maintenance. A youth trail-building program from Randolph, New Hampshire, the Trailmasters, rebuilt the old trail. It now gets considerable use because it is the most interesting ascent in the region to famed Table Rock cliff, still high above.

Climb steadily now but without undue effort, moving through bright openings marked by widely spaced trees and low growth and tight, dark spruce stands. Reach a junction on the right. A spur trail leads northwest down to Old King, one of the several prominent cliff faces on the extremely steep south flank of Mt. Gloriette. While Table Rock farther up the line is the usual destination point for all who come this way, Old King seems no less dramatic, except that, unlike from Table Rock, the view is a bit restricted to the west. However, the fear-inducing profile of Table Rock cliff is clearly visible from Old King.

Regain the Three Brothers Trail. The angle of the pathway increases, but no sooner than it does, the trail crests a bony knob, drops rapidly for 20 vertical feet,

Dixville Notch, eastern side

swings west, and levels out in forest teetering on the edge of sheer drops. In the flat now, watch the trail to the left of your feet. A great gash opens in the ground, a feature known as Ice Cave.

Here the mountain is literally pulling apart. If you study the rock wall directly over the gap in the rock below, you can see that the strata have slumped down and away from the main body of Mt. Gloriette. The cliffs of Dixville Notch over your shoulder are really quite unstable. Here the rock is on the move, ever so slowly. The chasm in the rock is of unknown depth. Are the depths 20 feet below, 40, 60? There is no way to know, because the gash is filled a great deal with ice 365 days a year. The ice, in turn, helps cleave the mountain apart. Someday, the forces will conspire to cause the collapse of

the cliff faces. When that happens, NH 26, in the bottom of the canyon far below, will fill with thousands of tons of rumble.

Just beyond Ice Cave, the Three Brothers Trail ends at a junction with the Table Rock Trail. At the junction, on the right, is a little flat with an opening in the trees. Step into the opening and have a good look at the rock formation that is the destination for anyone who reaches this elevation: Table Rock.

No reason to stop your progress now that the Tree Brothers Trail has come to an end. Continue west for a few feet and drop down a steep embankment to a saddle between the mountain and the Table Rock upthrust. Climb a set of stone stairs, the forest parts, and one of New England's greatest cliff environments shows itself. Hardy souls have been known to balk at trekking the 100 or so feet of narrow prominence out to the very pointlike edge of Table Rock. Most people manage to move out on the ledge two-thirds of the way; the route continuously narrows down until the utter lack of solid ground on either side makes it difficult to maintain equilibrium. The few people disciplined enough to narrow their focus to only what little rock stretches ahead can manage to reach the very last inch of terrain. Beyond is a 700-foot near vertical drop. If you choose to approach the edge, proceed very carefully, at your own risk.

Those who manage the feat without crawling have my respect. Whether you come to the brink of terra firma or not, the views from this perch are nonpareil, east and west. Eastward, the expansive forests of the Great North Woods stretch away into Maine, unbroken by human habitation. To the west, the view is more refined. Serene Lake Gloriette shimmers below. On its north shore stands the Balsams Grand Resort Hotel, with its bright whitewashed façade and acres of warm red roofing. Behind the edifice stands the expansive ledges of Mt. Abenaki. Farther off looms Vermont's Mt. Monadnock over little Colebrook Village. Beyond stretches the Green Mountains of Vermont and peaks across the international border in Canada.

Because of the waterfalls, the crossing at Clear Stream, Old King Cliff, Ice Cave, and Table Rock, the Three Brothers Trail represents, to my way of thinking, the best route to access the dramatic country on the south side of Dixville Notch.

31.

Canal Trail to the Lake of Floating Islands

Location: Dixville, NH

Distance: About 6 miles round-trip

Difficulty: Moderate short climb at first, then easy going the rest of the way

Trailhead: 44°52'19.48'N, 71°18'77.77'W

GETTING THERE

From Colebrook Village and NH 3, run eastbound 12 miles on NH 26 to Dixville Notch. Skirt Lake Gloriette on the left, and just as you pass the lake and just before heading into the maw of the great notch, turn left onto the entrance lane to the Balsams Grand Resort Hotel. Drive the lane to the hotel but continue past it. Round the corner of a large structure standing directly next to the road. Just beyond the building, look for a turn to the right, running uphill to a series of parking lots one above the other. Travel to the uppermost parking lot and park. To the left (west) side of the lot is a short grassy pitch. Climb it and continue to a service road. Turn uphill on that service road and you are on your way.

TREADING WATER

One of the rarest geological features on earth is a lake that drains down not one but two separate watersheds. Unusual, too, is stumbling upon a hand-dug canal deep in boreal forests where, logic would have it, there should be no such creation. Also rare is the opportunity to sneak up on a young moose, his head submerged in water to partake of aquatic vegetation, so that he might be approached within 25 feet.

Several miles north of the Balsams Grand Resort Hotel, at the head of rugged Dixville Notch, a small, low dam holds back a placid body of cold, black, but perfectly clear water that, today, goes by the rather unflattering name of Mud Pond. A century ago, the small lake had another name more fitting of its character: Lake of the Floating Islands.

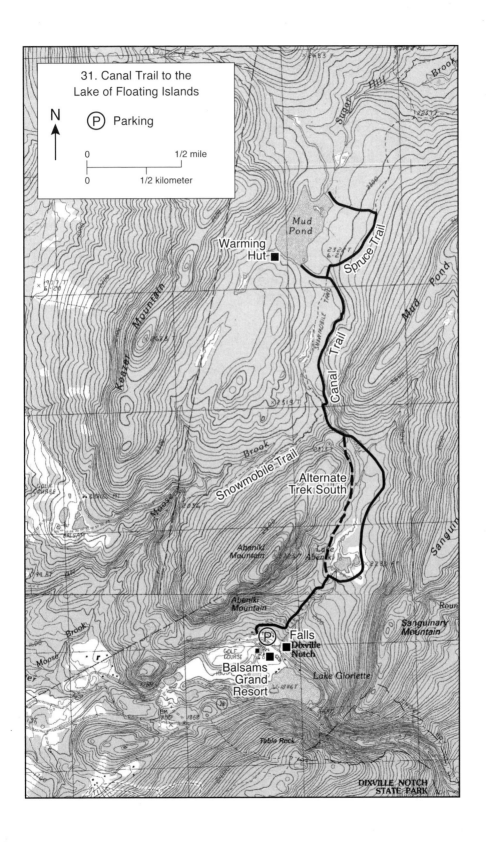

31. Canal Trail to the
Lake of Floating Islands

N

(P) Parking

0 _____ 1/2 mile
0 _____ 1/2 kilometer

Mud
Pond

Warming
Hut

Spruce Trail

Canal Trail

Snowmobile Trail

Mud Pond

Keazer Mountain

Brook

Snowmobile Trail

Alternate
Trek South

Abeniki
Mountain

Lake
Abeniki

Sanguin

GOLF
COURSE

Moose

Abeniki
Mountain

Roun

Brook

Sanguinary
Mountain

Moose

(P)

Falls
Dixville
Notch

GOLF
COURSE

Balsams
Grand
Resort

Lake Gloriette

Table Rock

DIXVILLE NOTCH
STATE PARK

The Canal Trail

I rather like that long-lost moniker, and I like the quiet walk that permits access to this quiet domain. The lake is reached by a path that is like few others in the Northeast, for it runs on an earthen berm created when laborers excavated a long, snaking canal and tunnel aqueduct designed to bring copious amounts of water down to the great resort in the notch.

To locate the Canal Trail and Mud Pond, turn off NH 26 at the hotel entrance and drive along the shores of Lake Gloriette to the marvelous world-class hotel. Drive past the main building and look for a second turn to the left to the upper parking lot above the hotel. Climb the hill to the upper lot and park at the upper end. Don a day pack and leave the parking lot uphill to the left (west). Climb the grassy bank and immediately encounter a dirt forest road that is gated and supports no traffic. Turn uphill (north) and walk on a modest incline for a few minutes, until a large, earthen dam comes into view. Below the dam, turn right and walk eastbound be-

neath the slope of the dam. Pass the spillway on the left and bend gradually left, northward toward the woods, gaining a view into the empty bowl of Abenaki Pond. The depression use to cradle a good-size pond, but the recently build dam didn't do its job well enough, so the water was drained.

Proceed to a pleasant grassy lane overshadowed by the crowns of large trees. Pass an indistinct trail junction, access to the Sanguinary Summit Trail on the ridge high above, and continue in gently undulating terrain northward. Ten minutes north of the dam, you'll pass a wide weed-filled lane on the right, and soon reach a junction where five woods ways meet within the span of 100 feet. Move straight ahead through a low gap in the terrain to a Y-junction. Take the right turn and drop immediately downhill. Below, you can see a narrow channel of water and hear water tumbling.

At the base of the hill, turn right and go to that ribbon of water: the Canal Trail. To the right there appears to be a cave in the side of the hill and the water in the canal runs into the dark recesses and disappears. Somewhere in the depths, water must drop enough to generate the canal's waterfall-like sounds.

The Canal Trail winds in somewhat level terrain, gradually swinging right and left through pleasant woodlands punctuated with towering spires of fir and spruce. The route is just barely wide enough to support a vehicle. The surface is easy on the feet, often filled with low tufts of grass.

As you move north, the canal keeps you company, its waters drifting by at a lazy pace on its way south to the hotel. On the floor of the canal, long green streamers of aquatic vegetation trail out with the current. In high summer, the algae and plants attract moose, which relish the food for its sodium content. If my experiences are any guide, you have a fine chance of coming upon a moose, standing chest deep in the water, grazing on the water plants.

A decade ago, I came upon a young bull moose as I rounded a bend in the trail. The creature's head was submerged. As he could not see or hear me with his head below the surface, I would jog along quickly toward the animal until he began to lift his head clear of the water. Then I would stop. When he dropped his head again, I repeated my advance. This went on five or six times, until I had closed the distance between him and me to about 25 feet.

Quite close to the animal now, I stood stone still as he pulled his head up, chewing his lunch. Now he finally noticed me. His eyes flared wide and his ears swept forward. He stopped chewing. Although moose don't talk, I could imagine him saying to me, "Huh! Where the hell did you come from?"

We spent a good minute eyeing each other. In truth, the creature did not seem to be the least bit put out by my being on his home turf. He stood his ground, waiting for me to end the standoff. I did. I left the trail, made a broad arc around the moose, and regained the trail. The moose simply turned his head over his shoulder to watch me as I walked away.

After a good mile on the watery way, you'll reach a crossroads. Pass directly through it. Five minutes beyond the junction, the canal ends at a low earthen and stone dam. Clamber up 6 vertical feet or so. Here Mud Pond comes into view, nestled beneath Van Dyke Mountain and Sugar Hill.

Settle in. Have lunch or a snack, and be quiet. Mud Pond is coveted real estate for waterfowl. Loons patrol here, moorhens on occasion, mergansers and ducks, too. Goshawks find the environment to their liking. Venture close to their nest and they will bomb your noggin, sometimes striking you a blow.

At the dam, the lake drains down the canal to the Mohawk River, a tributary of the Connecticut River. Its waters eventually join Long Island Sound in Connecticut. A mile away is a second spillway, albeit a small one, but the waters draining away there aren't bound for Connecticut. Instead, the flow eventually reaches the Androscoggin River watershed and empties into the Gulf of Maine. Well, so what of it? In fact, there are almost no other bodies of water on Earth that accomplish this feat.

The Canal Trail is as pleasant a walk in the forest as can be had in the Great North Woods. It is suitable for families with children. And it's certainly suitable for those who are wildlife aficionados. Because the regions supports a chain of small lakes, marshlike environments, alder swamps, streams aplenty, plus the canal, all sorts of birds and mammals thrive here.

In spring, hungry black bears roam the grassy lanes, wolfing down young shoots of grass. Barred owls rotate their heads seemingly around and around, just to keep an eye on you. Loons carry snoozing chicks on their back. After moving through this country a dozen times while building trails in the region, I rarely failed to observe some of the Northeast's most interesting denizens going about their business.

Peakbaggers may not care for a day hike that doesn't gain some craggy outpost in the clouds. The Canal Trail, though, is true respite from a harried world, almost a meditative experience. Quiet, flowing water at your side works wonders in powering down a hardwired soul. And if you need something to replenish your constitution at the end of the trek, you can always stop in at the Balsams Grand Resort Hotel and order a drink, or maybe even stay for lunch. If you do, be sure to sample one of its world-class desserts. Wow! Heavenly.

32.

Sanguinary Ridge Trail

Location: Dixville, NH

Distance: 1.2 miles one-way

Difficulty: Moderately steep in the east, steep in sections to the west over unstable rock scree

Trailhead: 44°51'33.65'N, 71°17'24.28'W

GETTING THERE

Travel eastbound from Colebrook Village on NH 26, near the top of the Granite State, and pass through Dixville Notch and down its eastern terrain to the first of the two Dixville Wayside pullouts, this one on the north (left) side of the highway. Or travel westbound on NH 26 from the hamlet of Errol. Approaching Dixville Notch in level terrain, pass the lower Dixville Wayside on the left, and look for its upper cousin on the right (north), 800 feet farther along.

Pull into the wayside and park in a small lot of broken pavement at the foot of a small flume in a northern branch of Clear Stream.

SIX CHANCES TO FREE-FALL

There is something exhilarating about standing at the edge of a cliff. The Sanguinary Ridge Trail, on the north rim of Dixville Notch, offers up six chances to test your mettle when tippy-toe to the very limit of terra firma. But rather than begin in thin air, the trail gets its start at the water's edge on the eastern edge of the mountain pass.

In Franconia Notch 50 miles to the south, torrents of glacial water carved a narrow chasm in solid granite, the famed Flume, with its tight vertical walls, turbulent jets of water, and well-designed tourist boardwalks. At Dixville Notch, similar geological processes carved an infant flume, not what one would call a spectacular feature, but a delightful one. Fill your bottles here if you haven't done so already. The Cave Mountain–Mt. Sanguinary watershed draining through the flume is virtually never

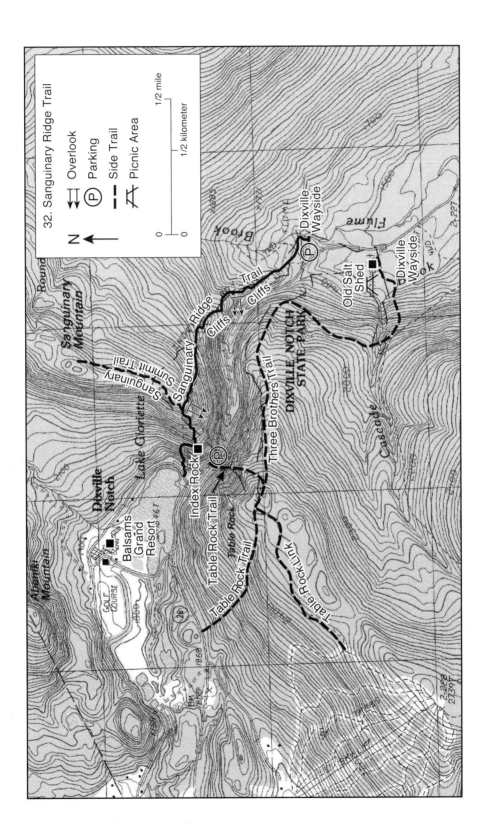

32. Sanguinary Ridge Trail

N

Overlook
P Parking
Side Trail
Picnic Area

0   1/2 mile
0   1/2 kilometer

hiked. Water is as clean here as a mountain stream can be.

The trail steps immediately uphill from a picnic table by the flume. Look for white blazes and a small CT (Cohos Trail) sign. Twist and turn uphill to an overlook into the flume, then cut away abruptly to the west. Level out, cross a little seep and a very old logging lane, and then begin a continuous pull uphill for nearly a mile. The going gets moderately steep, but the rewards for your effort come on quickly.

Just 15 minutes into the trek, the trail skirts a little granite shelf. Step off the trail and out onto it. Just a few feet from the path and the world falls away. Several hundred feet below and to the west snakes NH 26, rising on its way to the height of land deep within the ravine. Already, cars below look like toys.

Turn and study the very steep terrain that is the hallmark of Dixville Notch. On the north side of the highway rises Mt. Sanguinary. High along its flank you should be able to make out several rock outcroppings, each one higher than the next. You will reach each of them as you trek ever higher. On the south flank of the north stands Mt. Gloriette, marked by a series of rock spires and vertical drops. Later in the hike, you will come to intimate terms with that jagged real estate.

Back on the trail, the uphill pull is interrupted every five minutes by cliff edge after cliff edge. On the incline there are a total of four rock shelves, once of which is rather spacious and makes a good spot to stop and take in the views. To the south over the rim of Mt. Gloriette, the whaleback form of Dixville Peak rises. In the future, it's possible that wind turbine blades might be visible rotating in the near constant winds that sweep over that summit.

After leaving the fourth cliff ledge, the trail becomes considerably steeper, pushes away from the edge of the notch, and swings through several wide switchbacks. You'll gain vertical feet quickly and begin to work up a sweat when the angle of the path begins to moderate as the height of land approaches. But the trek gets easier and easier when it comes to a junction right at the height of land. Here the Sanguinary Summit Trail, the SST, cuts due north toward the true summit of the mountain.

At the junction continue straight ahead and immediately drop in elevation. The path drops downhill at a modest angle, swinging in S-turns, when it reaches a naked ledge with a fine view. But don't linger here, for just another 100 feet below, the trail becomes a great slab of rock that forms a sheer precipice.

North of the White Mountains, there are few more dramatic overlooks than from this shelf at the western gateway to Dixville Notch. First, directly 300 feet below, stands the red-roofed Balsams Grand Resort Hotel on the shores of Lake Gloriette. It seems one could almost jump off the cliff and land on one of the roofs of the great recreational complex below.

The hotel is framed by the tortured naked rock slopes of Mt. Abenaki. Farther west reposes the broad Connecticut River Valley, itself framed by the classic Appalachian Mountain form of Vermont's Mt. Monadnock. Beyond stands the long spine of the Green Mountains and a few summits across the border in Canada.

But the best vista here is the view directly across the chasm, Dixville Notch. Here you can get a full appreciation of the 700-foot vertical spire that holds up famed Table Rock. If you are fortunate to come here when someone is standing on the very upper edge of Table Rock, the true scale of the feature will come home to you. Visitors appear no larger than sweet ants on a kitchen counter.

HR Index Rock

Table Rock is only one of half a dozen desert bluff country–like spires large and small that grace the unstable north face of Mt. Gloriette. The place looks as though it is a raw wound of sorts. And indeed it is. Dixville Notch was carved by the sudden and repeated blowouts of vast glacial lakes. When the continental ice sheet was melting and receding quickly from this country at the end of the last ice age, unstable ice dams that overtopped the mountains periodically collapsed, allowing countless gallons of water to flood through minor gaps in the mountainous terrain. Dixville Notch suffered the worst of these catastrophes not once but numerous times, and was carved into its present form in just a handful of calamitous days.

If you are lucky, you might witness the movement of big raptors that occasionally use the notch to move between the Connecticut River and Androscoggin River watersheds. Ospreys and ravens have a habit of riding rivers of air that speed up in the narrow confines of the notch. No reason why other species wouldn't do the same.

Back away from the cliff edge and turn west down a narrow path that empties out at the head of a steep and unstable rock scree field. Turn south directly toward the notch and pick your way carefully downhill. A series of stone steps in the scree field have been buried by soil and rock slide. These are slated to be excavated, cleaned, and new stone steps put in place.

Descend to a point where the path bends west at the foot to two curious rock monoliths that have been give various names over the years, from Madonna and Child to Index Rock today. Descending gradually now, cut directly across the open scree field, with rock slide above and below, and make your way into the forest.

Once in the woods, the trail becomes a series of tight switchbacks that drop quickly in elevation. Use caution in several spots where there are not ready handholds, and make your way quickly out to the entrance drive to the Balsams Grand Resort Hotel, just a few feet from the junction with NH 26.

33.

Sanguinary Summit Trail (SST)

Location: Dixville, NH

Distance: 8-plus-mile loop hike

Difficulty: Easy to moderate, but lengthy once you reach the trail high on Mt. Sanguinary

Trailhead: 44°51'51.38'N, 71°18'11.05'W

GETTING THERE

Travel eastbound 11 miles from Colebrook Village on NH 26, near the top of the Granite State, or nearly an equal distance westbound from Errol. Reach the very confines of Dixville Notch. From the west, look for a sandy pullout on the right just uphill from the entrance to the Balsams Grand Resort Hotel on the left. From the east, cross over the height of land in the notch and immediately turn left into the small pullout. Park and walk downhill 200 feet to the entrance to the hotel, across the road. Enter the drive and look to your immediate right for a trail sign at the forest edge, half a dozen vertical feet above the lane.

ELEVATED RIDGELINE TOUR OF THE GREAT NORTH WOODS

The Sanguinary Summit Trail–SST for short–gets its start high on the upper south slope of Mt. Sanguinary. To reach the trail, climb the short, steep western leg of the Sanguinary Ridge Trail out of Dixville Notch. Swing through several wooded switchbacks before striding into the lower stretches of a scree field of rotting shale. Trek over loose stone to the east, then bend up a steep pitch to the north, mounting stone stairs as you go. Climb to a flat stone slab that ends in a 200-foot vertical drop seemingly onto the red roofs of the Balsams Grant Resort Hotel. Pass another cliff edge, then enter the woods and climb moderately for five minutes to the trail's height of land. At the highest point, you'll reach a trail junction. The Sanguinary Ridge Trail runs straight ahead to the

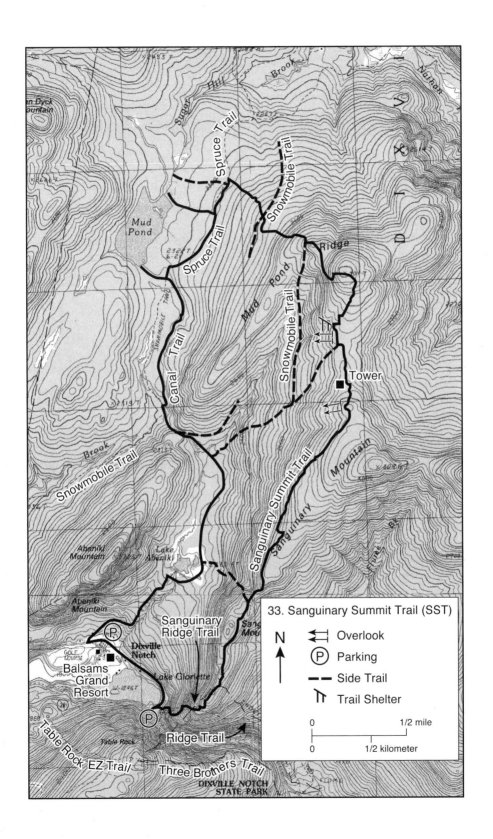

33. Sanguinary Summit Trail (SST)

N

⇄ Overlook

Ⓟ Parking

– – Side Trail

⛨ Trail Shelter

0   1/2 mile

0   1/2 kilometer

east, but the SST cuts away abruptly left and up an easy grade.

Swing onto the SST and start a long ridge run on terrain that ties Mt. Sanguinary to the distant, low main peak of Mud Pond Ridge. Despite the name of the trail, this path doesn't reach the true wooded summit of the mountain but skirts it to the west.

Walk north just a few seconds to an opening in the forest on the left. Continue to the edge of the little cleared area. Directly below sprawls the acre of red roof shingles of the Balsams Grand Resort Hotel. Leap from this outcropping and you'd have a room to yourself in a few seconds, or so it seems.

Set off northbound and thread open mixed forest on the elevated spine of Mt. Sanguinary, a ridgeline that rarely deviates from 2,800-feet elevation. Often, in the first mile, the forest thins sufficiently to the east to permit glimpses of peaks standing in the state of Maine, as well as of nearby Cave and Rice Mountains. The path is pleasant enough for hikers, but it is also a favorite with moose. I've met the big creatures along the route several times, including once when I had finished a long day of trail work and was heading southbound. Tired, I paced along, head down, until I sensed rather than saw something from beneath my broad-brimmed hat. I stopped and looked up to see a bull moose, standing still directly in the trail, about 30 feet away. He wasn't going anywhere, so I left the trail and wedged myself within a clump of trees. Satisfied he again had the thoroughfare to himself, the moose plodded forward and disappeared to the north.

Pass through a depression, cross a bog bridge, and rise to a trail junction. Signs in the junction state Low Route and High Route. For our purposes, continue straight ahead on the High Route, shunning the turn to the left. Continue trekking in open and fern-carpeted forest, drifting slightly toward the west away from the true summit of the mountain. Slab the low summit in the ridge on its left flank and enter an ancient logging skidway lined with spruce on either side. You'll reach a small, boggy area where a trail crew improved the footing five years ago. Cross the outflow, bypass a seep, swing downhill to the west, then cut north again and rise to regain the ridgeline. Pass through a stretch of infirm trail and eroded segments. Snake through a stand of tight young spruce growing in a 15-year-old logging cut. Rise out of the growth onto a minor knob. Here views open dozens of miles to the west and ahead to Mud Pond Ridge and Blue Ridge.

Dismount the rise and cross an open plateau marked by large but impoverished and dying white birch trees on the left and mature uncut forest on the right. You will suddenly emerge from the spruce and fir onto a gravel- and earth-filled lane. On the left stands a small tower erected so that wind speed could be recorded in the area. Turn right and walk on this ridgeline road for ¼ mile. The route reaches a dogleg turn to the left and falls downhill. Make the turn and descend just 100 feet. Look for a yellow-topped stake on the right. It marks the resumption of the Sanguinary Summit Trail. Drop downhill off and away from the road, fall 50 vertical feet, and level out. Turn north to a series of bog bridges over a seep running with water. Pass the seep and begin a short, steep climb that comes to a building capped with a dark green steel roof, located on a minor plateau.

A lean-to shelter named Panorama will materialize on the left. It's a big one, with plenty of capacity and a substantial roof overhang that allows visitors to sit on the edge of the floor in wet weather and not get wet. Some 3½ miles out from your parked car, Panorama is a logical place to take off

Building Panorama

your pack, have a bite to eat, rehydrate, and spend time taking in the sweeping view from the south to the north-northwest.

The lean-to opening faces east out of the prevailing winds. The finest vistas can be had from just behind the structure. The site sits high above the narrow Mohawk River Valley and the Connecticut River Valley. Mountains and hills rim the entire scene. The backdrop far to the west is the long spine of the Green Mountains. Peeking out of the forest to the south are the cliffs of Dixville Notch. The farther, northern vista ends at low summits across the international border in Canada. In that direction, 100 feet from the lean-to, is an outdoor toilet. It will be replaced in the future by a composting latrine.

Panorama is a fine facility, roomy and tall,

for spending the night. On clear, moonless nights at the lean-to, the night sky is spellbinding. There is no earthly light pollution to speak of to blemish the heavens. Satellites are often visible; occasionally the international space station, too.

The area is well traveled by moose, as well. There are plenty of piles of droppings about to mark their passing. I discovered a shed antler nearby, brought it home, and donated it to a children's summer camp. Once in a great while you might hear a moose plodding through the forest at night or eavesdrop on one snorting through its copious nose.

Refreshed, continue northward. A few paces uphill you'll reach a 90-degree turn to the right, cross two bog bridge spans, and soon turn hard left and uphill. Begin an easy uphill march to the nearby unnamed 3,000-foot summit of Mud Pond Ridge, a rather special little island of pure Canadian boreal forest plant communities.

You'll attain the summit just 10 minutes out of the lean-to. Swing onto the path that passes bright red property boundary blazes. Here you'll enter an interesting realm, only 5 or so acres large, that is a dead ringer for the Canadian Shield forest environments of central Quebec. This is the domain of spruce and fir. In the low light on the forest floor, green mosses carpet the landscape. The summit has an otherworldly feel to it, as if it were a movie set plopped down in the forest.

Slip over the summit and fall quickly in elevation to a long-abandoned field. Turn hard to the right and shortly pick up a very indistinct logging skidway that falls gently in elevation until it ends on a wide grassy forest lane, a snowmobile trail really, with soft footing. Turn right onto the lane, head north over a knoll, and then cut downhill and to the west. You'll arrive at a crossroad junction of snowmobile trails. Pace straight through the junction and drop into a woods trail that runs ¼ mile under the forest canopy to another snowmobile path. At that junction, turn downhill and soon you'll reach the valley floor, where an unused road cuts across your path.

This road goes by the name of the Spruce Trail. It is used by cross-country skiers and snowmobilers in the winter. Make a hard left, pass another junction on your immediate right, and move southwestward. In 800 feet reach yet another junction. The path you want runs straight ahead, but turn down this new lane for five minutes, until you encounter a body of water. Walk out onto a very small earthen impoundment that sports a culvert at its center.

This aquatic environment is Mud Pond, as seen from its eastern end. Van Dyke Mountain stands over it. Waterfowl thrive in this environment. Large mammals come to its shoreline in early morning and at dusk. This is a lonely spot, fully 3 miles from the Balsams Grand Resort Hotel. Few people ever come this way in summer and fall. You will have the lake to yourself. The spillway dam is a pleasant place to languish and fill up with fluids.

Return to the Spruce Trail dirt lane and turn right. In five minutes, you'll come across another crossroads. Turn left onto the Canal Trail, named for the hand-dug ribbon of water that follows this route for more than a mile. Tread along beside the gently flowing water in the canal until the flow disappears into a tunnel. Swing uphill to the left and come to a junction where many lanes come together roughly in the same spot. Move straight ahead through the junction and pick up the true access road ahead and to the right, or its grassy, soft-footed equivalent ahead and to the left, marked by yellow blazes. Both routes eventually meet at the large but defunct dam that holds back a very shallow Abenaki Pond. I favor the old grassy trail through hardwood forest. When the pond and dam come into view, pass directly beneath the dam, pick up the access road, and take that lane downhill to the rear of the Balsams Grand Resort Hotel. Turn hard right and walk the length of the hotel drive, Lake Gloriette on your right, to reach the western head of Dixville Notch and NH 26. Turn uphill to the left and return to your car parking across the highway 100 feet away.

VI. Connecticut River Headwaters

Mt. Covell and Round Pond

New England's mightiest river, the Connecticut, collects itself for a 400-mile run at Long Island Sound, among the beaver bogs, moose flowages, cold ponds, and huge lakes in the headwaters country in and around Colebrook Village and to the north toward the Canadian border.

Various large streams, including the Mohawk, Halls, Indian, and Perry, add uncounted gallons of water to the great river.

In the high country and bogs within the drainage, miles of new trails have been built to complement a few old and cherished routes that reach some of the more sweeping vistas that can be had anywhere in New England. Fire towers, eastern cedar swamps, canyons, and giant black lakes can all be explored now in an area that was once the exclusive domain of the logger.

34.

McAllister Road to Weir Tree Farms

Location: Clarksville, NH

Distance: 6.6 miles round-trip

Difficulty: Easy to moderate trek over largely abandoned farm lanes in beautiful rural countryside

Trailhead: 44°57'00.02'N, 71°23'51.03'W

GETTING THERE

Find your way to Colebrook via NH 3, NH 26, or VT 102. Toward the northern end of the community, NH 145 bears right, northeast and then due north, and soon begins snaking uphill through a tight wooded canyon. Pass a fine waterfall on the right and motor through numerous curves. Reach a tiny hamlet known as Stewartstown Hollow and a junction with Bear Rock Road on the right. Take Bear Rock Road nearly 4 miles, passing hardscrabble homesteads and abandoned farmland. Watch on the left for a green metal sign that indicates McAllister Road. Pull left but park at the edge of Bear Rock Road. Do not block the lane.

WHERE CHRISTMAS GROWS

Most of the hikes in this book feature treks up mountains or to remote geological features and falls. This hike to the remarkable Weir Tree Farms in isolated country in Clarksville, New Hampshire, is the exception. And what an exception it is. Who would guess that an abandoned Class VI farm lane in a region of northern Appalachian poverty and low hillocks could yield a world-class view, a haunted house, the skeletons of dead early 20th-century agriculture, and a stroll through one of the most innovative tree farms in North America. And if you time this hike just right in mid-June, the landscape explodes with yellow as hundreds of thousands of dandelion blossoms overwhelm the rich fresh greens of late spring.

This jaunt begins at the junction of Bear Rock Road and McAllister Road. Leave your

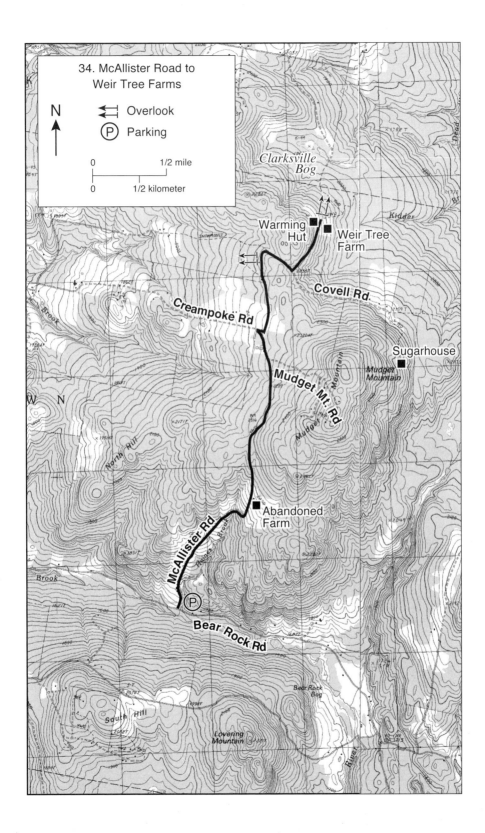

34. McAllister Road to
Weir Tree Farms

N

⇄ Overlook
Ⓟ Parking

0   1/2 mile

0   1/2 kilometer

Clarksville
Bog

Warming ■ ■ Weir Tree
Hut   Farm

Covell Rd.

Creampoke Rd

Sugarhouse ■

Mudget
Mountain

Mudget Mt. Rd

Mudget

W   N

North Hill

Brook

McAllister Rd

■ Abandoned
Farm

Brook

Ⓟ

Bear Rock Rd

South Hill

Lovering
Mountain

Bear Rock
Bog

River

Weir Tree Farms, Mudget Mountain   WILLIAM AND PAULINE WEIR

vehicle and immediately pace uphill. A working dairy farm stands to the left. Go straight uphill, pass around a metal farm gate, and climb on an easy but steady grade out of the valley. On both sides of the old farm lane, good, well-maintained barbed-wire fencing runs with the lane for some distance.

The way uphill is sometimes open, sometimes shaded by maples and evergreens. Old pasture acreage rather than forest predominates. Within five minutes, a high hill clearing to the north shows through the trees in the distance. In the opening stands what looks like a weathered farmhouse. You are headed in that direction.

The lane runs straight, crosses over a rivulet running in a culvert, and then bends to the right at the start of a long S-curve. In the middle of the turns, the route becomes con-

siderably steeper. With each step, you gain in elevation. Limited views stretch out of the valley below and the far ridgeline that frames it. For a few moments, the pitch becomes quite steep, but it moderates as that farmhouse you cast your eyes on below looms on the right.

Once a proud homestead seated in a cluster of farm buildings, the house and a small barn are all that remain. Both buildings are losing their battle with the North Country elements. They look haunted, malnourished. Vandals long ago broke out some the windows, and weather finished them off. Rain has little trouble finding its way into the building, so its timbers and framing is rotting. Who knows how long it will be before a winter with heavy snows brings down the porch, collapses a section of roof, or topples the whole of one or both of them. I don't recommend going into the house or the barn now, but curiosity is terrible thing. I paid homage to my curiosity. I suspect you might, as well; just take care if you give in to the temptation.

The last time I made the trek to the hillside, it was on the fifteenth of the month of June. The hayfields on all sides had not seen the blade of a sickle in some time, so the odd clusters of dandelion had spread their seed throughout the land. They'd taken over, literally. Every open area in full sun was a riot of dandelion yellow, an unbroken sea of it. It seemed like a beautiful falsehood, like something a graphic artist had conjured with Photoshop software. And me, I hadn't brought my camera, fool that I am.

Drift up the lane onto the flat ridgeline and walk on the level. Large cut stones hint at the outlines of big barns that once stood just off the lane to the left. Nothing remains of them except the stone. Given the foundations' former dimensions, they must have been something to behold. One of the cornerstones makes a good seat, perfect for stopping to rehydrate or have a snack.

Keep northward. The lane seems to narrow and grow rougher as trees close in on both sides. Pace in forest for ½ mile, where small camps with small patches of mowed lawn and flagpoles holding aloft American flags reveal themselves. A bumpy lane off Mudget Mountain swings downhill at an acute angle to meet McAllister Road. Pass it and one or two more camps before reaching the junction with Creampoke Road, a town road only maintained during the summer and fall months. At the junction, a view to the southwest opens down into the Con-

necticut River Valley. The blue peaks in the distance stand in Vermont.

Walk Creampoke on the level through fields on both sides. Pass a few more camps and come to a hard dogleg turn to the right. March around that bend and reverse direction on dirt road that infrequently sees the blade of a road grader. Once out of the turn, walk 100 yards and look for a birch on the right that sports a yellow-painted angle that points 90 degrees left.

On the left is a two-tire track into the trees. There is no sign to herald the approach of one of several of the big plantations of Weir Tree Farms, a nationally recognized grower of balsam fir and Frasier fir Christmas trees and a renowned hybrid tree that combines the genes of both species.

Walk downhill on a shallow grade when a great expanse of cleared acreage opens. Within the clearings, hundreds if not thousands of small, hand-trimmed evergreen trees stand in orderly rows. Uphill on the left, two small structures stand guard over this coniferous empire. One is a snowmobile enthusiast's snack shed that's open on some winter weekends and hosts scores and scores of sled riders.

But there is something else about this productive silviculture farm carved out of an isolated ridge in so sparsely populated a rural community. The vista to the northwest, north, and east is startling in its sweep. From this vantage point, hundreds of square miles of Pittsburg, the very largest township in the eastern United States, are visible, as are summits in Maine and a few in Quebec, Canada. The view encompasses almost all of the headwaters terrain of the Connecticut River.

35.

Mt. Monadnock Trail

Location: Lemington, VT

Distance: 6 miles round-trip

Difficulty: Moderate to moderately steep over most of its length

Trailhead: 44°13'36.60'N, 71°29'48.78'W

GETTING THERE

Drive into the town of Colebrook, the principal trading center at the top of the State of New Hampshire. NH 26 and NH 3 reach the community, as does VT 102.

In the very center of Colebrook, look for Bridge Street (NH 26 west) on the west side of NH 3. Turn down Bridge Street and travel ¼ mile to the bridge over the Connecticut River and VT 102 on the far side. Turn right (north) on VT 102 and travel about ¼ mile, until a large sandpit shows itself on the left. Turn into the sandpit and stay to the left. Drive to the far end of the opening and park.

TREK TO A RESTORED FIRE TOWER

There is nothing like the power of an idea and the determination of a clutch of willing volunteers to make an idea come to life, even if it means hauling a ton of material on one's back over 2 miles to the summit of a mountain.

The small trading center that is Colebrook, New Hampshire, population 2,305, is blessed to have a kindly if big neighbor. The town is shadowed on the west by a sprawling 3,148-foot peak by the name of Monadnock—not famous Mt. Monadnock of southwestern New Hampshire fame, one of the most climbed summits in the world. No, Vermont's mountain with the identical name and nearly identical elevation is much too far removed from the 'burbs of Boston to be trampled by legions of day-hikers.

But the Vermont version has a fine trail that snakes all the way to the summit and ends at the foot of a recently restored fire

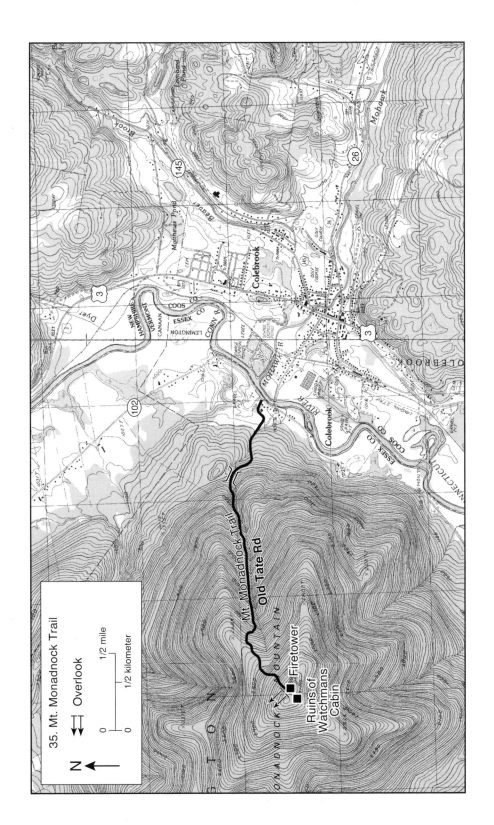

35. Mt. Monadnock Trail

tower, an 80-foot one that still supports the original watchman's cab, albeit without glass in the window frames.

From the streets of Colebrook, that tower is visible, something of a tiny quiet beacon watching over the town. But as in all structures that must withstand harsh winter environments exposed occasionally to hurricane-force winds, the wooden stair treads, landing decks, and cabin floor deteriorated to the point where the structure was dangerous to climb. That fact did not set well with some local folks at the Green Mountain Club who possessed a true love for the old fire tower. So they set about raising money and calling for volunteers to try to rescue the tower from a slow but certain death.

When the appointed day came to try to tackle the restoration, the organizers of the effort were stunned to find that 70 people had assembled in the sandpit parking area to help shoulder timbers up the mountain, one or two planks at a time. Among the motley crew were skilled carpenters, grandmothers in hiking shoes, businessmen and -women from the community, students, teachers, even a few kids not yet in their teens.

And lo, they did what they set out to do. Each made the long climb to the summit and fed hand-carried planks up the tower superstructure one after another to the skilled souls above. They sawed, drilled, bolted, and hammered, and, by God, finished the project in just a few days. When they were done, Mt. Monadnock tower was safe again, and one could climb all the way up into the cab and stand witness to an astounding 360-degree view of the northern ends of two states and the southern expanse of Quebec.

A good measure of the long trek to the summit is on the backbone of old logging lanes and an abandoned fire tower jeep road that bears little resemblance to a vehicle lane these days. But the first quarter of the jour-

ney is an overland trek through field and forest designed to get adventurers to that long-abandoned route up the mountain. The sandpit was carved out of a glacial till deposit that underlay an old farm pasture. Leave the sandpit to the west-southwest, moving toward the flank of the mountain. Cross in a zigzag through a brushy meadow marked with the odd end post and pink surveyor tape. At the woodlands margin, you'll begin to gain elevation as the track crosses over a low, indistinct ridge, cuts directly over, and follows a small stream in a draw, crosses the stream again on a recently built footbridge, and then rises abruptly onto the northeast flank of the mountain.

The route steepens and suddenly empties out onto an 8-foot-wide leaf-strewn track. Turn right, uphill, and begin a moderate to moderately steep climb. Like many fire tower roads of yore, this one rarely levels out. The incline remains quite consistent over much of the route. But unlike the unrelenting monotony of the ridge assault on Mt. Sugarloaf, 25 miles away to the southeast in Stratford Township, Mt. Monadnock's pathway is far more varied and interesting.

Also, the trail has recently undergone a full refurbishing by pro crews with the NorthWoods Stewardship Center at East Charleston, Vermont. It had eroded badly in some sections and held water in other sectors. Now the trail drains well, as new water bars and drainage ditching move water off the treadway. Some sections have been firmed up with rock and soils to improve the going.

The old jeep route is no longer recognizable as such. The way has softened to a true woods trail on the upper half of the mountain and is a pleasure to climb.

Mt. Monadnock presents a broad, flat summit. Near the top, the trail finally levels out considerably and the approach to the

Monadnock Fire Tower
NORTHWOODS STEWARDSHIP CENTER

half a dozen landings higher and higher above. On the summit, the trees reach to heights of 40 feet or so. The tower vaults twice as high into the sky. Halfway up, the view is revealed, and what a majestic one it is. Continue skyward into the steel cab that is little more than a big metal box without any refinements. It doesn't need any. The vista is refinement enough.

Below and to the east, all roads lead to Colebrook Village, the street layout easily traced from this altitude. Twelve miles beyond is a blue ridge with a distinct gap in its center. That's Dixville Notch. Ridgelines run north and south, increasing in elevation to the south. Big but virtually unknown peaks pop up, with such names as Lightning, Teapot, Savage, and Goback in the Stratford Range; and Gore, Notch, and, tallest of all, Bunnell at 3,724 feet, in the Northwest Peaks Range.

To the north, Quebec is only a few miles distant. Boundary peaks between Canada and the United States rise to form the divide between the watersheds of the St. Lawrence and Connecticut Rivers. To the west, the long spine of the Green Mountains undulates unbroken all the way from tall Jay Peak in the north to the vanishing point in the south. At the foot of the mountain shimmers Island Pond, at the head of big bog and timber county in the Nulhegan River watershed. Those who know what to look for can locate Mt. Mansfield, Vermont's tallest summit. The uppermost dimension of Mt. Washington in the Presidential Range can be observed on clear days, too.

With its perch so high above the Connecticut River, the view south down the river valley is like no other in the state, save, perhaps, the one from the topknot of Mt. Ascutney, near Windsor, more than two hours' drive to the south. The ribbon of water has been running in this domain for more than

tower through substantial spruce and fir stands is easy and very pleasant. The metal superstructure rears up out of the spruce and fir and commands attention because of its substantial height. But the tower is only the most visible improvement on the summit, for the cut-stone foundations of several former summit buildings can be traced amid the trunks of trees.

At the base of the tower, watch for shards of broken glass. If you are hiking with a pet, be sure to monitor its movements so that it does not cut its feet.

The handiwork of the volunteers is visible at the first step. New treads lead the way to

Mt. Monadnock over Colebrook

200 million years, and with the help of repeated influxes of glacier ice, it has carved one most beautiful valley.

Northern New Hampshire and Vermont are well known for being inundated with cloud cover for more days per year than any point in the continental United States outside of Seattle, Washington. If it is not a picture-postcard day in the region, don't necessarily turn down Mt. Monadnock as a destination. For more than one hundred days a year, its summit is a cloud forest. Don't be afraid to climb the peak when it is shrouded in overcast. There is no way to lose the trail in the woods, so there is no danger of getting lost.

When the summit is socked-in with clouds, the experience can be otherworldly. If there is little wind, most noises are thoroughly suppressed. It can be stone quiet except for the occasional peep of a bird. All trees appear as monotone ghosts. The tower superstructure disappears above in the mist. Although it may not be raining, moisture saturates everything, coating the face with a cool slick.

Climb the tower in cloud and leave the world behind. The trek can be disorienting. Once the trees are topped and disappear in the fog, there is no way to get your bearings. If the wind is up and moaning in the steel struts, the sound of it adds an element of eeriness to the environment. The physical world as we know it seems to have exited the stage. Nothing is visible, except the immediate steelwork and deck. Some may not find the experience pleasant, but some will thrill at the rare break from physical reality.

The only way down is to return along the path you ascended. Return to your vehicle and motor into the town of Colebrook, just a minute away. Gas up and get a snack for the drive home, or get a meal at Howard's Restaurant on the corner of Main and NH 145, or at the Wilderness dead center in the middle of town.

When you've paid your tab and hit the street, Mt. Monadnock will be over your shoulder.

36.

Hurlbert Swamp Trail

Location: Stewartstown, NH

Distance: 2 miles round-trip

Difficulty: Easy

Trailhead: 44°59'28.41'N, 71°27'2.31'W

GETTING THERE

Travel NH 3 north of Colebrook and north of the village of West Stewartstown. Roll into the tiny community of Clarksville, fronted by a general store and gas pumps. Just south of the store, West Road turns east and uphill toward high-elevation terrain. Turn onto West Road and motor less than 2 miles, until an artificial pond appears on the right with a dirt lane skirting it. At the junction is a Nature Conservancy (TNC) sign, emblazoned with a green oak leaf. Turn right onto this access lane and travel a long mile, watching for small TNC signs at a few back road intersections. Reach a Y-junction with a pronounced dog-leg turn to the left. Stay left on the level and soon you'll approach a grassy pullout on the left, before a large sign that designates the location of the 313 acres that encompass Hurlbert Swamp.

AN EXCEPTIONAL EASTERN WHITE CEDAR RESERVE

The small, sparsely populated communities of Stewartstown and Clarksville, near the very top of the Granite State, harbor an exceptionally cold boreal swamp, recognized by the National Park Service as a national natural landmark. Home to fine tall stands of eastern white cedar, tamarack and black spruce, rare plant communities, and regionally uncommon birds such as the black-backed three-toed woodpecker, yellow-bellied flycatcher, and Tennessee warbler, Hurlbert Swamp is itself a rarity. Because the underlying glacial soils provide good anchorage for tree roots, the swamp is laced with healthy

---

Hurlbert Swamp Trail

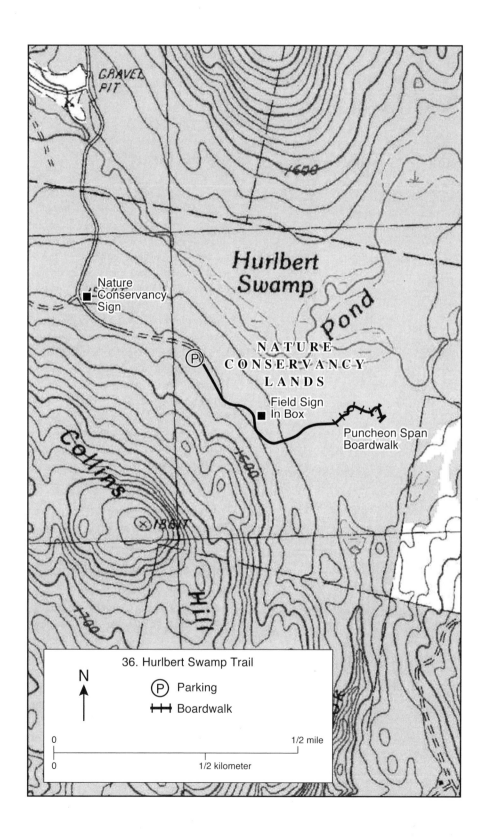

GRAVEL PIT

Hurlbert Swamp

Pond

Nature Conservancy Sign

Ⓟ

NATURE CONSERVANCY LANDS

Field Sign In Box

Puncheon Span Boardwalk

Collins

⊗ 1887

Hill

36. Hurlbert Swamp Trail

N

Ⓟ Parking

Boardwalk

0   1/2 mile

0   1/2 kilometer

Hurlbert Swamp cedar stand

60-foot tree specimens that grow handsomely straight despite the wet surroundings and resist tipping over, as often do their relatives in wetlands with heavy mulch and peat footings.

Into this unusual realm you will tread first on well-maintained, mowed trail; forest path; and on 800 feet of puncheon plank walkway. Leave your vehicle, dodge under a rope festooned with red caution tape, and enter a level 6-foot-wide path, perhaps once a farm lane surrounded by tightly growing spruce and fir. Move easterly on very good footing. The pathway soon swings lazily to the right and drifts uphill into a clearing that is kept tidy with the blades of a brushhog. At the top of the little opening is a sign-in station.

Beyond the sign-in kiosk, the trail runs through a narrow field filled with weeds. The path gets a little less attention here but is still easy to maneuver through. Slowly, the field narrows to the point where the path becomes a woods trek. No sooner do the trees close in than the trail jogs suddenly to the left and toward the northeast.

Make the turn. Ahead, at least for now, a goodly pile of cedar log rounds some 4 feet long stands on the left at the point where the first planks of a long bog bridge, or puncheon span, come into view. A few feet beyond the log pile, standing water becomes evident, and Hurlbert Swamp is at hand.

The trail now gets interesting, indeed. The architects of the plank bridge ahead must have had a joyous time laying out the long structure that runs deep into the swamp. Rather than exhibit the discipline and efficiency that urban planners might bring to the task, those that built this span let their creation wander and snake through the terrain.

Hurlbert Swamp Sign

Walking the dual-plank footway is a delight, like exploring a maze.

There is a purpose to this playfulness, of course. The bog bridge sections work with the terrain, looping and turning sharply as necessary to take advantage of the lay of the swamp. More toward the edges of the wetland, black and red spruce predominate. But the farther into the swamp you trek, the more the tamarack and then the cedar hold sway.

Hummocks appear, bumps of land a few feet higher than the surroundings. On these rises, cedars gather in clusters. The plank walk runs through a number of these congregations. Some of the cedars have substantial dimensions given their location and longevity. While their cousins all over New England were harvested extensively for telephone poles, fence posts, shingles, and more, these trees were never harvested. A good number of them are thought to be older than the first white settlements in the North Country. Some are 2 feet in diameter and over 60 feet tall.

When the bog bridge comes to an end at a double-back some 800 feet into the heart of the swamp, most of the denizens on all sides are the cedars. It is not often that hikers find their way into mature stands of such trees. Forest trails inevitably bypass swamps. Here the puncheon spans provide dry footing and an avenue into the enclave of the boreal giants. They and their kin have been residing here for at least 10,000 years. The waters of the first primordial swamp in the area could not drain away because of a glacial debris dam left behind when the continental ice sheet began wasting away 12,000 years ago. The natural impoundment proved to be a durable one, for Hurlbert Swamp is still with us and will likely remain for millennia to come. And because of property is protected now, perhaps these fine cedars will remain for millennia, as well.

The Hurlbert Swamp ends too soon. Retrace your steps and return to your vehicle. But on the plank walk, take your time about it. Watch for swamp orchids and the ruby-crowned kinglet. If you've been quiet, you might be lucky enough to encounter the largest mammal of the east, the moose.

On the return to Colebrook and points south, east, or west, turn right once you reach West Road again. Turn uphill and travel 1½ miles to NH 145 on high ground, at the Clarksville-Stewartstown boundary line. Head south (right) down NH 145. It is one of New England's more pleasant byways, with splendid views of farmland and blue peaks at many a turn. Even a 70-foot waterfall, Beaver Brook Falls, tumbles near the roadside once you cross the Colebrook town line. Don't pass this up.

37.

Lake Francis Trail

Location: Pittsburg, NH

Distance: 6.4 miles round-trip

Difficulty: Easy wood walk within close proximity to the eastern shores of 1,800-acre Lake Francis

Trailhead: 45°04'22.81'N, 71°18'09.22'W

GETTING THERE

Five miles north of Pittsburg Village on NH 3, motor into the tiny hamlet of Happy Corner. Well-known Young's Store rises on the right. Pass through the hamlet and travel about 1 mile farther north. Watch on the right for a good dirt lane, River Road, which strikes south downhill away from the highway. A sign for Lake Francis Campground heralds the turn.

Descend into valley where Perry Stream and the Connecticut River converge. After a long mile south, a small covered bridge just to the side of River Road comes into view ahead and the right. Before the bridge, on the left, Carr Road cuts 90 degrees left. Turn left onto Carr Road and travel a short distance to the point where a stringer bridge built for logging trucks spans the Connecticut River. Rather than cross the bridge by car, turn left or right into an informal pullout and park.

THE LAKE THAT DROWNED A TOWN

The artery of the community of Pittsburg, largest township in acreage in the eastern United States, is the Connecticut River. By the time the waters from dozens of brooks and streams collects in town and makes a run for Long Island Sound, the river is already a force to be reckoned with. The flowage of the big drink fills five of some of the largest lakes in northern New Hampshire, dozens of small ponds, and countless acres of bog. Thrown across many a body of water is a dam, large or small, many originally built by loggers to regulate water flow for the spring

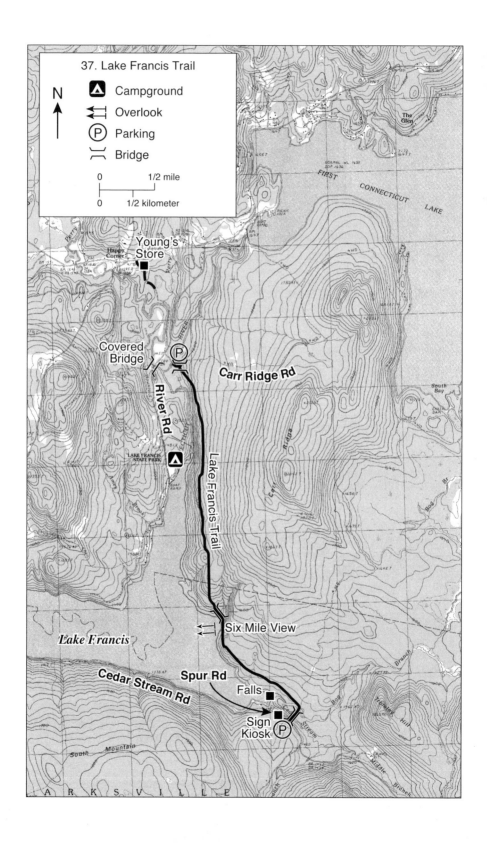

37. Lake Francis Trail

N

⬛ Campground
⬅⬅ Overlook
Ⓟ Parking
⟏⟍ Bridge

0 — 1/2 mile
0 — 1/2 kilometer

FIRST CONNECTICUT LAKE

The Glen

Young's Store

Covered Bridge

Carr Ridge Rd

South Bay

River Rd

LAKE FRANCIS STATE PARK ⬛

Lake Francis Trail

Carr Ridge

Lake Francis

Six Mile View ⬅⬅

Cedar Stream Rd

Spur Rd

Falls ⬛

Sign Kiosk ⬛ Ⓟ

C L A R K S V I L L E

Wild River

over boulders and ledges as the elevation recedes. The rumble of the river constantly fills the air for the nearly 10 minutes of the trek, but there is little opportunity to actually see the waters below, as the growth is too dense on the slopes above.

Watch for yellow blazes as the wide trail runs southbound. As the woods brighten, the path intersects a wider weedy lane below a woods-road intersection clearing and gradually begins to fall in elevation. The Lake Francis Trail, a snowmobile trail in winter, descends immediately into the woods and presses ever southward.

Walk easily downhill in cool mixed forest. On occasion, you might hear the sounds of people talking or playing at Lake Francis Campground, unseen through the woods and on the far side of the invisible Connecticut River. Loon calls trumpet through the trees, and the occasional putt-putt of a small-engine fishing craft can be heard. Canopy closes overhead once again.

Continue descending every so gradually until the terrain seems to level out and undulate gently. The old trail, once a logging road, is soft on the feet and on the eye. The way has mellowed with age into a fine foot thoroughfare. Wood sorrel and fern often carpet the waysides. Much of the shoreline forests here are protected by easements, so the trail should continue to serve trekkers well, and riders on snow, too, for that matter.

Much of the way south over the first mile, the path stays more than ¼ mile away from the eastern shore of Lake Francis. After that mile, the route begins to creep closer to the water as the shoreline of the lake begins to bend steadily to the east. Cross a seep, and cut alongside of the shoulder of low hill that pinches the pathway and finally forces it right out to the very edge of the shoreline. At trail's closest approach to the lake, the forest is a single tree or two wide.

log drives. The biggest of the water-control impoundments, a great earthen Civil Conservation Corps works called Murphy Dam, holds back 1,800-acre Lake Francis, named for a former governor. Along the entire eastern flank of the lake runs a trail that lets trampers become intimate with one of the great lakes of the North Country.

Start your journey to Lake Francis on the western bank of the Connecticut River. You've parked your car close to a wild stretch of river. Walk onto the Carr Road bridge and have a look up and downstream at the young river that is bound to grow ever larger in volume, until it becomes the king of New England's rivers before emptying into Long Island Sound in Connecticut.

Just across the bridge to the east, a wide trail slips right and begins to arc toward the south, closely paralleling a logging road that runs just a head in elevation above the trail. The path rises slightly at first, while the river below drops in elevation, quickly drifts away for a while, and then swings back close by. Once the Connecticut River reenters the realm, it does so loudly, as the waters tumble

Duck through an opening in the tree line and walk out onto Lake Francis's beautiful long shoreline that comprises sand, boulders large and small, rock outcroppings, and bleached and debarked driftwood. At this point, the view direct to the west is 6 miles in length, truncated by a thin ribbon of black in the distance: Murphy Dam. The vista is expansive and oh so bright after your eyes have been accustomed to twilight on the forest floor.

Lake Francis

Now is the time for a change in itinerary. Rather than continue south on the trail just now, explore what the shoreline ribbon of Lake Francis has to offer, provided the water level in the lake is not so high that the shoreline is inundated. Most seasons, there is ample room to wander.

Strike south and trace the shoreline as it arcs slowly toward the east. Much of the early going is akin to walking an ocean beach. Sometimes you might find whimsical rock cairns piled up by earlier visitors. Sometimes someone builds an illegal fire of driftwood. If trash has washed onto the shore, pick it up, stow it away, and carry it out.

Half a mile down the beach, the lakeshore swings hard to the east. The way gets increasingly boulder strewn and the boulders grow larger and larger. Picking a route gets a bit more difficult but worth the effort. The lake waters narrow to an eastern inlet. A camp appears to across the channel to the south, and the sound of falling water greets the ears.

At the very narrowest point where the lake waters terminate, a low waterfall plunges into the lake. Cedar Stream and Bog Branch join forces just upstream out of sight to form a fat brook. It has to cross a shelf of rock before dropping into the lake. No spectacle by any means, but the falls adds a pleasant touch to an otherwise quiet backwater inlet. The resident loon, patrolling

with its red eye fixed on any visitor, rounds out the scene.

Tread northward back to the entrance to the shoreline, gain the trail again, and drift southward. Drop down an incline, cross a snowmobile bridge that is in poor repair but should be refurbished before the next snows come, and enter terrain that is perfectly level. The trail is wide here with grassy shoulders that push off the forest margins. Round a bend and walk eastbound on a fairly straight course for over ¼ mile, when the trail abruptly swings to the right and south and comes to a bridge high above a small stream. Below is Bog Branch. Cross the bridge to reach an "island" between two streams. A camp shows itself on the right. Pass it and, in another minute, cross a second bridge, this one over Cedar Stream. Pass a gate and go to a sign kiosk placed in a clearing that is used by snowmobilers in winter.

The Lake Francis Trail ends here, on Bog Branch spur just off Cedar Stream Road. Anyone with a good map or a Google Earth download can find this location, and if you've planned ahead, you could spot a second car here and call it a day. Otherwise, a return trip the way you came is now the order of the day. Retracing your steps is almost as easy as the trek down. Although it's all uphill from here, the elevation gain is little more than 100 feet in 3 miles.

38.

Mt. Prospect Trail

Location: Pittsburg, NH

Distance: About 1.6 miles round-trip

Difficulty: Moderate climb

Trailhead: 45°06'11.39'N, 71°18'14.05'W

GETTING THERE

Roll northward on NH 3 to the town of Pittsburg, at the top of the Granite State. Travel through the community and continue north for 5 miles to the tiny hamlet of Happy Corner, with its must-stop general emporium, Young's Store.

Just before entering the small cluster of buildings at Happy Corner, look for Danforth Road on the left. Turn left uphill and travel north for about a mile, disregarding several spur roads uphill and to the left, until the dirt road appears as if it might end in the yard of a home. Just before the yard, look for a steep drive to the left. Turn uphill and climb a very steep, short pitch. Once over the hump, the lane climbs gradually. Travel about ¼ mile from the turnoff, Danforth Road, staying right at a Y-junction, and climb a hill to a private home perched on the crest of the hill. Turn left into a parking spot and stop.

BIG LAKE COUNTRY

Pittsburg, the northernmost community in the Granite State, is one of the very largest townships in the continental United States. At nearly 300,000 acres, it is big enough to encompass five large lakes and dozens of ponds, marshes, and bogs, all of which conspire to give rise to the Connecticut River.

This has always been big timber country. To this day, commercial logging is an economic staple here. In winter, the community is the snowmobile capital of the eastern United States. The motorized sled trail system is extensive and links with Maine, Canada, and Vermont.

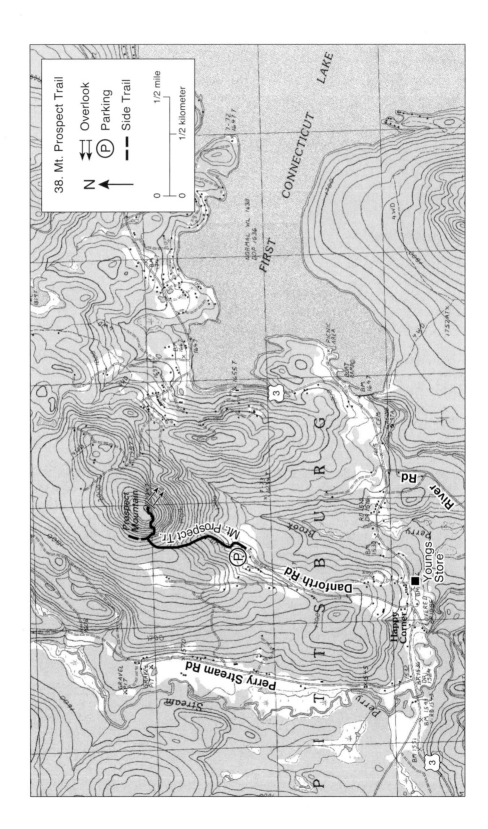

38. Mt. Prospect Trail

↙↘ Overlook
Ⓟ Parking
– – – Side Trail

N ←

0   1/2 mile
0   1/2 kilometer

Prospect Mountain

Mt. Prospect Tr.

Danforth Rd

Perry Stream Rd

PITTSBURG

Brook

River Rd

Perry

Happy Corner

Youngs Store

FIRST CONNECTICUT LAKE

PICNIC AREA

A stunning view from high above 2,800-acre First Connecticut Lake   ELLEN KOLB

This heavily forested environment was never a hiker's destination, but that is beginning to change. The state of New Hampshire holds easements on more than 150,000 acres of private timberlands, and for the first time, hiking is a permitted use across those many hectares.

And although the community does not boast peaks as tall as those in the White Mountain National Forest, more than an hour's drive to the south, some elevations boast dramatic views. One such hillock is little Prospect Mountain, a mile north of NH 3 and 2,800-acre First Connecticut Lake.

From the parking lot at the Castines' residence on the south flank of the mountain, turn away from the view across the Connecticut River Valley and pick up an ATV track that rises away from the home and enters the trees. In a minute, break out of the trees in a narrow clearing that was cut to create an access road to the top of the moun-

tain. The access road was never fully developed and has grown in to grasses and weeds. Turn right uphill and begin a gradual climb up the southwest flank of the peak.

The way is perfectly discernable and is marked on occasion with a yellow blaze. Sometimes white-tailed deer come into the cut to feed, and you may see one or more bound away, white flags waving.

The route becomes more steeply pitched in its midsection and it bends in a lazy S-curve as it climbs. But the going is good and never strenuous. Restricted views open on occasion through woodlands that are fairly young because the logging cycle.

Only 20 minutes into the climb, the path begins to level out near the summit. Watch on your left for a small collection of rocks that form a set of steps. Climb the steps, punch through an opening in a thin band of trees, and walk out onto a manicured summit that has been cleared of trees and outfitted with a gravel lot. On a granite rib in the clearing, a local family has set up a picnic table and some animal knickknacks.

The improvements leave a bit to be desired, but not the view. Mt. Prospect presents a showstopping vista, given the modest effort necessary to obtain it. Your eye will take in about a 160-degree panorama from the north-northeast to the south-southwest. No trees obstruct your view whatsoever.

The main attraction is placid, black, and cold First Connecticut Lake, all 2,800 acres of it. The vast body of water sprawls to the east, filling what seems like half the visible landscape. Above the lake, farther to the east, stands the region's mountain king, 3,360-foot Mt. Magalloway. Magalloway turns a classic Appalachian mountain profile here, and it stands out prominently against the horizontal lay of the lake.

This appears to be, by far, the tallest mountain in the realm. It isn't. The proximity to the big lake lends Magalloway a nobler presence than the summits around it. Just a bit to the northeast, above a rambling 3,000-foot upland called Diamond Ridge, stands Stub Hill, another 100 feet taller than Magalloway. Unfortunately for Stub, it carries a less than prestigious moniker, and its less-than-distinguished profile effectively hides its height.

That is not the case with Rump Mountain, farther still to the northeast. Only the west shoulder of Rump resides in New Hampshire; the summit ridge and true summit inhabit Maine. Unlike Stub Hill, Rump's profile is all business, and the peak commands attention.

On the northern horizon, the boundary mountains, with such names as Kent, D'Urban, and Salmon, rear up on the New Hampshire side of the Maine border. Salmon is actually 4 feet taller than Magalloway, but it looks like a long blue ridge without a true summit, from the viewpoint of Mt. Prospect.

Beyond, the upper real estate of Maine's Bosebuck Mountain, Mt. Aziscoos, and others are visible, as are fractions of boundary peaks in Quebec—Saddle and Marble.

Southward, 3,100-foot Mt. Pisgah rises above a jumble of lesser ridges and hills. On the southwestern margins, the land rises again to form the graceful profile of Vermont's Mt. Monadnock.

From your perch, you can survey what was once a sovereign nation known as the Republic of Indian Stream. The lands surrounding the headwaters of the Connecticut River were claimed by both Canada and the United States. What few settlers there were in the region became frustrated with taxation entanglements and land claim disputes to the point that, in 1832, they moved to form their own republic. They drafted a constitution, voted to adopt it, and for four years thumbed their noses at those who presumed to rule them.

One has to tip a hat to those flinty forebears for their brazen stand against greater forces. Can you imagine some ragtag group of stalwart malcontents doing the same thing today?

Given that there is a picnic table on the summit, there is little reason not to take a seat and have a little snack while drinking in one of the grandest of views in northernmost New Hampshire. In the fall, always on the last days of September, it is peak foliage season this far north. Come to Mt. Prospect on a bright Canadian high-pressure day and the forests are a sea of fire red bedecked with fringe of birch leaf yellow and green-black spruce and fir.

The way down from the little nubble is the same as the ascent. Because the trek takes so little time, plenty of hours remain to visit some of the other geological wonders that New Hampshire's largest township has hidden in its recesses.

39.

Mt. Covell Trail

Location: Pittsburg, NH

Distance: Nearly 3 miles to the summit, 4.4 miles to Round Pond Road terminus

Difficulty: Easy to moderate, but moderately steep in a few short stretches

Trailhead, west: 45°06'31.10'N, 71°17'11.09'W

Trailhead, east: 45°08'02.19'N, 71°16'11.07'E

GETTING THERE

Travel north on NH 3 or NH 145 to Pittsburg Village, at the top of the Granite State. Continue north through the village and motor 5 miles to a tiny hamlet called Happy Corner. Run through the hamlet on the highway and continue north. Pass First Connecticut Lake dam and the public picnic area. Cross over a height of land and descend to a tongue of lake water known as West Bay, on First Connecticut Lake. A wide view to the east opens across the huge lake to Mt. Magalloway. Round a broad bend to the right and watch on your left for Ramblewood Road. Turn left uphill on Ramblewood Road and drive 1 mile into a campground facility called Ramblewood Cabins and Campground. Bend left uphill into campground and reach a parking area near the main building of the facility. Park there.

Walk uphill, staying left on a campground lane. The lane bends to the right, but continue straight ahead to the north. The way levels out with an open area on the left and the tree line close on the right. Look for a wood trail that leaves right off the lane. It is marked with yellow blazes.

VARIED OVERLAND ROUTE REACHES A DRAMATIC SUMMIT VIEW

The creation of wholly new footpaths is something rare nowadays. The Mt. Covell Trail is an exception. Not a rail trail, not a restored old route nor an old logging tote road, this pathway is almost entirely new, top to bottom, in country where logging has been king for more than a century.

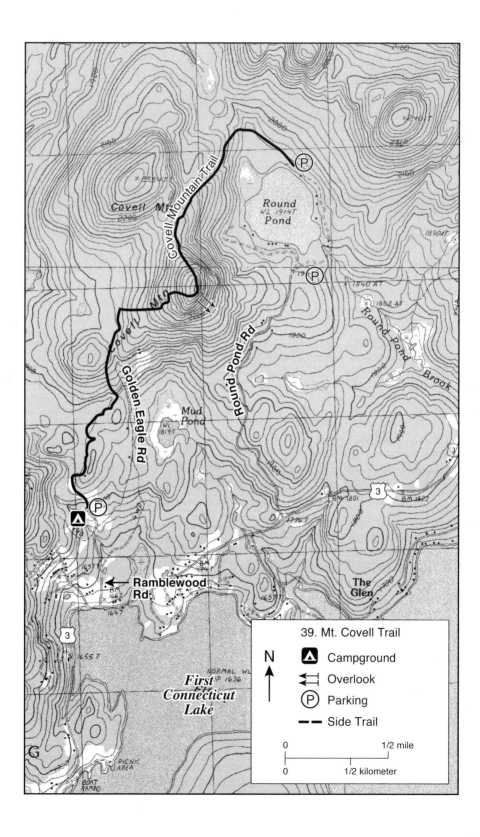

Covell Mt.

Covell Mountain Trail

Round
Pond
WL 1914 T

Golden Eagle Rd

Round Pond Rd

Round Pond Brook

Mud
Pond
WL
1819 T

BM 1801

BM 1822

3

1776 T

The
Glen

Ramblewood
Rd

3

First
Connecticut
Lake

NORMAL WL
1636

G

PICNIC
AREA

BOAT
RAMP

39. Mt. Covell Trail

N

⬆️

▲ Campground

⇄ Overlook

Ⓟ Parking

— — Side Trail

| 0 | | 1/2 mile |
| 0 | | 1/2 kilometer |

Mt. Covell view clearing

The Mt. Covell Trail is behind the northern edge of Ramblewood Cabins and Campground, a well-laid-out facility located on a low ridge 1 mile from the north shores of 2,800-acre First Connecticut Lake. From the parking area by the main buildings, stride uphill, keeping left on the west leg of a campground loop lane. Head north. The lane splits. Move straight ahead instead of taking the loop. Walk on a dirt-base track into a narrow clearing, the tree line close on the right. Watch on the right for a woods trail far narrower than the lane out of the parking area.

Leave the clearing, watching for yellow blazes, and move under the cool forest canopy, ambling in level terrain toward the east. A few minutes along, you'll reach a junction with another path that enters at an oblique angle on the left. Swing 130 degrees left and move toward the northwest, again on level ground. This path follows a very old logging skidder lane that no longer bears any resemblance to its original purpose. It passes a camp, barely visible on the right through the growth, and strikes left into pleasant young and mixed forest.

Several minutes beyond the camp, the trail jogs right off the indistinct logging lane and climbs a shallow grade through undisturbed terrain. The path undulates easily up and down, drops into a small moist saddle filled with grasses, then begins to climb uphill in earnest in spruce and hardwood. As the grade increases, a logging cut opens on the left, allowing light to flood in. The going becomes increasingly steep. Climb less than 200 vertical feet. Again the trail levels and soon runs dead straight, following the long western leg of a private property line, the logging cut still on the left.

After running 500 linear feet laser straight, the path bends abruptly 90 degrees toward the east, finally heading directly at the summit for which the trail is named. But the base of Mt. Covell is still a long mile away, the low summit visible through the trees once or twice.

Now the new trail follows a roughly straight course, level at times, rising here and there, but gaining very little elevation as it crosses a broad basinlike plateau. There are few distinctive features or well-organized water courses to cross in the area to mark your progress. But things change abruptly at the foot of the mountain.

Mt. Covell is a low, C-shaped upland formation with three principal summits that form a western and northern wall around one side of well-named Round Pond. The trail takes aim at the highest middle summit, and the terrain becomes steeper at once and stays that way all the way to the rather broad and flat summit.

Climb out of the plateau region in moderately steep terrain, most of it coated with maturing hardwood trees. The peak is only 2,300 feet high and the elevation gain from its base is no more than 500 vertical feet, so gaining the summit takes little time but some effort. On the way up, cross the mellowed remains of old skidder tracks from logging that took place 30 and 40 years ago.

Approached from the west, it's impossible to get a good sense of scale of the mountain, let along why it could be an attractive peak to bag. When viewed from Round Pond on the far eastern side, it becomes apparent why Mt. Covell works as a destination. The little peak looms over the pond and seems to stand alone among its two neighbors.

But it's the view from this heretofore unknown summit that gives this big bump in the landscape its stellar rating. Like Mt. Prospect, its near twin some 3 miles to the west, Mt. Covell surveys a good deal of northernmost New Hampshire, a good chunk of northwesternmost Maine, and mountainous boundary terrain in Quebec. At the eastern foot of the mountain sprawls 2,800-acre First Connecticut Lake, the biggest of five great lakes that inhabit the township of Pittsburg.

To gain more than just limited and intermittent views from the top of the peak, the timberland holder agreed to allow some half-dozen gnarly, weather-abused hardwood trees to be taken down, plus some small growth. They had little commercial value, so the company permitted the view to be opened.

Today, hikers to the summit enjoy a stellar vista from the northeast to the southeast over the lake. Directly east stands the classic eastern mountain form of Mt. Magalloway, its fire tower perfectly visible at the very top. On the summit are a log bench and a small stone outcropping to sit on, for those who wish to rest a moment and refresh.

It's been nearly 3 miles of trekking to attain the summit. You may wish to return now. If you want to put in a full day, continue north and then eastward down off the summit to Round Pond.

Cross the broad summit of Mt. Covell and follow its northeastern ridgeline off the heights, descending very gradually onto the lower, gently sloping flank of the mountain's lesser northern summit. Drop continuously in elevation, making a broad arc that swings slowly eastward through forests one minute, through narrow and grassy logging clearings the next.

Within the arc, the trail is a new woods path that is well cut, blazed with yellow paint, and easy to follow. It eventually intersects a logging skidway and follows it, always curving toward the unseen pond. Cross a wet spot on new bog bridges and shortly reach a sunny clearing and a cul-de-sac. This turnaround may be utilized as an eastern parking spot, should you choose to approach Mt. Covell from its shorter eastern route.

This is the end of the hike, but there is one last feature to take in, if you wish. Stride downhill across the circle and walk the road to the first camp. Staying close to the tree line on the right, walk down to Round Pond and take in the view. This pleasant body of water is graced with the fine profile of the little peak you recently climbed. It's a very pleasant scene, not spectacular, no doubt, but pleasing.

Now make your the return trip back over Mt. Covell and down to Ramblewood Cabins and Campground.

40.

Mt. Magalloway

Location: Pittsburg, NH

Distance: 3.5 miles round-trip, including a short walk to the cliff ledges

Difficulty: The Coot Trail is steep and eroded; the Bobcat Trail is moderate to moderately steep in places.

Trailhead: 45°04'09.7'N, 71°10'19.41'W

GETTING THERE

Travel north on NH 3 to the top of the Granite State. Pass through Pittsburg Village, and 5 miles farther north, the tiny hamlet of Happy Corner. Continue northward past First Connecticut Lake Dam and West Bay on First Connecticut Lake. Soon you'll cross the boundary of the Connecticut Lakes State Forest. In a mile, watch for a sign indicating Magalloway Road.

Turn right off the highway onto a wide, gravel-based logging road. After a mile, cross a plank bridge over the Connecticut River and continue straight ahead (east). Watch for small signs that say, TOWER. Travel 3 miles beyond the bridge on the Magalloway Road and watch for a major junction to the right. Turn right and begin a winding drive that climbs gradually and loops toward Mt. Magalloway. The lane ends abruptly at a large parking area at the base of the peak.

THE MOUNTAIN KING

A storied mountain, which goes by a Native American name, lords over northernmost New Hampshire. Rising gracefully in a classic form over the southern shores of 2,800-acre First Connecticut Lake, Mt. Magalloway can be seen far and wide. At 3,383 feet (most recent data), it is not quite the tallest peak in the region, but because of its lofty throne above miles of cold black waters, Magalloway seems like the Everest of the realm.

A trek of Magalloway is a loop hike that begins and ends at the parking lot. For this hike, I recommend climbing out of the parking area on the steep and unrelenting Coot

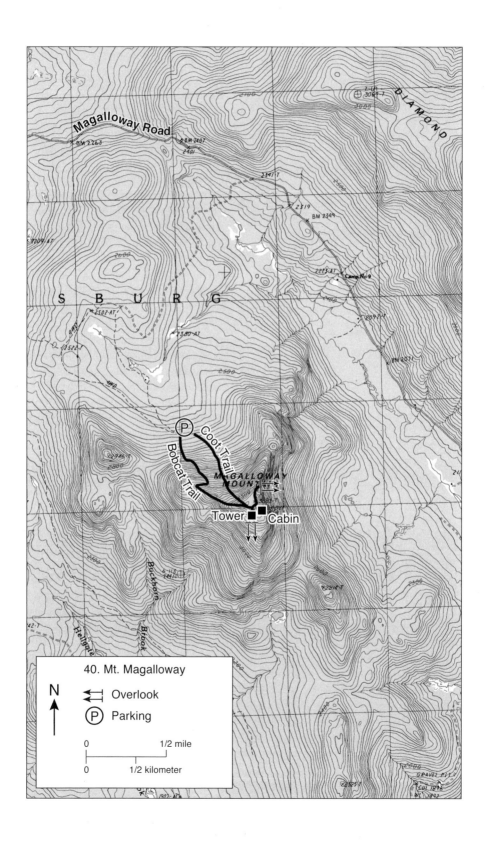

Magalloway Road

DIAMOND

BM 2263
BM 2407
2401

2341-T

2319
BM 2344

2209-AT

2600

2223-AT
Camp No 9

S   B   U   R   G

2502-AT

2093-T

2380-AT

2522-T

BM 2071

4WD

2500

2346-T

P

Coot Trail

Bobcat Trail

MAGALLOWAY
MOUNT

Tower ■ ■ Cabin

Buckhorn

2113-T
2414-T

2814-T

2300

Hellgate

Brook

42-T

1903-AT

2825-T

GRAVEL PIT

40. Mt. Magalloway

N

Overlook

P Parking

0   1/2 mile

0   1/2 kilometer

Trail and descending on the longer, more gradual, and much more pleasing Bobcat Trail. It's best to get the hard work out of the way early on, because there is much to enjoy upon cresting the broad summit.

Mt. Magalloway has long been home to a working fire tower. Even today, the tall, steel tower with its classic cab is manned during periods of high fire danger. Today, there are very few manned towers in all of New England, but of those few, three are in Coos, New Hampshire's vast northern county. Magalloway's is, by far, the northernmost of the trio, and it resides on top of the tallest summit of the three, as well.

At the base of the mountain, in the parking lot, approach the Coot Trail to the left, a few dozen paces to the south of the Bobcat Trail. Immediately, the path pitches uphill at a fairly steep incline. The route is not a woods path. It was originally built as a pack road to haul materials to the summit and to accommodate four-wheel drive vehicles that could ferry the tower warden up the peak. For many decades now, the lane has been eroding, despite some real effort occasionally to heel in heavy timber water bars or old cleat treads to divert water off the trail.

Nothing has worked, and it looks it. The Coot Trail exhibits a heavily eroded surface. The incline never moderates until near the summit, so water can collect and run with impunity, sweeping soils away and continuously roughing up the surface. The only positive thing about the Coot Trail is that it can be climbed in under an hour.

After giving you a 45-minute workout, the pitch of the old lane moderates and then nearly flattens. Soon, high above, the cab of the tower looms out of the spruce and fir, followed by the spidery steel superstructure that stretches far above the tops of the boreal forest canopy. The tower stands in a lawnlike opening of an acre or so. To the left,

as you approach the tower, a small, rustic cabin nestles among spruce. For years, this structure was home to the warden who manned the tower. Today, it can be rented overnight from the State of New Hampshire, which apparently does a brisk business for this accommodation during the high summer months.

Magalloway fire tower is a magnet. Who can resist climbing the half-dozen stairways to the many platform landings one above the other? Often the cab is closed, locked. But no matter. The views in every direction from above the forest are stunning, of three states and the Canadian province of Quebec. There may be detractors, but to me, the vista atop Magalloway is as breathtaking as any that can be had in New England. It takes a long, long drive to get into this domain, but the view makes the trip ever so worth the effort.

Of particular interest is your being able to see from the tower the boundary country between Canada and the United States. To the north, a big lake shaped like the flower of a bleeding heart ornamental plant pools in the landscape. Directly behind stands a long, rambling ridge, Mt. Salmon, which carries the border on its back. And beyond that is massive formation on the horizon—a ring dike, geologically speaking—called Mont-Mégantic, which rears up in Quebec. With binoculars, you will be able to see a pair of astronomical observatories atop that massif. Once of them houses Canada's largest telescope.

Come down off the tower and have a seat on the "lawn." Open your pack, take out a snack, and prepare for a show. The resident performers in these parts are big Canada jays, striking gray birds that know no fear of humanity. They are food hounds, because people have been trying to entice them to eat from outstretched hands for decades. They will always oblige. But if you can't resist the urge to feed a jay from your fingertips, please

Magalloway Tower PAPA BEAR

come prepared with unsalted, unsweetened sunflower seeds or something of that nature. Wildlife doesn't need a diet of junk food, not that we do, either.

Leave the company of the birds and walk behind the cabin. Pick up a trail that gradually drifts downward to the east perhaps 800 feet. The path soon approaches thin air, as much of Magalloway's eastern flank is cliff face, a long one. Slip along the edge of the precipice until the path swings right and abruptly terminates at an opening in the brush. Ahead is a vertical drop of several hundred feet that ends in a chaotic wonderland of talus rock, the largest such deposit of fractured boulders north of Franconia Notch's famous Cannon Mountain. Since the glaciers receded from the region millennia ago, Magalloway's flank has been shedding

rocks large and small. The calving of stone goes on to this day, as the freeze-thaw cycle deftly chisels away at the peak one chunk at time.

Climb back to the cabin and tower and turn to descend. Now, however, cut to the left at a signpost tree and pick up a true woods footpath, the Bobcat Trail. An old trail, it has grown in and been cleared several times over the years. Today it receives occasional maintenance, enough to keep the way open. The last time I was down the Bobcat Trail was six or seven years ago, and it was in fine condition, with nary a blowdown to block the path.

Unlike the Coot Trail that leaps almost straight up the mountain, the Bobcat Trail meanders down a northeastern ridgeline, descending gradually at first and then a bit more steeply. But the going is never truly steep or difficult. About halfway down, in a location where the trail bends in a fairly tight loop away from and then back to its allotted course, you'll come to an area of a blowdown swath on the left that afforded a restricted view for some years over immense First Connecticut Lake. Gradually, the route bends to the right, falls moderately, and suddenly reaches the parking lot. Your vehicle should be within a few dozen feet.

As long as I can remember, Mt. Magalloway was listed as 3,360 feet in elevation. But recent GPS satellite data is beginning to rewrite the books on the heights of many a peak in the Northeast. Magalloway is one of them. I have the number 3,360 burned into my Swiss-cheese brain, and I can't seem to warm up to the new 3,383 figure.

Many people I've known find a way to return to Magalloway. The mountain, as distant as it is from the warrens of the eastern megalopolis, is alluring. I call the peak the Mountain King, because of its majestic shape and its favored location at the edge of big First Connecticut Lake.

Also, I was fortunate 35 years ago to have lunch with the fire tower warden—Lamontagne, I think his name was—who introduced me to the Canada jays and the fire tower cab. This man could point to any peak on the horizon and name it. Visiting him was an education in and of itself. I was hooked on this vast northern world known almost exclusively by loggers, a few hunters, and expert fishermen. Hiking down off the mountain, I had this world to myself. Oh, how I liked it. I've been back may times since.

41.

Indian Stream Canyon

Location: Pittsburg, NH

Distance: About a 2.2-mile loop, if you include a jaunt southward down an unofficial trail and a road walk back to the parking area

Difficulty: Easy, but a bit complex if you bushwhack down into the very heart of the geological feature

Trailhead: 45°13'36.60'N, 71°19'16.98'W

GETTING THERE

Motor to the top of the Granite State, to the town of Pittsburg, on NH 3. Cross the Connecticut River at the southern end of the community. Several miles north of the river, watch on the left for Indian Stream Road, just south of Indian Stream Eatery also on the left side of the highway. Turn onto Indian Stream Road and drive on a good logging tote road for just under 16 miles. Mile markers are plainly displayed along the route. At a one or two confusing intersections, be sure to simply stay in the valley, in the lower terrain, and travel nearly due north at all times. Indian Stream will be on your left the entire way north. Just before the mile marker at Mile 16, a large brown sign appears on the right, marking the parking area for Indian Stream Canyon. The actual trail to the cleft in the landscape is on the left side of the road, directly across from a large sign kiosk with cedar-shingled roof.

BACK OF YONDER

In New Hampshire, you can't put much more space between yourself and civilization than by making the long trek into Indian Stream Canyon, a few miles from the boundary peaks on the Canadian border. First of all, you have to drive to the northernmost town of Pittsburg. But instead of your motoring into the village and taking a tour of the many big lakes in the huge township, Indian Stream Canyon beckons from its forest frontier far off the paved highway.

Indian Stream Road wanders nearly 20 miles north of blacktop, and you have to drive

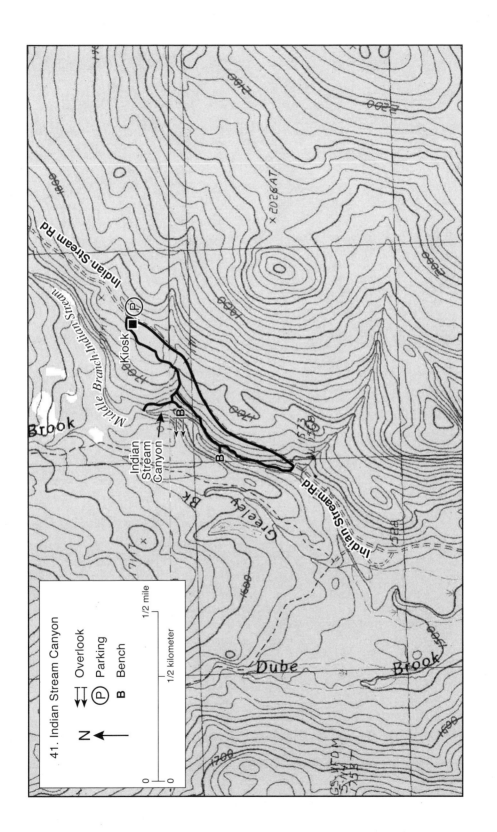

41. Indian Stream Canyon

N

	Overlook
(P)	Parking
B	Bench

0   1/2 kilometer

0   1/2 mile

Indian Stream Canyon gorge   PAPA BEAR

most of it to get to this short hike into a wild geological feature. Fortunately, Indian Stream Valley is beautiful, contained by two sinewy ridgelines that hover at the 2,400-foot elevation, and which are level almost every foot of the way. Between the ridges, the board stream rolls with authority off the Canadian line all the way to its junction with the Connecticut River.

This territory is fabled ground. It was once a good chuck of a tiny independent nation known as the Republic of Indian Stream, founded by settlers and farmers who were caught in the teeth of an international border dispute between the nascent United States and neighboring Canada in the early decades of the 19th century. Subject to two

sets of laws and taxed by both powers, the settlers revolted, drafted their own constitution, voted to adopt it, and thereby founded their own sovereign nation. The experiment lasted for four years, until the small nation state was incorporated into the United States, once the boundary dispute was formally settled at the signing of the Webster-Ashburnham Treaty of 1836.

Regardless if you are a rebel or a upstanding citizen, you have to drive those 16 miles deep into country that is primarily logging terrain, broken only by a presence of a few dozen hunting camps and a farm or two on the south end. Take your time traveling north. The way is quite pleasant and the road is good over most all its length, except where recent flash floods severed the lane and new, hastily bulldozed fill was introduced into the traveled way.

Tick off the miles one by one. Well into the 15th mile, climb a long hill and watch on the right for a New Hampshire Parks and Recreation sign on the right. Pull of the road and park in a rough lot that can accommodate quite a few vehicles. Just to the north is the roofline of a large, shingled sign kiosk. Walk to that kiosk. When I was there, not a single bit of information graced the structure. But up ahead on the road, mile marker 16 nods.

The foot trail in the canyon begins directly across the road from the kiosk, and the path is well trodden. Cross the lane and enter the woods. Turn southwest immediately and begin an easy descent just above a small branch brook running on the right. Light blue blazes in the trees mark the way. Pace downhill in mixed forest cover to an indistinct junction. A trail cuts away to the left, but stay to the right now and drop down a set of log stairs to the little rivulet. Cross it on a few stones and mount a second set of steps on the far side.

Within a few paces you'll encounter another junction and reach a ridgeline that falls away dozens of feet to Indian Stream below. Right this minute, turn left and walk 50 feet to a well-fabricated log bench. Have a seat. Below and upriver to the right, the maw of a jagged rock cleft can be seen. This is the lower granite framework of Indian Stream Canyon.

When the glaciers melted away from the region 12,000 years ago, impoundments of ice-jammed lake water backed up behind a low ridge here, maybe many times before the climate stabilized. As the ice dams collapsed, the lake waters above sawed their way through this depression and formed a short but rough gulch in an otherwise placid landscape.

Leave the log bench and resume your hike high above the stream. Move away from the steep edge of the ridge and walk in rather level terrain in spruce and fir, skirting well to the east of the rock formation. The path slowly bends in an arc to the west and approaches the river, ending abruptly at a large flat rock right at stream edge. There is little to see here, or so it seems.

It is not advisable to step into the stream. However, if the water is low and not rushing along so powerfully as to drag you, you might want to take a moment to seat yourself securely on the bank, take off your shoes and socks, and dabble your toes in the cooling waters. Then dry off, clamber back into your socks and boots, and move back along the trail from whence you came.

Retreat from the water course and work back to the point where you again approach the steep high banks at the south end of the gulch. Those with bushwhacking skills can, if careful, squeeze down into the maw of the canyon just as it opens out at its southern end. The drop is very steep, but trees offer good handholds and the distance downhill isn't much of a challenge. I picked my way down onto a flat slab atop the last falls before the waters organized themselves into the familiar stream you saw through the windshield on the way up Indian Stream Road. This spot atop the slab seemed to me to be the best location within the canyon, well worth the trek down to it.

Climb to the trail again and turn to exit. Pass the spur to the log bench and the short log stairs over the branch stream. You'll arrive at that first junction you passed on the way down. Instead of turning left back to the parking area, turn right now and follow the woods way south, moving along with the river but 20 or so feet above it. The trail is quite well built, with a string of puncheon spans over moist soils. Much of the way, the route is straight. Some 600 feet from the junction, the path edges up to an old, obscure logging skidway. Make a note of it, but focus your attention on yet another log bench. Go to that and have a seat. It's a quiet spot along Indian Stream to tank up with fluids or have a snack. It is pleasant for its isolation and the sound of the stream rolling.

The log bench is the end of the formal trail system at Indian Stream Canyon. But an outlaw trail follows the logging skidway farther south. Strike off on it. Rather than its being undeveloped and rough, someone has actually taken some effort on this trail to place stepping stones and bog bridges in places where the soils are quite wet. Mosey downstream with waters on your right, pacing along on the old logging way that was cut right on the lip of the ridge above the stream bank.

The shady way lightens ahead as the trail approaches the road. You'll come out on the thoroughfare near the base of the long hill in the middle of Mile 15. Turn left, uphill, and pace back to the parking area about $\frac{4}{10}$ mile

away, or simply duck back into the shade of the forest canopy and return your vehicle that way.

I suggest that, if you visit Indian Stream Canyon, you do so with the intention of getting at least your feet wet. By putting in a little extra effort, the canyon is far more enjoyable than if you simply trek to the log benches and have a seat. For the intrepid, there is a rarely trampled path across the stream from the point where the formal trail ends at the northern rock at the stream bank. A few people do cross the stream, mount the bank, pace off into the forest, and approach the canyon from very steep terrain on the far side. However, I don't recommend that. Although moving downstream within the water is the best way to get up close and personal with Indian Stream Canyon, one slip and you might become a permanent fixture of the elements. Be advised that staying on dry ground alongside it is a safer and still satisfying way to experience communion with Indian Stream.

VII. Dead Diamond Country

Garfield Falls

In the northeasternmost corner of the Granite State, mountainous terrain gives way to hills and slack-water backcountry where human population is an afterthought and townships are unincorporated and possess such names as Wentworth Location, Dix Grant, and Second College Grant. Rivers and lakes that moisten this region come with interesting or tongue-twisting monikers, too, such as Parmachenee, Aziscohos, Magalloway, Dead Diamond, and Swift Diamond.

With the exception of one glacier-tortured half-mountain and the trail thereon, the Dead Diamond Country hides within its folds a series of features that only water can carve, two of which routinely claimed the lives of river drivers one hundred years ago, men trying to sluice logs through impossibly tight clefts at the top of wild waterfalls.

42.

Little Hellgate Falls

Location: Pittsburg, NH

Distance: Nearly 3 miles round-trip

Difficulty: Easy to moderate with a difficult short descent at the falls

Trailhead: 45°02'48.29'N, 71°10'32.34'W

GETTING THERE

Travel north on NH 3 to Pittsburg at the very top of the state. Pass through the village and the hamlet of Happy Corner, 5 miles up the line. Continue north past First Connecticut Lake Dam, and several miles later watch for Magalloway Road, a major logging tote road, on your right. Turn onto Magalloway Road and motor 3 miles to Buckhorn Road on the right. Buckhorn is also a wide logging road, with a good gravel surface. Now drive 3 miles to Cedar Stream Road (unmarked) on the right. Soon, Cedar Stream Road begins a very long and moderately steep grade downhill into a narrow valley behind Mt. Pisgah. Eventually you will bottom out and run on the level for a short distance. Pass a camp on the right and on the left and then look for a large, two-legged, roofed sign kiosk on the left side of the road. Pull over to the kiosk and stop. There may or may not be information posted on the kiosk when you get there. The trailhead is down the road 25 feet and the trail cuts left into a very weedy and grassy corridor.

LOGJAM HELL

During the heyday of logging at the turn of the 20th century, the men whose job it was to move 100 or 200 miles downriver dreaded sluicing logs through narrow "squeezehole" formations in the rivers and streams in the North Country. One such strangle point, a falls in Hellgate Brook, was tagged with the name Little Hellgate, and for good reason. The stream is very tightly pinched at the head of a 30-foot, near-vertical cascade, and the

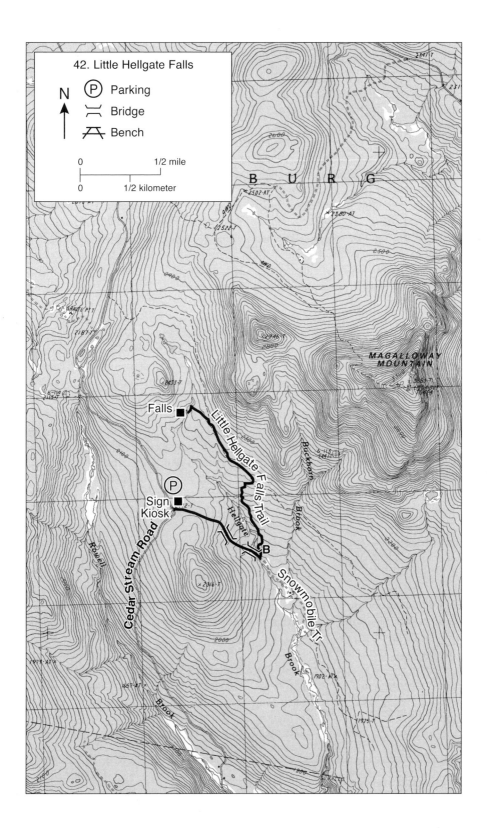

42. Little Hellgate Falls

Ⓟ Parking
⊐⊏ Bridge
🏕 Bench

N

0 — 1/2 mile
0 — 1/2 kilometer

BURG

MAGALLOWAY MOUNTAIN

Falls ■

Little Hellgate Falls Trail

Ⓟ
Sign ■
Kiosk

Hellgate

Buckthorn Brook

B

Cedar Stream Road

Rowell

Snowmobile Tr

Brook

Brook

granite structure of the place caused logs to jam at the time of the year when the falls and rocks were covered with rotting ice and snow. It was a formidable environment to work in. It was deadly. Many a river man lost his life at Little Hellgate Falls.

Little Hellgate Falls is deep in the folds of the south flank of hulking Mt. Magalloway, the classic peak that dominates the landscape in the town of Pittsburg. To get to the falls requires a lengthy drive from NH 3 on logging roads where large, heavily loaded trucks have the right of way at all times. Once you arrive at the large kiosk, the only feature that marks the trailhead location, the falls is still 1.5 miles away, well uphill into the forests of Mt. Magalloway.

Leave your car and walk downhill 10 paces from the kiosk. Turn 90 degrees to the left off Cedar Stream Road and enter a wide, weed-filled corridor with a barely discernable trail through the growth. Walk straight on the level to a snowmobile bridge across a branch brook and continue. The route begins to bend gradually to the right in an easy arc, runs straight again for several minutes, and reaches yet another snowmobile bridge over another branch stream. This bridge is in some need of repair, but it can hold snowmobiles. It's perfectly safe for a hiker to cross.

On the far side of the second bridge, look to the left beyond a fire ring on the ground. Watch for an opening in spruce bows. That's the start of the woods trail uphill. It is not marked with a sign or a blaze, but is distinct enough to call attention to the trail.

Turn left and immediately begin to climb an easy grade uphill, the brook on your left. You'll come to a log seat and a log trail stairs and begin to move up and away from the stream in a nearly pure spruce stand filled with perfectly straight 6-inch trunks and carpeted with what looks like millions of spruce saplings, all trying to compete for what little

light there is filtering through the spruce canopy above.

The trail meanders quite a bit but hugs the valley wall of the brook that is now out of sight. The layout of the trail is interesting, running with the contours of the land, rather than cutting a straight line. All the while, the path continues to climb. The going is never difficult but the gain in elevation is continuous.

As the route gets steeper, it swings through a series of switchbacks and reaches an old logging skidway that cuts obliquely cross the path. Turn a hard left onto this dead-straight, man-made lane, now a pleasant trail underfoot, and strike off on a beeline up the valley. The route crosses several seeps bridged with single-span puncheons and climbs very gradually in mixed hardwood and softwoods. After a few hundred paces on the skidway, the path cuts abruptly away from it to the left, runs on very gently undulating terrain, crosses over an indistinct height of land, and begins to descend toward the stream. Quickly the chatter of water fills the woods. Red surveyor tape appears in the trees at about the time the running water comes into view.

This locale causes confusion. It is obvious by the foot wear on the ground that folks don't know quite what to do when they reach the brook. Red flag tapes show across the stream and disappear into the forest. Many a soul has picked his or her way across the stream and followed the red tape to a dead end a few hundred feet away. When I was last at this point, the confusion was enhanced by a number of blowdowns along the brook.

Don't cross the stream. Instead, turn 90 degrees left and follow the trail downstream. Once you make the turn, it's obvious where the course of the pathway is supposed to go.

The roar of water becomes an enticement to draw you on. The trail begins to pitch

Little Hellgate Falls

downhill gradually at first and then on a steeper grade to another log bench. Below the bench, the trail falls steeply downhill for 30 feet on soils and rocks that can be slippery and unstable. The path now needs the serious attention of a professional trail crew, if it is not to deteriorate to the point of being unusable in future. The descent is complicated by fallen logs and uprooted trees whose branches form obstacles.

But no matter. The falls are at hand, and who doesn't want to clamber down into the basin below the cascade, obstacles or no obstacles. With some effort, you can reach the outflow rocks and turn to look upstream. A fat jet of water appears at an impossibly narrow opening 30 feet overhead and fans out into a bridal veil of mist and foam. At times of high water, this falls rumbles with noise. In times of low water, a narrow snake of white liquid wiggles down the very steep granite face. At the very foot of the falls is a small, cold pool of crystal-clear water that is excellent to the taste.

Little Hellgate Falls boasts its fascinating river-drive history, but its magnetism today has to do with the fact that it is a very isolated feature in the vast forests of New Hampshire's Great North Woods. The cascade isn't close to anything. It takes some real time and effort by car and on foot to get into this watery realm. Without question, if you decide to make the long trek to the top of the Granite State to find Little Hellgate, you will have it to yourself. Most all the other falls and flumes in the region are far more well known and easier to access.

Because Little Hellgate hides so effectively in the topography and in the cool boreal forests, I found this falls enchanting and a tad mysterious, if a little rough around the edges. No sounds of civilization intrude. The forest and ancient rock slabs appears primordial. It isn't a far stretch to imagine Paleo-Indians moving in the shadows, coming down to the falls to drink.

I stayed awhile, completely confident in the knowledge I would be alone. I tested out the shallow pool under the cataract by dunking myself into it, submerging for a second, but the water in July was frightfully cold. Good thing the sun was shining and the air temperature in the high 70s.

On the way up out from the falls, take care on the wet rocks and retrace your steps back to your vehicle. But before you leave, cut down a few paces off the trail to the top ledge and have a seat on the granite slab, just above the point where the water squeezes through its "nozzle" and drops away. Peer down into little gorge that frames the falls and enjoy the surroundings. And think what it must have been like to be a logger with a pike pole in hand, trying to sluice logs out of a logjam tangle and over the falls, all the while standing on blue ice running with water.

Now, that had to have been a "when men were men" job, eh?

43.

Garfield Falls

Location: Pittsburg, NH

Distance: Less than 1 mile

Difficulty: Easy walk down to the falls, but challenging to get into the gorge above the falls

Trailhead: 45°01'48.15'N, 71°06'52.92'W

GETTING THERE

Finding Garfield Falls is an adventure, and as interesting as the falls itself. Travel north on NH 16 north of Gorham and Berlin to the tiny community of Errol. Or roll east from Colebrook or west from Upton, Maine, on NH 26 to Errol. Once in town, take NH 16 north on the east end of the village and motor through the isolated valley of the Magalloway River. Drive to the remote New Hampshire community known as Wentworth Location, pass the Mt. Dustin Country Store, and cross the Maine–New Hampshire line and over a Magalloway River bridge. Continue north through the tiny, unincorporated communities of Magalloway Plantation and Lincoln Plantation, passing historic one-room schoolhouses, granges, and town halls spaced far apart.

Ten minutes north of the Maine line, watch for a major dirt road intersection on the left, fronted by a sign for Bosebuck Mountain Camps. Turn off NH 16 and travel on a major logging truck tote lane known as Parmachenee Road, which runs deep into forests surrounding the headwaters of the Magalloway River in the remote northwestern corner of Maine hard by the Canadian border.

Mile markers appear in the trees on the drive north. Near Mile 4, keep to the right at a major intersection and continue on to Mile 6. At that point, Magalloway Road breaks left off Parmachenee Road. Turn left, northwest bound, drive 3 miles on Magalloway Road over a low height of land, and enter a narrow valley drained by a branch of the Magalloway River. Cross a bridge over the stream and reach yet another intersection on the left.

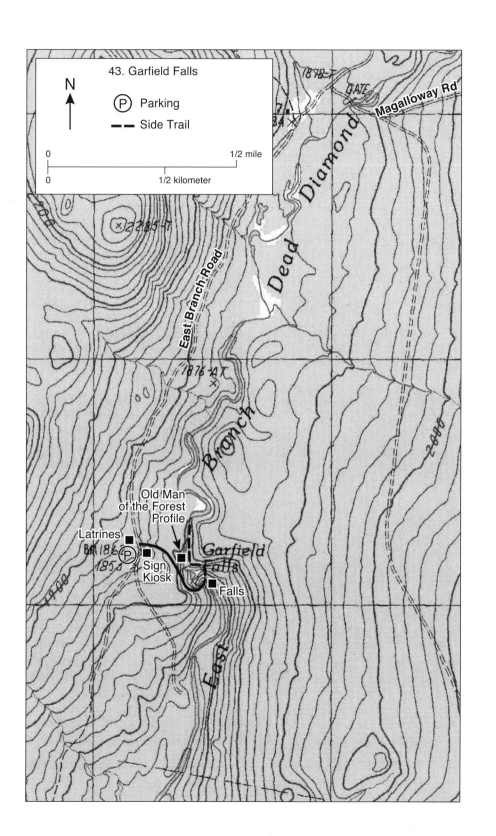

43. Garfield Falls

P Parking
- - Side Trail

0   1/2 mile

0   1/2 kilometer

N

Magalloway Rd
GATE

Dead Diamond

East Branch Road

Branch

Old Man
of the Forest
Profile

Latrines
BM 186
1854

P

Sign
Kiosk

Garfield
Falls

Falls

East

A sign at the junction points the way to Garfield Falls.

Turn left onto this much narrower dirt lane and travel several long miles until a large, free-standing sign kiosk with a cedar-shingled roof appears. Pull up to the kiosk and park in a cleared lot. At the top of the clearing is a set of latrines. The trail to Garfield Falls begins at the edge of the kiosk and falls immediately downhill away from the parking area.

WILD WATERS

Northern Coos County's forests hide numerous wild watery features spaced great distances apart. One of the most remote, yet one of the more compelling, is Garfield Falls. The cascade is a fine, fat jet of foaming water that falls 25 feet into a confining granite vestibule, but the long, rugged gorge above the falls steals Garfield's thunder. A visit to the falls, without exploring the dramatic gulch, is akin to leaving a blockbuster movie in the middle of the show.

At the edge of the sign kiosk, the trail slips into the woods, bends to the southeast, steps over a few water bars, then swings southwest on a narrow, long-abandoned logging track. The path runs arrow straight under a dense canopy of trees and slowly approaches a gash in the landscape on the left. The sound of tumbling water rises in the woods. Through the trees, you'll catch glimpses of a tight canyon 50 feet below. Herd paths radiate from the main trail, but stick with the path now.

Soon you'll drop more steadily in elevation and swing in an arc to the left to a little ledge at the head of the gorge. Thirty feet of space separates you from a palisade that forms a barrier across the gorge. Waters above have no choice but to push through a narrow gap in the rock and fall unimpeded in a well-defined funnel-like form into a cold

Garfield Pool and Hanging Rock

pool at the base of the ledges.

The terrain where Garfield Falls tumbles is tightly restricted by the geology. Instead of the outrun stream running directly forward and away from the falls, the waters are bottled up and have to squeeze sideways through a rock cavity hemmed in by sheer walls. Because of this, it takes some effort to try to get down into the base of the falls where the real action is.

Continue on the path downhill to the branch stream that drains through the area. Here the formal trail ends. The steam bed is pocked with rocks large and small, and these can be used as stepping stones to try to approach the falls. Facing upstream now, stay to the left side of the brook and work your way under a sheer rock face, using the natural elements, including downed logs, to pick your way forward. Your spine to the rock face, inch along until the stones and a low rock shelf come to an end at the large, crystal-clear pool at the base of the falls. Now the full force of Garfield Falls can be appreciated, and its somewhat classic beauty, too. Most falls in the North Country tumble and slide on rock ledges, but Garfield Falls cascades without being disrupted into its terminal pool.

Because the falls environment is so confined, the granite walls reverberate and augment the sound of the falling water.

It is tempting to think of slipping into the pool below the falls and taking a pummeling shower, but the water here never warms up; unfortunately it's frightfully cold all year round.

Many who visit Garfield Falls never venture any farther than this point. That's a mistake. Treasures await above the falls, though getting to them takes a bit of a scramble and some luck not falling in the stream.

Retreat to the point where you first reached the waters. Now try to find a way across the brook on exposed stones. Sometimes it is no problem whatsoever, but when the water level is high after heavy rain, it can be a daunting task getting to the far stream bank without getting wet or needing to remove your boots.

Once on the opposite shore, climb directly up a steep slope around jutting rocks and attain the ridge above. Turn toward the stream, follow a short herd path, and carefully move out onto a wide bed of exposed rock above the falls. There is considerable room to maneuver in the tight canyon you are now in. Soils have long ago been scoured away by violent spring freshets brimming with snow melt and grinding blocks of ice, leaving a rough-and-tumble granite highway that runs gradually uphill to the northeast.

In the gorge, the footing is quite good for the length of a football field, although in one or two places you have to retreat to the woods to jimmy around a barrier. Exploring this rock grotto reveals kettle holes, numerous cascades and flumes, cobble deposits, bark-stripped fallen trees, and a delightful rock profile that I like to call the Old Man of the Forest. The profile graces the full length of the rock strata on the left (west) side of the stream, not too far upstream from the falls.

In the midst of the canyon, the wildness of the place seeps into the senses. Twenty-first-century sensibilities are of no use here. The place is positively primordial. Here, amid rock walls, dark boreal spires, and rumbling noise, time becomes malleable. It could be 10,000 years in the past, for all you know or care. Nothing man-made encroaches. The natural world rules completely here. That's mighty refreshing. Good for the soul, I'd say.

To leave Garfield Falls and its gorge, you can retrace your steps or bushwhack out at several points within the canyon and climb up to the access trail above. But before reaching that thoroughfare, stop at a herd path that traces the lip of the gorge. From there you can obtain fine views down into the rock chasm that leaves you with final impressions of the wild environment that encompasses Garfield Falls.

44.

Magalloway River Trail

Location: Umbagog National Wildlife Refuge, Wentworth Location, NH

Distance: 1 mile of loop trails, one of which is still under construction.

Difficulty: Easy and handicapped accessible even in this remote area

Trailhead: 44°50'17.69'N, 71°03'13.83'W

GETTING THERE

Travel NH 16 north of Gorham and Berlin to the little hamlet of Errol. Or motor east from Colebrook or west from Upton, Maine, on NH 26 to Errol. Once in town, turn northbound on NH 16 at the eastern end of the village and drive into the Magalloway River Valley, an isolated stretch of backwater terrain that has a 19th-century feel to it. Drive to the remote New Hampshire hunting camp community known as Wentworth Location. A mile or so beyond the more dense cluster of small buildings, watch for a large sign on the right announcing Umbagog National Wildlife Refuge. Pull off the highway and park in a small lot.

SLACK-WATER COUNTRY

It is remarkable what a small water-control dam can do to change an environment. Just above the village of Errol, a very modest New Hampshire impoundment stretches across the Androscoggin River, bucking up its flow and the discharges from the mammoth lakes in the Rangeley, Maine, region and from Lake Umbagog, too, into a vast shallow fluid expanse that straddles both states.

The little flood control structure backs up an immense watery habitat that encompasses thousands of acres of national wildlife refuge. Marshes and bogs spread out for miles. The Magalloway River flowing down from the north slows to a crawl and meanders wildly as if not knowing where to go. Umbagog Lake expanded in girth once the dam was in place, flooding acreage beyond its original shores to form a sprawling wetlands.

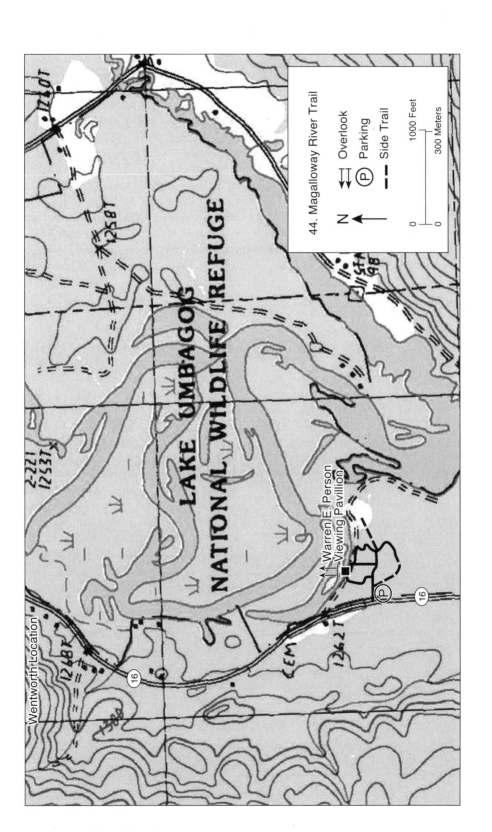

Wentworth Location

LAKE UMBAGOG
NATIONAL WILDLIFE REFUGE

Warren E. Person
Viewing Pavillion

44. Magalloway River Trail

N

Overlook
℗ Parking
Side Trail

0   1000 Feet
0   300 Meters

Magalloway Trail from the observation deck

Into this rich biotic realm flock myriad species of songbirds, raptors, and waterfowl, and mammals and their predators, too. There is food for all, and anyone with a pair of binoculars and a few hours to kill can spot scores of different denizens going about their wild lives.

At the northern margin of this watery world, the U.S. Fish and Wildlife Service has created the Magalloway River Trail above the isolated hunting camp hamlet of Wentworth Location, a community that boasts no more than a few dozen residents year-round.

The Magalloway River Trail has been in existence for years, but a good deal of work is under way to expand the network. Originally, there was a short path over an old logging thoroughfare to accommodate wheelchair-bound citizens and the general public. The early pathway followed the logging route a short distance, then veered down a newly built path that ended at a small viewing station on the shores of a Magalloway River marsh.

Today, that original trail has been married to a series of new woodland loop paths, one of which is still under construction. When complete, the new footways will quadruple

the hiking and provide additional access to the river environment and lowland spruce stands.

At the parking lot beside NH 16, head eastbound over dead-level terrain, walking on pea gravel intermingled with ground-hugging greenery and grasses that are kept mowed. The walking surface is exceptional for such a remote location and could support electric wheelchairs and handicapped scooters. The path, once a tote road, runs straight for a few minutes, then gradually bends toward the southeast, the entire way lined by young spruce and tamarack trees. Once through the bend, the trail straightens again and seems to want to run to a vanishing point in a far sunlit clearing.

Reach a T-junction on the left. The main trail veers 90 degrees left, while straight ahead is cut off by a low pile of dead branches placed in the path. Take that left turn and the well-groomed surface continues a short distance to another T-junction marked by a few sections of split-rail fence. You could turn in either direction, but for now make a hard left and follow the path a few hundred feet to a small but very well-built viewing shelter. The structure is enclosed somewhat, but its northeastern and eastern facings are fronted by large openings that present a fine view of a modest marsh fed by the Magalloway River. Here binoculars come in handy, as wading birds and waterfowl can usually be seen from the confines of the building.

The viewing station was dedicated in honor of the late Warren E. Pearson, former partner of the Balsams Grand Resort Hotel who worked tirelessly on behalf of the residents of the North Country and who was an advocate for healthy forests and wild tracts of land.

At the entrance to the viewing station, a new trail swings left and parallels the margins of the marsh. The surface of the new path is ground softwood bark. The red-brown bark provides a soft surface to walk upon, so much so that footfalls are silent.

The path runs in softwood stands crowding the margins of the marsh. It soon turns abruptly away from the wetlands and heads directly away on a straight course. In a few minutes, the path meets the access trail and ends.

Turn left and retrace the original route to its left turn. Pace out to the split rail fence once again. Now, instead of taking a left turn, swing right and begin a far longer loop. The western end is still under construction at the time of this writing, but likely to be completed in a year.

This new loop path follows the course of the Magalloway River, but no closer than 50 feet from it. Cross a new plank bridge and enter a spruce and ground moss environment. So little sunlight reaches the forest floor in this area that understory plants simply can't survive once they germinate. So mosses dominate the terrain, filling in most niches around the tree trunks. This is pure boreal forest, so utterly different from the bright hardwood forests that populate most of the Northeast.

The trail designers have let this new pathway meander on purpose. It swings in lazy arcs through the forest, never running straight. The new route crosses directly over the old logging road and reenters the woods. Where it does, a large pile of ground bark sits, its contents waiting to be shoveled aboard wheelbarrows and moved up the trial.

The meandering nature of the path continues on the far side of the logging road.

Westbound now, the route draws closer and closer to the highway, then swings to the north, keeping the asphalt at bay. Where the trail turns northward, the soft bark threadway ceases and the way becomes a flagged route with, at this time, minimal improvements. But the course that the trail will take is easily discerned, easy to follow. Long yellow-green and red surveyor tape streamers hang from the trees and some preliminary saw work has been carried out.

As the unfinished route runs northward it crosses what looks like a silted-in canal, a distinct depression in the soils that runs perfectly straight north and south as far as I could ascertain. Sometime in the early history of the settlement of the area, some hardscrabble farmer probably ditched the poor soils of his land to try to increase the amount of arable acreage that was not so susceptible to saturation during periods of heavy rainfall or snowmelt.

The path roughly follows this depression until it ends at the access trail quite close to the parking lot. Granted, this loop is obviously a work in progress, but all indications point to its completion sooner than later. Besides, only a little more than ¼ mile of pathway remains to be finished.

The Magalloway Trail is a nice prelude to a hike into Diamond Peaks in the Second College Grant, not too far up NH 16. This hike is ideal for families with small children and trampers who double as birdwatchers. I, for one, am always enchanted with boreal forest environments. My only complaint about the Magalloway River Trail is that it is not long enough and does not provide enough footage along the very banks of the beautiful Magalloway River.

45.

Diamond Peaks Trail

Location: Second College Grant, NH

Distance: 6.2 miles round-trip

Difficulty: Easy to moderate hike, with one or two very short, steep pitches

Trailhead: 44°51'51.50'N, 71°03'04.93'W

GETTING THERE

Find your way north to Errol on NH 16 or NH 26. Errol is the last town of consequence close to the northeasternmost quadrant of the state of New Hampshire, well above the small city of Berlin and 20 miles east of Cole-brook. Continue north on NH 16, roughly following the Magalloway River. Pass through the tiny hamlet of Wentworth Location and by the Mt. Dustin Country Store situated there. Little more than a mile north of the store and just feet before crossing the Maine state line, look for a cemetery on the left and a gravel road beside it. Turn left onto that gravel lane. In a short distance reach a bar gate across the road. There is a parking pull-out to the right. Park there. You will be walking on the gravel road into the domain of the Second College Grant. The public may enter the Grant on foot or bicycle.

A MOUNTAIN VIOLATED

One of the most famous peaks in all of North America is Half Dome, in Yosemite National Park. The towering bald peak is, quite literally, half a mountain. Ice-age glaciers gnawed away, destroyed, and carted off the missing half. On the other side of the continent, there is a small, almost entirely unknown mountain that suffered much the same fate as Half Dome.

At 2,017 feet elevation, Diamond Peaks may be a poor cousin, indeed, to Half Dome, but the 1 1/10-mile pathway to its summit ledges is a heady experience if you like heights—that is, true vertical drops that measure in the hundreds of feet.

Dead Diamond Country

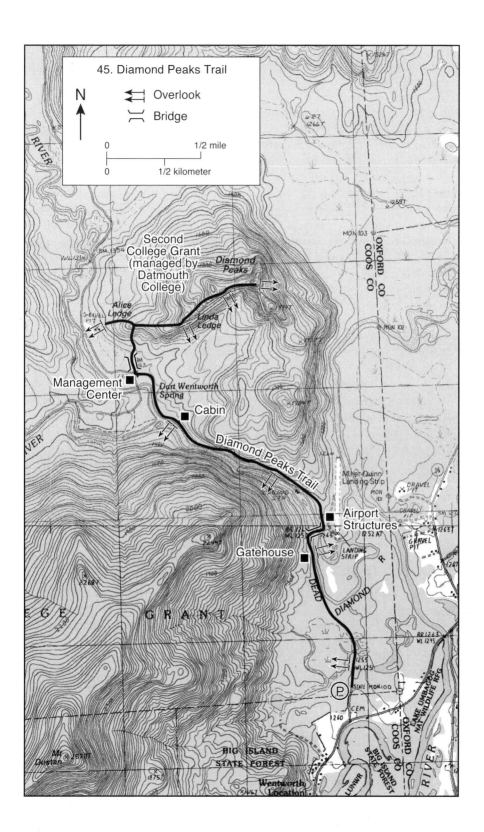

45. Diamond Peaks Trail

N

⇇ Overlook

⟩⟨ Bridge

0   1/2 mile
0   1/2 kilometer

RIVER

Second
College Grant
(managed by
Datmouth
College)

Diamond
Peaks

Alice
Ledge

GRAVEL
PIT

Linda
Ledge

OXFORD CO
COOS CO

MON 103

MON 102

Management
Center

Dart Wentworth
Spring

Cabin

RIVER

Diamond Peaks Trail

Miller-Quinn
Landing Strip

MON
IDI

GRAVEL
PIT

16

GRAVEL

SM 127

GRAVEL
PIT

1263T

Airport
Structures

1252 AT

Gatehouse

LANDING
STRIP

DIAMOND R

RR 1263
WL 1245

EGE   GRANT

DEAD

DIAMOND

1255
WL 1251

STATE MON 100

P

Mt
Dustan

BIG ISLAND
STATE FOREST

Wentworth
Location

CEM

260

OXFORD CO
COOS CO

BIG ISLAND
STATE FOREST

LUNWR

LAKE UMBAGOG
NAT WILDLIFE REG

RIVER

Diamond Peaks is nearly invisible. It is hidden from view from any highway in New Hampshire by Mt. Dustin, which rises over the hardscrabble community of Wentworth Location near the Maine State line. Moreover, the gravel road that skirts the west flank of the mountain is gated 2 miles to the southeast. You have no choice but to approach the mountain on foot. Even then, you can't see Diamond Peaks over the trees that line the road.

The bar gate, just a few hundred feet northwest of NH 16, walls off a township-size parcel of land that has long been under the stewardship of Dartmouth College. The domain is known as Second College Grant. The acreage was given to the college in 1807 so that resources harvested from the land might be sold to offset the cost of tuition for indigent but promising students. Today, the college manages the forest well, conducting all manner of research into sustainable timbering practices, water resource protection, ecosystem and climate change, and more. Dartmouth maintains a few camps within the Grant that its students and alumni get away to.

The walk into this wild environment is equally as appealing, as is the hike up Diamond Peaks. Within the first minute, after passing around the bar gate and heading north, the road breaks into the clear. A broad marshland opens on both sides, with a fine view to the left of Mt. Dustin. My last trek through here, a bald eagle sat perched on an evergreen snag next to its massive stick nest, about 80 feet west of the road. The bird of prey assailed me with high-pitched screams for as long as it took for me to walk out of its sight, but it never moved from its post. While I was scolded, two otters made appearances now and again in the marsh waters.

At the ½-mile mark, the Dartmouth College gatehouse appears on the left. A large kiosk features all manner of posted information and maps. Pause here and study the informative material; you may use it to your advantage on your trek.

Just above the gatehouse, the road swings 90 degrees to the east for a minute and crosses a large, steel stringer bridge over the Dead River, one of the Northeast's fabled log-driving rivers when ax and cross-cut-saw timbering was king, more than one hundred years ago. Wide and free flowing here, the Dead is a product of two wild and handsome tributaries that converge just out of sight a mile upstream, the Swift Diamond and the Dead Diamond Rivers, which drain a vast region of northeastern New Hampshire. The rivers were given their names by logging crew roughs who relished fast-moving water to move logs downstream with little effort. The Swift Diamond was just that, swift. But the Dead Diamond meandered and was slow moving, and logs often jammed in the river bends. It was a better assignment to work the Swift than the Dead.

The road swings back to the north once across the bridge and passes the "international airport," a grass airstrip on the right. A new facility to accompany work sheds was being built at the time I last passed through. Close by is the Airport Trail, but it is rough, weed choked, and unmarked. Stay with road.

The lane rises in elevation beyond the airstrip, and as you climb the air fills with the sound of fast-moving water. At the height of land, a small clearing appears on the left. It is a little rock ledge perhaps 70 feet above the river below. Here the stream cut a small, rugged canyon through a low east–west ridge once the glaciers retreated from the area 12,000 years ago. The view into the canyon raises the pulse rate. The ledge is a nice place to spend a few minutes rehydrating or enjoying a snack.

Move north again, drop off the rise, and

Dead River

proceed to the broad flats near the confluence of the Swift and Dead Diamond Rivers, where there is a view to left. To the right is a well-maintained camp dedicated to two doctors who lost their lives in a small plane crash in the Pemigewasset Wilderness decades in the past. Around the bend from the cabin, the north end of the Airport Trail opens on the right. Pass that and walk another ¼ mile to a cluster of buildings on the left. This is the Management Center of the Grant. Across the road stands a well-fabricated sign with bright yellow letters, pointing the way to the Diamond Peaks Trail.

Leave the Management Center clearing to the right (east) and enter the forest immediately. The Diamond Peaks Trail begins as a trek over flat, and in a few places, moist ground spanned by aging log and plank puncheons. Soon, those bog bridges will have to be refurbished, but they still do their appointed job.

The flat terrain ends abruptly at the base of the mountain. The trail pitches uphill at a moderate incline and leaves the valley for good for a series of higher and higher crags that make this little mountain and its pathway well worth the visit. The first pitch is the longest and steepest along the route. Near the upper stretches where the going becomes more moderate, about ⅓ mile into the trek, a side trail exits left and runs to an overlook called Alice's Ledge. The view is down to the Management Center and the valley of the Dead and Swift Diamond Rivers, but every time I've been here, this vista has been socked in with low, ground-hugging clouds.

Return to the main trail and continue uphill. After snaking back and forth through

Diamond Peaks Trail

mixed hardwood and softwood forests easily gaining altitude, the path works its way to the first of many narrow, south-facing ledges. This first is a sample of what is to come, although the view is a bit restricted. The rounded northern and western slopes of the mountain end abruptly. Southern slopes don't exist, bulldozed away by glacier ice millennia ago. In their stead are sheer precipices one after another, collectively encompassing ½ mile.

Cut uphill from first exposed ledges and hike within close proximity to the cliffs for the remainder of the trek. Every few minutes, a fresh ledge appears on the right. At each one, the view expands and improves. Be sure to check as each new opening comes your way. One of them presents a ledge that is a bit larger than the others, and it offers a view directly along the dramatic south face of the mountain. From this vantage point in the vicinity of the flat topknot of the first summit elevation, it is possible to see the remarkable damage done by a moving continental ice sheet. The full vertical dimensions of the cliff walls are visible, particularly of the terminal cliff still well up the line. Estimating now, using the height of trees as a guide, it seems to me that the longest drop to the forest below approaches 200 feet.

Drop in elevation ever so slightly and continue to another trail junction on the left, an outrun trail to the north that is in poor condition. Pass the junction, climb over a blow-down or two that block the main trail to a small degree, and push on to the prize at the end of the trail. Along the way, take advantage of blueberries in season. The plants thread the margins of the cliffs much of the way toward the end of the trail.

The Diamond Peaks Trail continues to rise very gradually to a height of land. The path pitches down a few feet to a terminal ledge that offers good footing and area enough for a few people to sit. This last crag reveals the finest view of all into the very sparsely settled valley of the Magalloway River, to Mt. Dustin and other nearby summits, to extensive spruce bogs, and to Sturtevant Pond and the fringes of Lake Umbagog. Look over the edge of the ledge and the drop is perfectly vertical; the tree canopy is a long way down.

Lowbush blueberries crowd this last ledge, a good thing late in July. You should have the berries to yourself, and the cliff ledge, too. Because Diamond Peaks is such a long distance removed from the heart of the White Mountains, and because access to the trailhead requires the 2-mile walk in, the pathway gets little use other than from the Dartmouth crowd, what few there are up here at almost any time of year. But the fact that it is a lonesome outpost ought to be attractive to those veteran trampers who have had their fill of the most popular hiking trails in the eastern part of the country, from here a good deal more than an hour's drive to the south.

VIII. Boundary Mountains

Deer Mountain fire tower PAPA BEAR

Toward the very northern extremes of the Granite State, a series of serpentine ridges divide two great nations, the United States and Canada. The most remote terrain in the headwaters country that gives rise to the Connecticut River, these boundary mountains are far removed from the daily hustle and bustle in the Lower 48. This is moose country, and even the main asphalt artery, NH 3, goes by the name of Moose Alley up here.

Virtually unknown as a hiking destination, the boundary mountains are just beginning to attract the unorthodox characters among us who wish to get into places that will never attract those who like their hikes prepackaged so they know precisely where they will end up once a day of tramping is done. Some will come because they want to add the largely trail-less 3,000-footers–D'Urban, Salmon, Trumbull, Kent, and Deer–to their conquest list. Some will want to see the thundering falls and flume in a stretch of wild Connecticut. A few will just have to find the very source of that same river hard by the Canadian border. And maybe a handful will want to bushwhack to the Crown Monument boundary pylon at the junction of New Hampshire, Maine, and Quebec, or to the high-elevation bog and deteriorating steel superstructure of the former Deer Mountain fire tower.

46.

Falls in the River Trail

Location: Pittsburg, NH

Distance: 2 miles to the junction with the Moose Alley Trail

Difficulty: Easy to moderate

Trailhead: 45°08'32.17'N, 71°10'53.79'W

GETTING THERE

Travel north on NH 3 through Colebrook and continue due north to New Hampshire's northernmost community, Pittsburg, a 300,000-acre heavily forested township that harbors numerous large streams that make up the headwaters drainage of the Connecticut River. Pass through the village and continue on the highway 5 miles to a hamlet called Happy Corner, where the last market on the road, Young's Store, resides. Motor ever northward another 5 miles, passing large First Connecticut Lake dam and Magalloway Road before swinging around a curve and reaching another impoundment, Second Connecticut Lake Dam. Turn off the road to the right and park before the dam. Facing the dam, look 90 degrees to the right. There is a large sign with bright yellow raised letters at the woods line that signals the start the newly constructed Falls in the River Trail.

IN WILD RIVER COUNTRY

The Falls in the River Trail, built recently by Lainie Castine of Pittsburg and a host of volunteers, brings day hikers in contact with a truly wild stretch of New England's greatest river. The river is almost always close by, sometimes placid and peaceful, sometimes torrid and roaring loudly.

On the south side of the grassy parking lot at Second Connecticut Lake Dam, immediately enter the woods where the fine, large sign stands, and amble along a low ridge directly above the river. Here the trail follows a long-abandoned anglers' path that until recently was full to brimming with blowdowns

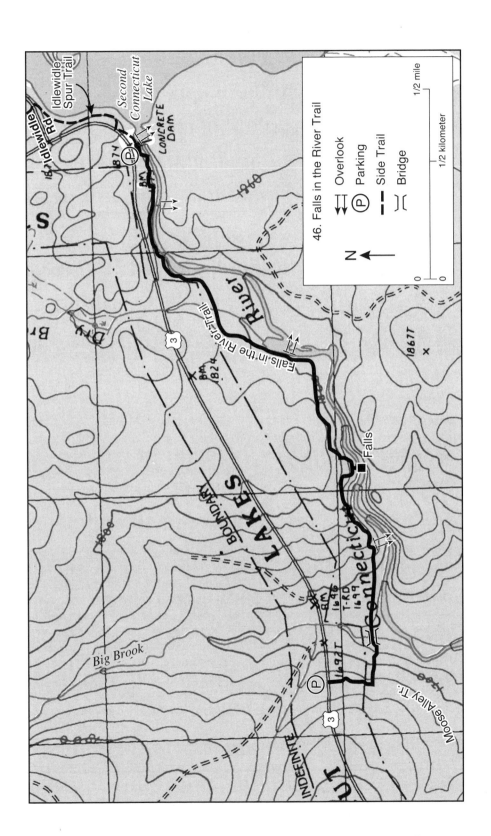

Idlewidle Spur Trail

Idlewidle Rd

Second Connecticut Lake

CONCRETE DAM

BM 874

P

BM

1860

Dry Br

3

Falls in the River Trail

BM 1824

1867T

Falls

LAKES

BOUNDARY

1880

Connecticut

T-RD 1699

BM 1646

1692T

Big Brook

P

3

INDEFINITE

UT

Moose Alley Tr.

1700

46. Falls in the River Trail

Overlook
P Parking
Side Trail
Bridge

N

0
0

1/2 kilometer

1/2 mile

Falls ledges and flume   STEVEN D. SMITH

and forest debris. Always close but above the river's northern bank, descend ever so gradually on fine footing in maturing forest. For a few minutes, NH 3 is close by over the right shoulder, but the path descends away from the ribbon of asphalt as the elevation drops. At several points along the way in the first 10 minutes or so, you can dodge down openings to the river itself to have a look at the fast-moving waters.

The trail soon levels out in flat terrain and turns to the right away from the river for a while. In five minutes, you will approach an alder thicket and cross the first of several bog bridge spans over various narrow branches of Dry Brook. Pass through tight spruce and an S-turn at a forest opening, to another bog bridge string over moist ground. Walk across the span, and in a minute, cross yet another one, this time at another alder patch and another branch of the brook.

The trail reaches the river again a little over a mile from the trailhead and parallels it on flat ground. Here the waters open out into a quiet backwater inlet that is a favorite haunt of wildlife and waterfowl. When the trail was built, cutters found most of the skeletal remains of a moose along the proposed pathway.

The pathway runs with the river in the flat for five minutes, then bends uphill into a region of tight dark spruce. The way zigzags briefly in this cool, shady environment before reaching a height of land where the forest lightens abruptly and roaring noise greets your ears. Descend a moderate decline in very pleasant surroundings, pulled along by increasingly loud sounds of great volumes of falling water. Round a bend and rock ledges come into view, along with foaming river water.

Descend to a great spur of granite ledge that juts out directly into the path of the river.

Everyone who comes this way can't resist walking out onto the rocks and having a seat just a few feet above a big and powerful step falls that swings in an arc around the visitor and falls in a tumult into a long, narrow flume gorge boiling with frothy waters.

Remarkably, this feature of the Connecticut River was virtually unknown before the trail was built. No one I have ever talked to in the region knew of its existence. I simply stumbled upon it nearly a decade ago, while bushwhacking upriver to try to figure out a route for a future trail. I was smitten as soon as I reached the falls and flume and revisited often. Fortunately, the Cohos Trail Association was able to obtain permission to develop a trail in this area, and this falls is now a favorite spot for hikers and tourists tramping through the region.

There is no better spot on the trail to stop for lunch or a snack and relax for a time. Because of the noise of the falls and flume, no other sounds encroach on the visitor other than the voices of companions, perhaps. Be sure to take all trash with you when you leave, and if anyone has been careless enough leave trash behind, pack it out so that the falls environment remains pristine.

Leave the cataract and continue south, taking several quick turns and several short spurts uphill. Soon the trail levels out again in mature spruce, but this time you are directly above the river thundering 70 or more vertical feet below. Fallen spruce needles render the trail red underfoot. Stay high above the river for five minutes, when the trail suddenly loses elevation as the river turns away from the trail. Bottom out in the narrow valley of Big Brook. Soon you'll reach the brook and the long, narrow span over it.

Big Brook bridge is built on a 26-foot steel truss obtained from the state by headwaters forest-easement manager Sandy Young of Pittsburg. The steel creates a rigid frame on which heavy planks have been laid. Heavy rope guides have been strung along each side of the bridge, giving the span a secure sense.

Cross the bridge and begin a lazy climb out of Big Brook valley. Within a few minutes you'll be at a trail junction with the Moose Alley Trail, where the Falls in the River Trail ends. You may turn right (northwest) here to get to the shoulder of NH 3 in just a few minutes, retrace your steps back to the car at Second Connecticut Lake dam, or follow the highway shoulder north. Better yet, turn left (southeast) at the trail junction and trek the Moose Alley Trail 2 miles to its terminus on Magalloway Road, just 100 feet from the big stringer bridge over the Connecticut River.

In the headwaters region of the great river, the Falls in the River Trail has rapidly become a must-destination hike. Easy to access and easy to walk, and with the dramatic falls and flume in the middle, it has become a favorite not only with hikers but among families with children, and moose watchers and fishermen and -women.

If you wish to hike only ½ mile, the Falls in the River Trail can be accessed from the trailhead of the Moose Alley Trail, which is just off NH 3, about 500 feet uphill and south of the Big Brook highway bridge. The Moose Alley Trail is fronted by a large sign with raised yellow letters, similar to the sign at Second Connecticut Lake Dam. Walk down the Moose Alley Trail for a minute or two, to the junction with the Falls in the River Trail. A left turn downhill gets you on your way toward the falls, ½ mile away.

If you are a fan of moose viewing, try hiking the trail at dawn or dusk. Moose frequent the trail and the surrounding terrain then. But remember, moose are wild animals. Keep your distance and do not disturb them. In the fall, the mating rut season, bulls can be temperamental. Give a bull a very wide berth.

47.

Deer Mountain Trail

Location: Northern Pittsburg, NH

Distance: About 4.5 miles to and from the bog, about 6-plus miles to and from the fire tower

Difficulty: Moderate terrain most of the way. This hike is presently a well-flagged bushwhack. Expect uneven surfaces, fallen trees to step over, forest debris clutter, and some evergreen branches at eye level. But tracing the route is easy, and it will soon be formally cut, improved, and extended.

Trailhead at Route 3: 45°11'41.16'N, 71°12'05.79'W

GETTING THERE

Motor up NH 3 to the very top of the Granite State. Four miles south of the Canadian border, round a bend and look up ahead for a large sign that flags the entrance to the Deer Mountain Campground on the left. One hundred feet before that sign, cross a bridge over the Connecticut River and take an immediate right into a large pull out alongside the highway. Park there.

Walk across the highway to the west, stride south across the bridge over the Connecticut River, and then make an immediate right onto an old logging tote lane that is fronted by a bar gate. Pass through or around the gate and trek west on what is known locally as Sophie's Lane. Pass a wide trail on the left and a sign kiosk on the right. Continue west and then swing around a bend to the north. Walk ¼ mile to where the lane splits. Turn off Sophie's Lane to the left and walk uphill on a short spur lane. Near the height of land, look on the left for red surveyor flagging waving in a small, weedy clearing. Leave the lane and follow the red tape westward uphill.

THE DISAPPEARING ACT

A few miles south of the Canadian border rises an isolated peak whose lower eastern flank seems to disappear into the waters of 800-acre Third Connecticut Lake. Seen from the eastern shore of that lake, Deer Mountain presents a pleasing profile with an indistinct southern summit and a lower but far more prominent northern summit.

This lonesome peak once supported an

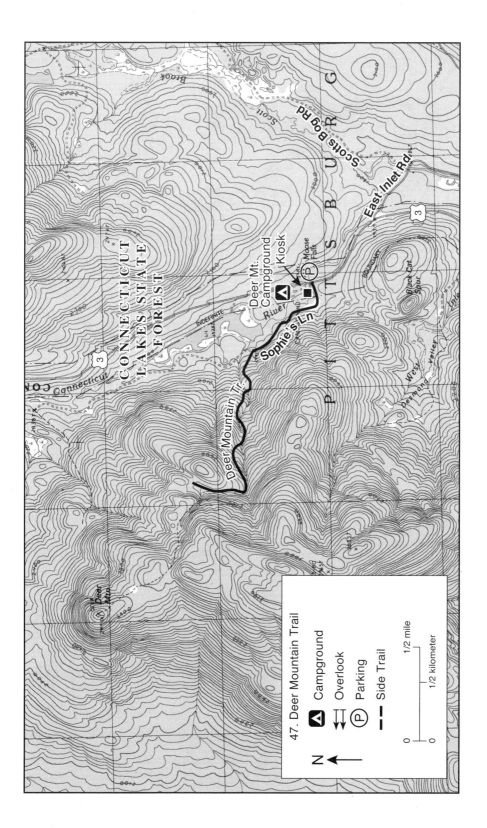

N

47. Deer Mountain Trail

▲ Campground
⊤⊤ Overlook
Ⓟ Parking
▬ Side Trail

0   1/2 mile
0   1/2 kilometer

Deer Mountain hut

active fire tower on the northern upland. Much of the superstructure is still in place but it's difficult to locate from the east. Less difficult to find is a high-elevation bog. This hike focuses on the route to the bog, but provides some direction to the fire tower on the summit.

The original Deer Mountain Trail has long been obliterated by logging. But this bushwhack follows quite closely the original route, which was overtaken and overwhelmed by logging equipment years ago. The mountain has reclaimed the logging skidway, yet it is quite easy to trace. Not only that, the route has recently been flagged well with red surveyor tape.

Having left Sophie's Lane below on a spur lane, walk uphill gradually to a point where the lane reaches a crest south of a brook. Just before the height of land, a modest clearing opens on the left. In the clearing, red surveyor tape waves. Cut left uphill across the clearing, watching underfoot for a few odd, decaying logging debris sticks. Approach the tree line and listen for the sound of informally named Deer Mountain Brook, hidden in the trees to the right. Enter the trees on a long-abandoned logging skidder track that has eroded and softened but at times makes for very uneven ground. This skidder path roughly follows the obliterated old pack trail that ran up to the north summit of the mountain. That old route above is unrecognizable, having been overrun by repeated logging operations decades ago. Much of the way up the mountain is defined by depressions in the earth that often run with water that smoothed the soils and also eroded the terrain long after the heavy logging ceased across the peak.

Rise on moderately steep ground at first, following the red flagging. Drift toward the mountain stream. The terrain levels out for a moment and crosses directly over the brook. Gain the north bank and in a moment turn uphill, following the course of the water some 50 to 100 feet from its confines.

The angle of ascent is never acute but steady over nearly half the length of the track. In the lower section the forest is predominately maple. The woods are well lit and pleasant to trek through, although you must step over the occasional fallen tree or push aside a few small spruce.

Cross the stream again and soon you'll make a third crossing, as spruce and fir begin to intermingle with the hardwoods. The skidway narrows and the softwoods crowd in about the corridor. The growth is an infrequent nuisance, but as the way is so well flagged, there is no need to worry about losing the path.

In the years to come, this trail will no longer be a bushwhack. The Cohos Trail Association is planning even now to restore the old historic route. The flagging you are following was put in place by that organization all the way to a high-elevation bog on the east flank of the elongated peak. But in coming seasons, the hiking group will push the trail farther up the mountain, cross an eastern ridge, and attain a second, taller ridge, following that to the remaining superstructure of an abandoned fire tower that stands at the 3,005-foot elevation.

The high bog is now your destination. Several miles into the climb, the incline moderates and becomes nearly level. The waters in the stream slow down. Cross a moist patch on your left, and drift into quiet country with open and level forest to the right and very steep terrain to the west.

Make yet another crossing of the now placid stream and slip along just above its west bank. Numerous blowdowns form minor barriers in this stretch, hemmed in by

the steep slope on one side and the stream on the other. Use caution in one 10-foot section where the treadway is very narrow.

Ahead, the way brightens considerably just as alders try to pinch off the path. Suddenly the forest gives way to a 10-acre boreal bog with a limitless northern horizon and walls of spruce growing on steep hills to the right and left.

Step across the outlet of the bog, keeping to the east side of the wetland. Pace in grasses on the driest surfaces and you can skirt the fringes of the bog, stepping over sun-bleached logs and passing naked snags. Work your way toward the northern reaches of the wetland and find a seat on a log.

This remote bit of real estate virtually never sees human traffic. If you wish to experience solitude, Deer Mountain bog is as tranquil a destination that can be found in the far north.

Across the bog, two subsummits of the mountain rise, separated by a shallow saddle. Try as you may, you won't obtain a glimpse of the spidery, cabless steel superstructure of the long-lost Deer Mountain fire tower. It stands just out of sight behind the northerly ridge. The taller of the two subsummits presents rock outcroppings, very steep slopes, and a crown of healthy spruce and fir.

The bog is frequented by moose, the inrun into the bog heavily trodden by their hooves. Moose droppings are plentiful on the ground here and there. A few moose "highways" meander through the opening in the forest.

When I was at the bog, a canine track also appeared in the mud, probably made by a large coyote. At night in this realm it is common to hear a coyote pack howling in the late hours.

In a year or two, the flagged bushwhack will be cut and cleared all the way to the bog,

Deer Mountain Bog

if not to the north summit where the tower steel still stands.

If you are comfortable with your backwoods and orienting skills, reaching the summit is a no-brainer. But the way up is a real challenge. The eastern mountain ridge above the bog is very steep, fraught with big fallen trees and countless branches, not to mention a million small evergreen saplings competing for every scrap of sunlight. There are no blazes or flagging to find.

From the far side of the bog, you will see a depression in the ridge. The old trail ran through that col, but the way is virtually impossible to locate. Yet that saddle is the path of least resistance and the obvious lane to the next ridgeline that is the upper spine of the mountain. Once at the height of land, it is only a matter of turning north and following the highest terrain right up to the site of the fire tower.

The old structure still looks impressive, despite the fact that the watchman's cab is long gone, as are the stairs and railings. Of the few people who manage to reach this spot, virtually all come up the west side of the peak, utilizing more recent logging tracks

and moving through more open forests.

The steel is only the latest incarnation of structures that once stood on the north summit. The very first was an impossible tower built of logs stacked into a 30-foot crib held in place by cables. The only way up was a rough-built wooden ladder.

As bushwhacks go to the bog, this one presents little difficulty. There is no getting lost, given the many red tape streamers and the old, eroded trackways. Also, the stream is always with you. If you lose the trail for whatever reason, just perk up an ear. You can always hear the sound of water running.

Return to your vehicle along the same track. But before leaving the area, why not visit the little Deer Mountain Campground and Third Connecticut Lake, just 2 miles up the road. At Third Connecticut Lake, you get that fine view of the Deer Mountain over the big, moody lake. Continue north and reach the brand-new U.S. Border Patrol and Customs station. The border itself is marked by two pylons housed in a tiny corral. They share the plot with two flagpoles, one displaying the Stars and Stripes, and one the Canadian maple leaf.

48.

Fourth Connecticut Lake Trail

Location: Pittsburg, NH

Distance: 3 miles round-trip

Difficulty: East to moderate, but steep in the first five minutes

Trailhead: 54°15'10.52'N, 71°12'17.30'W

GETTING THERE

Travel on NH Route 3 all the way to the Canadian border. Look for the U.S. port of entry offices on the left side of the road. Just beyond and on the right side of the highway is a parking pullout.

Please note, at this writing, construction work is nearing completion on a new and much larger port of entry facility at the border; parking arrangements may change, and most likely will change. For information updates about this situation, go to www.cohos trail.org and read the latest material regarding parking for the Fourth Connecticut Lake Trail.

STRADDLE THE CONNECTICUT RIVER WITH YOUR FEET

At the very top of the Granite State, moisture collects in the Canadian border country hills for the 400-mile run to Long Island Sound in the guise of the Connecticut River. In a hollow on the south flank of an unassuming peak called Prospect Hill, a 2-acre fen, a puddle of clear, never-stagnant water creates an opening in the spruce and fir forest. This tiny body of water carries a lengthy moniker: Fourth Connecticut Lake. The pond is nearly 1,500 times smaller than its cousin, First Connecticut Lake, a dozen miles to the south. But Fourth Lake, as the natives call it, has a substantial job to do. It is the true headwaters of the Connecticut River, New England's mightiest.

Fourth Connecticut Lake is reached by a short trail, much of which threads within the international boundary clearings that snake

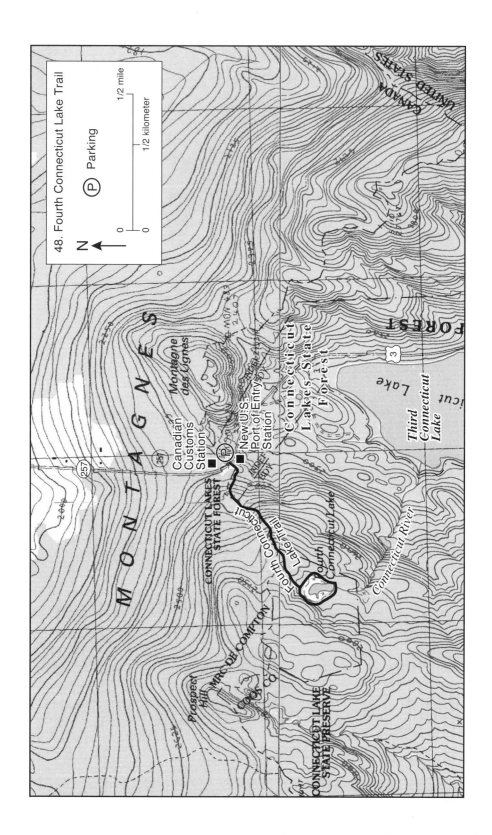

48. Fourth Connecticut Lake Trail

Ⓟ Parking

N

0 — 1/2 mile
0 — 1/2 kilometer

CANADA
UNITED STATES

M O N T A G N E S

Montagne
des Ugnes

MON Pk 2,407

Canadian
Customs
Station

257

New U.S.
Port of Entry
Station

INDEF. BDY.

Connecticut Lakes State Forest

Connecticut Lakes State Forest

CONNECTICUT LAKES STATE FOREST

Fourth Connecticut Lake Trail

Fourth Connecticut Lake

Prospect Hill

PARC DE COMPTON

COÖS CO.

CONNECTICUT LAKE STATE PRESERVE

Third Connecticut Lake

Connecticut Lake

3

FOREST

Connecticut River

along the U.S.-Canada border. The trailhead rests just to the northwest of a huge, metal ionized-particle detector standing within feet of the border. That machine was installed in 2010 as first line of defense against the importation of dangerous radiological material or a crude nuclear weapon. Looming as it does in a cold mountain environment, the device seems positively alien, as if it was deposited here from another world, albeit one dreamed up by Hollywood screenwriters.

Just to the east of that mammoth bit of technology is a little picket-fenced yard. Inside the fence stand two flagpoles, one displaying the Stars and Stripes, and one waving the red Canadian maple leaf. Between the two poles poke up two border pylons—boundary monuments—that fix the dividing line between the nations precisely in place. Many people who come to the border to hike to Fourth Connecticut Lake can't resist posing for a photograph, standing beside the little courtyard that houses the flagstaffs and castings that each look like a miniature Washington Monument.

Just up a little knoll from the high-tech machine and the port of entry headquarters, a well-made Fourth Connecticut Lake Trail sign and sign-in box herald the start of the trail. Leave the mowed grass that surrounds the border patrol facility and step onto what appears to be a well-used foot trail. Rather than swing into trees, the path runs in a cleared swath sometimes 40 feet wide, sometimes as wide as 60 feet. This clearing actually stretches from the St. Lawrence River in New York State across Vermont. It meanders as if drunk on the height of land between the two nations to form the boundary of New Hampshire, and continues for hundreds of miles to round out the dimensions of the state of Maine.

The trail traverses protected Nature Conservancy acreage. That land conservation society maintains the trail and does a good job of it, too.

Almost immediately, the trail climbs into steep terrain marked by small ledges and exposed rocks. Scramble uphill to the point where the effort puts some load on your heart and on your rate of breathing. Just when sweat breaks out, the angle of the trail moderates and the going gets considerably easier.

To the right against the tree line in Canada, small signs sing out in French, warning against illegally entering the country. To the left, nothing indicates that you are slipping along an international border. However, at your feet, small, round, and flat bronze markers appear infrequently. Their purpose is to mark precisely where the boundary runs. You will find you are occasionally hiking in the United States, sometimes in Canada. Not to worry. Because your intent is to visit the fen that is the headwaters of the Connecticut River, no one is going to arrest you for ambling back and forth between two sovereign nations.

That is not to say that you are not being watched, so to speak. In various places along the boundary, particularly in areas that are known smuggling routes or where people are believed to have slipped across the border illegally, there are seismic instruments that can pick up the pressure waves of footfalls on the ground or even snowmobiles on snowy trails. Moose moving across the border at a good trot must make the seismometers wail.

On occasion, at night, helicopters loaded with infrared scanners have been known to buzz a few miles off from the border. Local residents have reported watching flying machines hovering in the night sky for hours during times of high alert. And self-appointed citizen patriots from southern New Hampshire have more than a few times set up lawn

U.S. port of entry   STEVE D. SMITH

chairs on the border and sat scanning the hinterland with binoculars, handheld radios in hand, a sort of civilian early-warning system.

Lest I go to unnecessary lengths about the terrorist threat on our northern border, let me confine my verbiage to the peaceful pursuit of hiking.

The Fourth Connecticut Trail gains altitude quickly. Since it trips along in the boundary clearings, views open out to remote terrain. Turn around and face east. Below you can see the saddle where the highway crosses into Canada. Beyond, wooded peaks roll off to the horizon, first Lignes (Line Mountain), then Mt. Salmon, followed by Mt. D'Urban, Saddle Mountain, Marble, and on and on.

Twenty miles to the north stands a conspicuous shape surrounded by Quebec farmlands. The sprawling mountain is Mont-Mégantic rising out of Notre-Dame des Bois Township. Atop the massive hump on the horizon stand two astronomical observatories, one of which houses Canada's largest telescope. Mont-Mégantic isn't so much a mountain as a hulking geological formation known as a ring dike, a nearly circular magma intrusion formed eons ago that stands on the countryside now because the landscape above it and around has eroded away over millions of years, leaving the dense formation exposed for hikers to see from the Fourth Connecticut Lake Trail.

Continue uphill to the northwest in the clearings when the path veers suddenly to the southwest. Leave the boundary cut and enter the realm of spruce and fir. Come upon a string of split-log bog bridges built in moist terrain. Cross the bridges and begin an easy descent down off the height of land. No more than five minutes removed from the clearings, light begins to invade the dark woodlands ahead.

Come upon a T-junction a few feet before the shoreline of the 2-acre puddle the trail is named for. The junction marks the beginning

Boundary Mountains

Fourth Connecticut Lake Trail cut PAPA BEAR

of a loop path that circumnavigates the little fen. Turn right and begin the jaunt around the waters.

Shortly good vistas open across the pond. It is apparent that Fourth Connecticut Lake is very shallow and marshlike. Plants that can tolerate wet feet thrive in the margins and in shallow standing water. Mosses prevail and build up mats of decayed matter that provide a substrate for seedlings to gain a toehold.

Fourth Connecticut Lake sits in cold country most of the year. At 2,600 feet of el-

evation, the border country here receives snow six and sometimes even seven months a year. Snow can pile up to astonishing depths for the eastern United States and the temperature in winter can plummet to more than 40 below on a few Canadian high-pressure nights. The forest surrounding the fen is no different than that which blankets the Canadian Shield, hundreds of miles to the north.

In 2002, I visited the pond on October 5 in a fog of heavy, wet snow that piled up at blinding speed. I had come to see the damage inflicted on the forest by a severe ice storm several years earlier, but there wasn't much to see, caught as I was in the grip of near blizzard conditions.

Slip around the ½-mile loop that circles Fourth Connecticut Lake. Cross a minor drainage where, when water is very high, the fen leaks from a second outlet. Toward the end of the loop come upon a little stream, this one the primary outlet of the pond. This rivulet is the mighty Connecticut River. Yes, it is. Without too much trouble, one can straddle the brook, one foot on one side, one on the other. Do that and you have a fine story to tell your grandchildren in your old age.

The loop hike around the fen is over too soon. In fact, you'll wish this trail were twice as long. It is not every day that you get to tramp in true boreal forest. Most residents of the eastern United States rarely, if ever, experience an environment completely dominated by closely growing spruce and fir and punctuated with white birch.

Some do not enjoy hiking in these cold, dark woodlands. Cheerier, brighter hardwood stands seem more inviting, less threatening. But boreal environments have a charm all their own, and no forest on earth smells as good during a warm summer day.

49.

Mt. D'Urban to Crown Monument

Location: International border, NH

Distance: About 8 miles

Difficulty: Moderate, and somewhat steep in one section, with a short bushwhacking stretch down an old smuggling route

Trailhead: 45°17'03.62'N, 71°05'55.34'W

GETTING THERE

Drive to within 5 miles or so of the Canadian border on NH 3. A few miles north of Second Connecticut Lake Dam, turn right down East Inlet Road and begin a long journey on a dirt logging road into one of the more remote recesses in all New Hampshire. You'll come to the beautiful finger lake and black spruce bog that bears the same name as the road. Continue on, enduring a long climb up and over the west flank of Mt. Kent and a long descent into a lonely, unlovely valley spread out below the long boundary ridgeline peak called Mt. Salmon. With this peak always on your left, pass the terrific moose habitat known as Snag Pond, where a bull moose once chased a friend of mine who was fortunate to outrun the creature by pedaling his trail bike like mad downhill. Begin another long but easy climb out of that valley, passing T-junctions, when the road eventually splits at a Y-junction. Turn off East Inlet Road and climb a moderately steep grade to the left. Continue uphill until the spur lane comes to an abrupt end at a parking clearing ¼ mile east of a quiet mountain tarn named Boundary Pond.

GOING TO THE ENDS OF THE EARTH

It's time to test your mettle. If you have hiked a few of the trails outlined in this tome, and you are still game for a real adventure, then I'm going to send you to the very tip on the Granite State, where one step too far is a step into the netherworlds of Quebec or Maine, or both. I'm going to land you at marker 475, a granite monolith that will

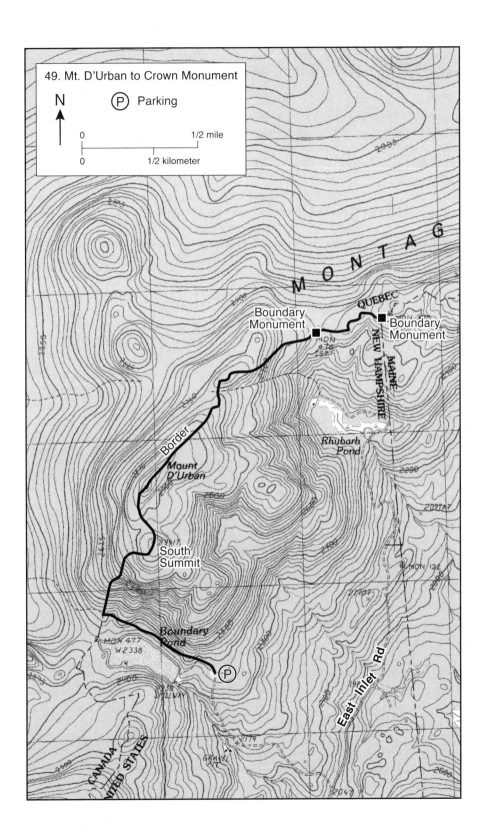

49. Mt. D'Urban to Crown Monument

N

ⓅParking

0 — 1/2 mile

0 — 1/2 kilometer

MONTAG

QUEBEC

NEW HAMPSHIRE

MAINE

Boundary Monument

Boundary Monument

Rhubarb Pond

Border

Mount D'Urban

South Summit

Boundary Pond

Ⓟ

East Inlet Rd.

MON 477
W 2338

CANADA
UNITED STATES

MON 122

forever denote the boundary between two states and that foreign country called Canada.

Although there is no formal trail to that most isolated vanishing point where the monument marker stands, the route is easy to follow. If bootleggers could do it, you can. And besides, both the United States and Canada now keep the international boundary well trimmed, at least periodically and more so since 9/11, and trekkers can hike across the very top of New Hampshire and Maine within what are termed boundary swath clearings, which snake wildly along the heights of land that separate the watersheds of the St. Lawrence River from the watersheds on the U.S. side that drain to the Atlantic Ocean.

Before setting out from the Boundary Pond parking lot, pack plenty of water, a good ration, a rain poncho, and a warm fleece, just to be on the safe side. Leave the lot toward the west-northwest and follow a good old angler trail/pond access track toward one of the loneliest bodies of water in the state. Walk nearly ¼ mile. Just when you can sense that there is an opening ahead (where the pond reposes), look to your right. When I was last here, I had to take some care to identify the old "smugglers' route" on the ground to the right. But I understand the way has been reopened, because boundary clearing cutters fairly recently did a good deal of work on the flanks of Mt. D'Urban to the northeast and Mt. Trumbull (Snag Pond Peak) to the northwest of the pond. If the way has been cleared, it would be a straight northerly walk to the boundary swath 10 to 15 minutes away. If the route is still overgrown and full of blowdowns as it was in 2005, you should be able to make out a long-unused woods lane on the right that cuts away from the main trail at a 90-degree angle and ventures due north. Tuck the location of this side track in your memory bank for few minutes. You'll be back here in no time.

Instead of turning off the trail right now, continue ahead for a minute to reach a small, earthen dam with an old deteriorating spillway, which holds back a narrow body of water confined tightly by the boundary peaks hugging both shores. Walk out on the dam and have a look around. The last time I was in to Boundary Pond, I spent some time watching beaver patrol the waters and an osprey coming and going to a nest in a tall snag near the far end of the lake.

I have never encountered anyone at Boundary Pond, but a few oar boats are flipped upside down on the shore, so some people do make the journey into this corner of the world, apparently. One who did come to this watery outpost is memorialized by a bronze placard affixed to a flat rock. The memorial is to one Gary E. Waterhouse, a well-liked New Hampshire conservation officer fondly known as the Jolly Green Giant, who died while in the line of duty at Boundary Pond.

There is something odd about Boundary Pond; at first, it's difficult to discover what it is that's unsettling. But if you look north across the entire length of the pond, you'll notice that there is nothing but infinity beyond the far shore. You will be able to make out nothing but clouds and sky above a low belt of green. It's as though over there, on the far side, the earth ends, and if you go over there, you will drop of the edge and never be heard from again. But, take it from me, the earth is round and you won't fall off.

After having had a good look at the lonely lake, walk back to that indistinct track in the woods (remember, it may be clear now) I asked you to commit to memory. If you've found it, fine. If not, it doesn't matter. Turn off the main trail and head north to the international boundary through the woods.

Mont Megantic from border PAPA BEAR

Boundary Pond's eastern shore will always be close by. If you've located the long-lost track, let it be known that it has served as a logging skidway, but more interestingly, it has also functioned as a smuggling route, most prominently during Prohibition, or so it is alleged. It is easy to imagine old woodsmen with a taste for fast money and hard liquor walking horse pack trains through the woods here, the animals weighted down with kegs or cases of bottled whiskey. Cigarettes might slip by the other way. Who knows.

Today, the United States government knows. The border is supposedly arrayed with seismic sensors that can easily pickup the footfalls of moose and human beings. Every once in a while I fall into a conversation with the local natives who tell me stories about helicopters and/or drones hovering south of the border at night, no lights running, their crews (on board or somewhere in a high-tech bunker in Utah or Nevada, perhaps) watching images filmed by infrared cameras mounted on the metal dragonflies. I suspect that when you come this way, someone may, literally, be watching you.

When I came through, my intent was to hike where most people never did. My conscience was clear. I suspect yours will be the same. Whatever your intent, trek north amid forest debris and fallen trees until the way suddenly clears at a 60-foot-wide boundary swath clearing. The boundary cut has been in place for decades, but it was full to brimming with young growth on that September day when hijacked airliners rammed into the World Trade Center towers and the Pentagon. Today, the border is well trimmed. Not only that, but a busy Quebec hiking club known as the Sentiers Frontaliers, based at Lac-Mégantic in the Eastern Townships, occasionally does some cleaning up within the clearings to create a border trail that runs for dozens of miles.

Turn right, uphill, away from the moist backwater of Boundary Pond and begin a moderately steep climb out of the saddle toward the first of two summits of Mt. D'Urban, a mountain that was, until very recently, just a foot shy of being 3,000 feet tall. The peak has benefited mightily from the advent of new GPS technology and has grown 11 feet in stature to a 3,010-foot elevation over the past few years.

Mt. D'Urban is virtually invisible from almost any point in New Hampshire; it is so remote and largely hidden from the south by Mt. Kent. That is not the case on the Canadian side. In the high farm fields of Chartierville, Quebec, Mt. D'Urban stands full bodied over the valley, presenting a fine profile for Quebeckers to enjoy.

In the early going out of the Boundary Pond col, you are confronted with the steepest incline of the entire trek. The slog is easier now because the heavy growth that was once evident on the west flank of D'Urban's boundary swath has been knocked down. The grind is also punctuated here and there by the appearance of hunting stands at the edge of the woods on the Quebec side of the swath. Brimming with low browse, the swaths are prime habitat for deer and moose, so hunters take advantage of that fact. In the tiny Quebec farming and logging villages nearby, far from Canadian cities and commerce, a dollar is not easy to come by, so bagging a deer in the fall is no small matter for a family. At the village of Notre-Dame des Bois a dozen years ago, not terribly far from the Canadian flanks of Mt. D'Urban, I watched skilled

fellows skin and butcher a deer in a dooryard right in the middle of town one blustery fall day. It was serious business, and the fact of that was not lost on me.

After some effort, climb onto the 2,941-foot west summit of mountain. Behind, to the west, get a good look down into the Boundary Pond saddle 600 feet below and out to pointy Mt. Turnbull several hundred vertical feet higher. That peak carries no name whatsoever on recent topographical maps, but 1916 broadsheets are said to show the name. Beyond is the very lengthy ridgeline known as Mt. Salmon, which tops out at 3,364 feet. It is the highest point on New Hampshire's boundary with Quebec. To the north, the Quebec countryside is visible, pocked with farm fields and peopled with small villages. The little settlement of Chartierville huddles far below, its finely appointed church at the center of things.

I once attended a meeting at the municipal hall to meet members of the Sentiers Frontaliers club and talk about joining two trail systems together to form an international trail. I know a little French, but that rapid-fire Québecois discussion was too much for my Anglophone ears.

But I do remember one thing about Chartierville that I will never forget. It was life-size cartoon image painted on a storefront right in the middle of town. The image? A bull moose copulating with a Holstein cow. Certainly, the delightful folks of Chartierville have a sense of humor.

Walk off the minor summit eastward and take an easy stroll up to the true, rather level summit of D'Urban. The clearings now permit a good view to the east-northeast along the swath out to some inviting country, particularly that of Mt. Marble in the distance, with its raw and dramatic cliff face.

The summit—in fact, the entire woodlands boundary that rambles far into Maine and down to Beechers Falls, Vermont—was legislated into existence with the signing of the Webster-Ashburton Treaty of 1842, establishing once and for all a permanent boundary between these two great nations. Before the signing, the boundary had been in dispute, so much so that a few citizens in what is now Pittsburg Township seceded from both the United States and Canada and formed their own sovereign nation they called the Republic of Indian Stream. It flourished as an honest-to-god independent country for four years, until the citizens voted to throw in their lot with the United States once and for all.

Three years after the signing of the treaty, surveyors from both nations and working as a team established the boundary by setting up monuments at the heights of land between the watersheds. In some cases, the crew set out native stone to mark the boundary. Today, the line is marked with small, round U.S. Geological Survey markers of bronze and belly-button-tall boundary monuments of cut granite.

The final destination on the border is monument 475, known as the Crown Monument. It rises precisely on the boundary between New Hampshire, Maine, and Quebec. Monument 475 stands about 1.5 miles from the summit of Mt. D'Urban. Luckily, the way out and back is over rather easy terrain. Along the route, the way is marked on occasion by red and white triangles, the blazes of the Sentiers Frontaliers hiking club. Pass by monument 476 and keep moving eastward. Finally, in an indistinct patch of wilderness, monument 475 shows itself. I couldn't resist walking around it a few times, just so I could say I was in two states and two countries all within a few seconds. Tourists who flock to the Four Corners monument, where Utah, Colorado, Arizona, and New Mexico butt up against one another, do much the same foolish thing. We humans are all alike under the skin, now, aren't we?

The granite monolith marks the end of this trek. The way back is actually a bit easier than the way in, because you can now descend the steep pitch down to Boundary Pond, instead of climbing it. On the way out, take a minute to walk an extra few steps to the backwater wet at the northernmost end of Boundary Pond and have a look at the handsome but oh-so-lonesome body of water one last time.

I'm not sure why I have come here half a dozen times over the years, to a placid pool so very far removed from anything downstate or down–New England. But I have a hunch. Sometimes one really has to get away from it all, you know, and I do mean *away*. In the Granite State, Boundary Pond is way, way away. That suits my particular pool of genes quite well, apparently. Perhaps it will suit yours.

IX. The Cohos Trail

Presidential Range from Owl's Head JOHN COMPTON

The final hike in this guidebook isn't a day hike. No, sir. The just-completed Cohos Trail is the longest hiking trail built in the Northeast in decades. It wanders through New Hampshire's largest and most remote county—Coos County—for 165 miles, from the southern county border on the Saco River to the Canadian border.

Below US 2 and NH 115, the Cohos Trail is largely confined to existing trails within the White Mountain National Forest. But north of those two highways, the Cohos Trail becomes a wilderness jaunt, a footloose freeway to a whole new universe of hiking in New Hampshire.

Here, in this guide, the trek begins at the Starr King Trail trailhead in the town of Jefferson and winds up beside a 2-acre fen on the Fourth Connecticut Lake Trail, within spitting distance of Canada. For 90 miles, the Cohos Trail rambles without encountering a settled community, until it reaches Young's Store among a tiny cluster of structures known as Happy Corner, in the northernmost town of Pittsburg. Beyond that hamlet, three more days of hiking await until you nose up to the Canadian border.

Lace your hiking boots on, don a well-thought-out pack with tent, and be off with you. Get good and lost on a yellow-blazed pathway into New Hampshire's great unknown . . . and love every step of it. Unless, of course, it rains (or snows) for a week.

50.

The Cohos Trail

Location: Jefferson to Pittsburg, NH, and the Canadian border

Distance: 120 miles from Jefferson to Fourth Connecticut Lake on the Canadian border, 165 miles from southern Crawford Notch to Canada

Difficulty: Very lengthy and isolated, with occasional sections that are steep and challenging

Trailhead: 44°25'13.14'N, 71°27'43.67'W

Alternative Trailhead, Davis Path Southern Terminus: 44°07'07.47'N, 71°21'05.02'W

GETTING THERE

Travel US 2 to the village of Jefferson. Just east of the Jefferson Village Store, at the crest of a knoll in the highway, watch for an international hiker symbol sign on the north side of the road. If eastbound, turn left; if westbound, turn right and travel uphill on a gravel lane. Stay to the left at any junction and soon you'll be at a parking lot at the base of the Starr King Trail. This path is the first of many trails, new and old, that have been chained together by the Cohos Trail Association to create a 165-mile footpath that transits the entire length of New Hampshire's largest and most isolated mountainous county: Coos County.

GO THE DISTANCE

The longest new trail system developed in the Northeast in decades snakes the length of Coos County, New Hampshire's huge northernmost county, home to Mt. Washington and the spawning ground of the Connecticut River, the Saco River, and the Androscoggin River. The Cohos Trail, developed by a tiny trail association that goes by the same name, rambles 165 miles from southern Crawford Notch to the Canadian border and links with Sentiers Frontaliers trails in Quebec, Canada, to form a second international trail system in eastern North America.

In the White Mountains region, the Cohos Trail follows existing White Mountain National Forest trails over the Montalban Ridge, Mt. Eisenhower in the Presidential Range, and the Dartmouth Range. For this guide, we begin our trek north of NH 2, where the

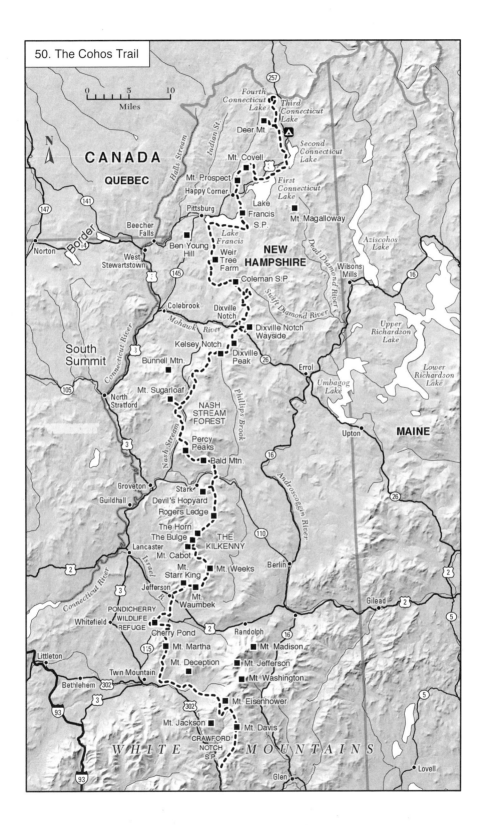

0   5   10
Miles

N

CANADA

QUEBEC

CANADA

Fourth
Connecticut
Lake

Third
Connecticut
Lake

Deer Mt.

Second
Connecticut
Lake

257

Mt. Covell

First
Connecticut
Lake

147

141

Mt. Prospect

Happy Corner

Pittsburg

Lake
Francis
S.P.

Mt. Magalloway

Border

14

Beecher
Falls

Norton

West
Stewartstown

Ben Young
Hill

Lake
Francis

Weir
Tree
Farm

NEW
HAMPSHIRE

Aziscohos
Lake

145

Coleman S.P.

Wilsons
Mills

16

Colebrook

Dixville
Notch

Mohawk
River

Swift Diamond River

Dixville Notch
Wayside

Upper
Richardson
Lake

South
Summit

3

Kelsey Notch

Bunnell Mtn.

Dixville
Peak

26

Errol

Lower
Richardson
Lake

105

North
Stratford

Mt. Sugarloaf

NASH
STREAM
FOREST

Umbagog
Lake

3

Nash Stream

Percy
Peaks

Phillips Brook

Upton

MAINE

Groveton

Bald Mtn.

Stark

16

26

Guildhall

Devil's Hopyard
Rogers Ledge

The Horn
The Bulge

THE
KILKENNY

110

Androscoggin River

2

Lancaster

Mt. Cabot

Mt.
Starr King

Mt. Weeks

Berlin

2

Israel R.

Jefferson

3

Mt.
Waumbek

Gilead

2

5

Connecticut River

PONDICHERRY
WILDLIFE
REFUGE

Whitefield

Cherry Pond

Randolph

16

Littleton

115

Mt. Martha

Mt Madison

Mt. Deception

Mt. Jefferson

302

Twin Mountain

2

Mt Washington

Bethlehem

302

3

Mt. Eisenhower

5

93

Mt. Jackson

Mt. Davis

CRAWFORD
NOTCH
S.P.

WHITE   MOUNTAINS

93

Glen

Lovell

Jefferson Meadows, Jefferson Dome region RICHARD CHARPENTIER

influence of the high peaks regions of the White Mountains begins to recede and the former logging terrain of New Hampshire's Great North Woods begins to assert itself.

What follows is a sketch of the 120-mile route that begins in the township of Jefferson and doesn't end until you reach a 2-acre fen high in the border country with Canada, a small body of water that is the true headwaters of the mighty Connecticut River. For complete information about this long trail system, go to www.cohostrail.org and review the many pages of that website.

The Cohos Trail trek in these pages begins in Jefferson, at the Starr King Trail trailhead parking lot. The journey starts with a 25-mile circuit of the Pliny and Pilot Ranges and a visit to the tiny community of Stark. Climb the Starr King Trail, a historic foot trail that was once an old bridle path, to a viewpoint at the summit and continue on, ridge running, to the 4,006-foot summit of Mt. Waumbek.

At the Mt. Waumbek summit cairn, pick up the Kilkenny Ridge Trail and stay with this

path all the way to South Pond Federal Recreation Area in Stark. Pass over the Weeks peaks, South, Middle, and Mt. Weeks, and descend to Willard Notch, a deep divide between the Pliny and Pilot Ranges. Leave the Pliny massif behind and climb the first Pilot peak, Terrace Mountain, with its three summits. Descend into Bunnell Notch and the junction with the Bunnell Notch Trail, and begin a moderately steep and steady climb up Mt. Cabot, the farthest-north 4,000-footer in the state. Visit Bunnell Rock outlook ledge and then the Mt. Cabot cabin, a former fire tower watchman's hut. The 4,170-foot wooded summit is another ¼ mile to the north.

Cross over Mt. Cabot, obtaining views from blowdown patches, and descend steeply to a col between Cabot and The Bulge. The Bulge has no views, but the next peak to the north, The Horn, boasts one of the finest summits north of the great White Mountain peaks, with a 360-degree vista. Descend steadily on well-designed trail to Unknown Pond, one of the more isolated and high-elevation lakes in the Northeast.

From Unknown Pond, descend through extensive white birch glades to a beaver drainage called Kilback Pond, pass the Millbrook Trail junction and Rogers Ledge campsite, and climb to Rogers Ledge itself, a large, exposed granite outcropping. The view from the cliff is a stunner. No human habitation is visible. The final 4 miles along the Kilkenny Ridge Trail is a pleasant woods walk that passes a spur trail to the Devil's Hopyard, an ice gulch, and reaches a placid body of water and recreation area known as South Pond.

The next leg of the Cohos Trail system is through the Nash Stream Forest, 39,601 acres of land that encompasses a great jumble of rugged features, including a waterfall, blueberry barren, a vast bald summit, cliff faces, high-elevation wildlife meadows, a large bog, and excellent moose and black bear habitat.

Enter the Nash Stream Forest at Percy Road, just north of NH 110. Climb to Bald Mountain Notch, cross Rowell's Brook, and climb the Old Summer Club Trail to South Percy Peak. Its bigger neighbor, North Percy Peak, is a massive domed peak with very steep sides and dozens of acres of exposed ledges and naked slopes. Although a challenge to climb, the summit is rather large, and flat and acres of blueberries straddle the peak.

Descend through the beautiful valley of Long Mountain Brook on the Percy Loop Trail. Pass the Percy Loop campsite to get to Nash Stream Road. Soon you'll find your way to a big step and slide cascade called Pond Brook Falls. Cross wild Nash Stream on the big Trailblazer bridge, swing over Sugarloaf Arm to the new lean-to on the east flank, and descend to a junction with an old spur trail to the exposed summit ledges of Mt. Sugarloaf at 3,701 feet in elevation. The peak offers splendid views of remote terrain, the Green Mountains of Vermont, and the Connecticut River Valley.

Moving ever northward, skirt around 70-acre Nash Bog, the basin of a lake that drained catastrophically in 1969 after its earthen dam failed. Rise out of the bog lands and climb steadily to a 3,000-foot elevation at Gadwah Notch, passing through a series of ever-higher meadows that are haunts for wildlife. Slink through narrow and dark Gadwah Notch on bog bridges and make for Baldhead Mountain and its lean-to high above the Phillips Brook Valley. The view from the lean-to stretches 40 miles to the south and takes in the Presidential Range and the Carter-Moriah Range, as well.

Beyond the lean-to, the Dixville Notch country prevails. Descend Baldhead to remote Kelsey Notch and the old tote road there. Cut east, then north, onto a wide, newly constructed thoroughfare designed to move huge wind turbine towers to the upper ridges off Dixville Peak. Climb the peak's southern face, taken in expansive views, then dodge down a new summit bypass foot trail and emerge on an old fire service lane on the north flank of the mountain. Descend to Mt. Gloriette and the upper slopes of the Balsams Wilderness Ski Resort and take in fine views of northern New Hampshire, Vermont, and southern Quebec.

Pace a mile north to a rendezvous with 700-foot Table Rock cliff, one of the loftiest rock ledges in the eastern United States. Trek eastward on the fringes of Dixville Notch and descend nearly 3 miles to a rugged and narrow gorge that cradles two separate waterfalls one above the other, known as the Huntington Cascades. Cross NH 26, go to Dixville Flume gorge, then rise on the northern cusp on Dixville Notch on the Sanguinary Ridge Trail. Pass four cliff outcroppings before reaching the height of land and a junction with the Sanguinary Summit Trail (SST).

Stride northward on the SST, running on an elevated ridgeline for miles. Breeze over a little service road, pick up the trail again, and continue to the Panorama lean-to shelter, with its expansive view from the southwest to the northwest. Climb over a "boreal island" summit called Mud Pond Ridge Peak and descend into chain-of-lake country. Trek old grassy logging lanes through Tumble Dick Notch and descend to Coleman State Park campground at Little Diamond Pond. There are modest facilities at the park, including toilets and showers.

Road walk on old farm roads away from Coleman State Park. One of them, McAllister Road, is a beautiful farm lane confined by good fences and pastures. After you come to an abandoned farm near the height of land, you'll reach what is loosely called the Stewartstown plateau, a region of small camps, farm fields, and views down into the Connecticut River Valley. Swing through a few hard dogleg turns and visit Weir Tree Farms, a Christmas tree grower's business, and behold one of the most expansive views that can be had in northern New Hampshire.

Follow old logging tote roads through aptly named Deadwater country and intersect with Cedar Stream Road, which rides the south shore of 2,000-acre Lake Francis. Walk the old road with the lake over the shoulder for 3 miles, then leave it for the Lake Francis Trail. Swing north near the eastern shore of the lake, reach Six-Mile View, then continue on to a crossing over the Connecticut River and the a junction with River Road. A south turn on River Road brings you to Lake Francis Campground, a fine state facility. Turn north and follow River Road for a short distance. The trail then turns off it, crosses Perry Stream, and ambles up to Young's Store, the first easily reached supply depot in nearly 90 miles.

Resupplied, trek up Danforth Road to a trail to the cleared summit of Mt. Prospect and take in its panoramic view of northernmost New Hampshire and northwest Maine. Four miles to the northeast, attain the summit of Mt. Covell and yet another dramatic viewpoint. Descend to Round Pond and follow its outlet stream to NH 3 and Camp Otter Road. Locate the Camp Otter Trail through moose habitat, cross an 800-foot bog bridge span, and reach the Connecticut River.

Cross Magalloway Road, a major logging lane, and enter the Moose Alley Trail named for its native residents. Pace across Big Brook bridge and pick up the Falls in the River Trail, a gem of a pathway that follows wild stretches of the Connecticut River and reaches a big step falls and flume gorge thundering with white water. Continue upriver to Second Connecticut Lake Dam and enter the Connecticut Lakes State Forest bound for Deer Mountain Campground and the international boundary country. Climb a restored historic trail up Deer Mountain or continue to the border and the U.S. port of entry station. Climb the border clearings to Fourth Connecticut Lake, a 2-acre fen that is the source of the Connecticut River.

That little body of water marks the end of the Cohos Trail. From Jefferson now far to the south, the journey should take at least a week. Trek the entire trail, beginning at Harts Location below Crawford Notch, and the hike may take as little as nine days or as long as two weeks.

The Cohos Trail stitches together scores of isolated Great North Woods features into a single recreational entity. Prior to its construction, many of the peaks, cliffs, falls, and other locations were out of reach or considerably more difficult to get to. Get a hold of a guidebook and map from the Cohos Trail Association, and go get lost . . . and love it.

The Cohos Trail